looking beyond labels..

Becoming a Mindful Parent!

Reena Singh

Author: Reena Singh

Title: *Looking Beyond Labels.. Becoming a Mindful Parent!!*

Edition: 1st Edition

Publication Date: August 2020

Price: ₹ 1500

ISBN: 978-93-5408-218-4

Language: English

Published by: Self – Publish
C/304, Satellite Park,
Caves Road, Jogeshwari East,
Mumbai – 400060
Website: www.khushi.net.in
Email: info@khushi.net.in

Printed at: Jayant Printery LLP
352/54, Girgaum Road,
Murlidhar Temple Compound,
Nr. Thakurdwar Post Office,
Mumbai – 400002
Tel: 022-4366-7159/7171

The contents of this book are my opinions, experience, thoughts, and personal conclusions. It is for information purposes only.

Parenting is a journey. Each parent tries to do his or her best to raise their child. Parenting a child with special needs requires special skills. Such parents need to be equipped and empowered with knowledge and information about the condition.

This book is for anyone who works with neurodiverse children- parents, grandparents, or therapists - and has made a commitment to partner in the developmental gains of a child.

The purpose of writing this book is also to try and cover as many frequently asked questions that my clients ask me during consultation sessions. I have seen a lot of parents searching for answers to their particular situations. This book will not end that search but will give you an opportunity to understand your kid better, especially if you are struggling to raise a neurodiverse child. Not just that, this book will help you to enrich your parenting experience.

The information provided here is for informational purposes only and is not a replacement for medical advice from a physician, pediatrician, occupational therapist, or speech therapist but to support it. Please consult with a medical professional if you suspect any medical or developmental issues with your child. Readers of this publication agree that neither the authors nor their publisher will be held responsible or liable for damages that may be alleged or resulting directly or indirectly from the reading of this publication.

Do not rely on the information in this book as an alternative to advice from your medical professional or healthcare provider. You should never delay seeking medical advice, disregard medical advice, or discontinue medical treatment as a result of any information provided here.

I am humbled and privileged to offer this book to you.

-Reena Singh

DEDICATION

"The risk of labeling is that it changes the way we perceive things."

~ Jennifer Eberhart
(Social Psychologist – Stanford University)

Twenty years back, on the 23rd of June, 2000, I started working as an Occupational therapist...I was 21 years old then and the child I first worked upon was an eleven years old boy diagnosed with Autism. From then until now, I have changed remarkably.

My soul has been colored beautifully by neurodiverse kids, my eyes have shed tears in pain, sadness, and joy.

My ears have been privileged to listen to the first words that the non-verbal kids started speaking...and the countless blessings their parents showered on me...

My heart has wept and sobbed at nights to see the kids deteriorate. My heart has experienced fulfillment to see my approaches to help kids and their families. My soul has attained an immense depth of wisdom through my interactions with these children...

I used to see them as children with challenges, but my understanding has now been transformed.

I now see them as "Gurus" who have come to teach me and their families some amazing virtues of patience, hope, and faith.

I see them all as "change-makers" who have the capacity to change the "collective consciousness" - making schools more receptive and adaptive - and revolutionize the "organic food" movement.

They rely on and trust the language spoken from the heart - feelings, and emotions- as words lack the power to convey their message.

They just want "love" and have managed to pull me out from the machine mode of running from one task to another and CREATING stress.

They are teaching me to "just be" and to "live in the present moment" with a full 100%. Neurodiverse children, at the soul level, are asking people around them to evolve and learn.

Thus, every time, I see a new child, I see a new "guru" with new lessons stepping into my life.

The soul of these children registers all of their mentor's emotions, intentions, and actions.

Intentions are most important to them. At the deepest levels, they cannot be tricked.

This is true for even the most so-called "severest" kids that I have worked with. They talk not with words, but from their hearts. They connect at a soul level where words are not important and unable to convey what their hearts want.

Each child I have worked with has the "seed" of something special in them. It may be music, art, or any such thing. When we say, a child is not good at something, that fault is partly because of our lack of commitment to explore that child. Surprisingly, I have witnessed abilities flowing at any age, even after I have stopped exploring or looking for them.

These children teach me to "never give up"...the seed will eventually grow when they mean to, not when I want them to.

These kids have taught me that it is not important to fit into something but to gracefully express your uniqueness without caring about the world.

These kids have helped me to travel the longest journey of my life, a journey from my head to the depths of my heart.

They have taught me to believe my intuitions and gut feelings, for these are not luxuries but gifts of the soul.

They have taught me that the best medicine to transform and heal the human body, mind, and soul is "unconditional love". Something that they shower in abundance.

These kids have taught me to explore the "space inside" me, for answers I cannot find in books. These kids have taught me to connect with the cosmic internet, to trust myself, and express what I truly am.

I am blessed to have been working uninterrupted, despite many ups and downs in my life.

I am really blessed to have been in great health, to have always received the support, and to have access to resources as and when needed.

Today, I thank each and every one who crossed my path and touched my life to make me into who I am today.

Namaste! My soul honors your soul. I honor the place in you where the entire universe resides.

CONTENTS

ACKNOWLEDGMENTS

I have been blessed to have invested two decades of my life working with neurodiverse kids. I have worked as an Occupational therapist with children of varying ages and abilities in all areas of pediatrics. The majority of kids on my caseload- I would say around 60% - have been on the Autism Spectrum and the remaining of them had other diagnoses such as ADHD, ODD, Fragile X, Cerebral Palsy, Sensory Processing disorder, behavior problems, and emotional disorders.

That's the reason I wanted to write this book so that I can share all that I have learned working with them in the last two decades.

While writing this book, I decided to rely heavily on my twenty years of experience. For me, the kids that I have worked upon have been like textbooks on learning and development. I can learn more about a child by getting a chance to know him rather than by reading a list of computer-generated test scores. In fact, whenever I participate in the clinical evaluation of a child, I see some facets of brain function that I have never seen before.

In this book, I want to share what I have learned from my students, their parents, and their teachers. Although I follow the research in the field very closely, I think it appropriate to write this book based purely on objective clinical observation. A volume in which children, their families, and teachers tell most of the story (the names and identifying details, all changed of course). I am referring to all the kids as 'he', 'him' or 'his', just for the sake of simplicity; it does not mean that I am referring only to a male child.

I would love to thank all the kids and their families who touched my life and made me into who I am today. It was and still is an amazing process of evolution which is spiraling me up in my spiritual journey. I learn new concepts every single day and every single hour that I invest in them. Thanks to all of them for allowing me to enter their lives and it has been my honor to work with them. Each child and family has influenced my thinking and shaped my perspectives for intervention. This book is a summation and distillation of my experience of two decades.

I would love to thank my son, Neel (my little guru who immersed me in this lab of parenting), and my husband, Mandar, for being supportive and my solid pillar. Most importantly, I would like to thank my parents, my dad, Surinder Singh who always believed in me and sculpted me into who I am today and my mom, Jaswinder Kaur, for unconditional love and support that I always receive from her. I would also like to thank my mother-in-law, Shilpa Varadkar, for being there for me to the best of her capacity. I am thankful to Mohit Lakhani for the book cover image. He is an abstract expressionist & was diagnosed with Autism at the age of 3. Mohit is here to teach us a valuable lesson about peace & love & he doesn't require any language to do so. Lastly, I would like to thank my editor, Dr. Praachi Verma for editing my manuscript.

On top of everyone else, I would like to thank, my readers, for making me an author.

First Steps in The Journey of Being an Occupational Therapist...

"I am not okay, you are not okay, but that's okay"

-Elisabeth Kubler-Ross

Reena: "Daddy, I am finding it difficult to work with neurodiverse kids. It's just been 2 months and I feel that I am not doing so great!"

Daddy: "What about your work is so difficult? Are you not enjoying being with them?"

Reena: "I have seen so many kids, but they are all so different from each other!! When I feel I understand them, another child who is totally different from the previous one comes to shake that faith."

Daddy: "So what's wrong if they are all different?"

Reena: "I don't even know if they will respond to what I do or say. Also, there are not many follow up studies. It is such a new thing and many people do not know how they will grow up and if they will be able to talk, communicate, socialize, study, settle down, or do things that we can do… Some of them do not talk yet and the ones who talk just repeat what I say. Some don't even listen to what I say!"

Daddy: "So, are you working to find results, and are you trying to attach yourself to the outcome?"

Reena: "Yes, daddy! I want them to get better and do what all of us can do and be happy."

Daddy: "Yes, that is what you want, but have you ever thought about what they want?"

Reena: "I don't know and I sometimes feel stuck. I am doing my best, but everyone responds so differently. I really don't know what to expect. Some are improving at a faster pace while others are really slow."

Daddy: "What's the reason you feel stuck?"

Reena: "Because I am not getting the results and changes in some of them."

Daddy: "Reena, you know what, you need to know the power of consistency. When we lower a bucket into a well to draw the water out, we stay unaware of the power of the rope to make impressions on the rock. But that power needs time and consistency to show its effects.

Reena: "You mean I am the rope and if I am consistent, I will see the changes?"

Daddy: "The rope is just doing its work and not expecting to see the impressions, Reena."

Reena: "So, I just have to do what I feel is right and not get attached to the outcome. That is so difficult, daddy."

Daddy: "That is what your teachers are trying to teach you."

Reena: "You mean these kids are my teachers?"

Daddy: "If you see them that way. No one in this world can predict anything. No one knows the potential of a seed until you nourish and nurture it. You have always been intuitive so, once again, just believe in the universe and embrace hope."

Reena: "Daddy, parents trust me and expect me to bring changes in their kids."

Daddy: "So, trust yourself and your skills and move ahead. Rely on new knowledge that you gain, but be open to the guidance that you receive from your heart."

Reena: "Daddy, there is no science in intuition or the language of heart. Nowadays, doctors don't believe in such things. Maybe, I have been trusting the wrong things since childhood."

Daddy: "Science teaches you to see and believe, but you must also believe in order to see. Be transparent and establish trust with those parents and honestly and genuinely convey to them what you feel about their kids. But remember, never try to take away their hopes. You are not God to predict anyone's future. So, set out intentions, but never underestimate the power of prayers. Instead, help them to convert their hopes and dreams into reality."

REENA SINGH

CHAPTER 1

WHAT IS NEURODIVERSITY?

Looking past the labels....

"Things are as they are. Looking out into the universe at night, we make no comparisons between right and wrong stars, nor between well and badly arranged constellations."

- Alan Watts

During my childhood, I had never interacted with any child who had a medical label of Autism. During my occupational therapy course, I worked with kids who had medical labels like delayed milestones, autism, cerebral palsy, ADHD, and learning disabilities, etc.

Through my initial years as an occupational therapist, I learned to understand the medical model of classifying and segregating the individuals on the basis of deficits and strengths. According to the medical model, kids with autism, ADHD, learning disability, and sensory processing challenges come under the label of disorders, dysfunction, and disabilities.

While I was still trying to understand this system, I heard the word "Neurodiversity". The word Neurodiversity was coined in the late 1990s by two individuals: journalist Harvey Blume and autism advocate Judy Singer. Blume wrote in the September 1, 1998 issue of The Atlantic: "Neurodiversity may be every bit as crucial for the human race as biodiversity is for life in general. Who can say what form of wiring will prove best at any given moment?"

The above statement taught me not to focus on the deficits, but the differences of the neurodivergent individuals. I love this model of seeing people as being just "different," this approach really provides a paradigm shift in how we think of mental functions. People who are neurodiverse are diagnosed with a learning disability, ADHD, Autism Spectrum disorder, or other such disabilities. Just like people have different hair color, eye color, body types, body structure, skin color, and so on, some people come with brain differences or neurodiversity. I personally like this model and this perspective of seeing individuals.

I witness biodiversity whenever I go for treks or nature trails. I always get fascinated by the diverse plants and animals that exist on our planet. Every single form of life on earth is valued for its strength, ability, and will to survive and thrive in this world. Virus, bacteria, fungus, flora, and fauna, all contribute to making our ecosystems diverse and resilient.

The encompassing model of neurodiversity taught me to recognize and respect these variations, the medical model, on the other hand, creates a divide between normal and the various disorders, disabilities, and dysfunctions that it considers abnormal. When I implemented the medical model, my clients grew up to realize that they belonged to a category of deficits, it made them feel less able and broken. Seeing these individuals with a deficit model makes us recognize them as the ones with impairments and limitations. This makes professionals like me to believe that they need to be "fixed" or made "neurotypical" or "normal". But seeing them through the lens of Neurodiversity celebrates them for their uniqueness while we work on the deficits. This helps them to make them shine with their differences. I am not against the label, but I am against focusing on JUST the label and trying every possible thing to get rid of it.

As Temple Grandin (adult with Autism) once said: "Autism and other developmental disorders still have to be diagnosed with a clumsy system of behavioral profiling provided in a book called the DSM, which is short for Diagnostic and Statistical Manual of Mental Disorders. Unlike a diagnosis for strep throat, the diagnostic criteria for autism have changed with each new edition of the DSM. I warn parents, teachers, and therapists to avoid getting locked into the labels. They are not precise. I beg you: Do not allow a child or an adult to become defined by a DSM label."

Getting rid of the medical label means to encourage parents to love and accept their child as he is and not to search for a Utopian world. When it comes to mental disorders like autism, dyslexia, attention deficit hyperactivity disorder, intellectual disabilities, and even emotional and behavioral disorders, it is still uncertain when a neurologically based human behavior will cross the threshold from a normal variation to pathology.

'We need to admit that there is no standard brain,' wrote Thomas

Armstrong in his pivotal work The Power of Neurodiversity. The term Neurodiversity indeed refers to the infinite range of differences in individual human brain function and behavioral traits.

We do not have to only work on changing the child so that he fits into the environment, but also work on changing the environment so that these children can fit in more easily. Most kids have a special interest or a skill that they excel in or it is the job of us as parents and professionals to help them find those areas of interest. We can help them to shine with their strengths while we work on their deficits.

David Neeleman told the ADDitude magazine, "If someone told me you could be normal or you could continue to have your ADD (the original name for what is now called ADHD), I would take ADD. I can distill complicated facts and come up with simple solutions. I can look out on an industry with all kinds of problems and say, 'How can I do this better?' My ADD brain naturally searches for better ways of doing things."

Ray Coyle, CEO of Auticon's British offshoot said, "Some of the most loyal, capable, and dedicated employees I've had have been on the autism spectrum. We've got to be really careful with the language we use: we don't want to give people the impression that all autistic people are IT geniuses, or that there are not neurotypical people who can do all of these things. But in the right role, and with the right support, an autistic person will significantly outperform a neurotypical person doing the same job. We have lots of evidence to back that up."

Billionaire Richard Branson credits his dyslexia for his success as an entrepreneur, noting that people with the condition possessed the "skills of the future." He says. "My dyslexia has shaped Virgin right from the very beginning and imagination has been the key to many of our successes. It helped me think big but keep our messages simple. The business world often gets caught up in facts and figures — and while the details and data are important, the ability to dream, conceptualize and innovate is what sets the successful and the unsuccessful apart."

When I share the above statements, I am not saying that living with autism, ADHD or dyslexia is very easy or it is just about strengths. I am not even saying that we need to lose sight of the deficits. All that I am trying to convey is that we need to also see the strengths which are most often missed whilst we focus only on attaining the "neurotypical" state. There is a lot of struggle and stress bringing up and raising kids who learn differently. Meanwhile, the expectations of reaching for utopia does hinder parents from loving their child. I have seen countless parents crying out saying they did not see their child for who he is and have only focused on his therapy and academics; they wonder how they lost that connection to the essence of their child.

I am also not trying to say that neurodiverse individuals do not have impairments, but the problem is to presume that neurologically different behavior is a problem. Just because the child receives a diagnosis, it does not mean that those deficits change the person's right to dignity. Therapies are important and they help to alleviate the difficulties but that does not mean that all the child has to do is attend therapies and go to school. They too have the right to have a "downtime," to unwind themselves and also play. Their plays might be different from other neurotypical children but are not any less important. As they grow up, it is important to know that they too have the right to choose their career path. I have often seen that when most little kids assert themselves or express their opinions, they are labeled as "non-compliant" and parents look for strategies to stop those so-called "tantrums" or "meltdowns". I have tried to elaborate on this topic throughout this book.

It is important that we as caregivers empower ourselves and change the way we see neurodiverse kids. There are some kids who may never learn to write or talk, but they may be good at other skills. Honing their hidden skills brings with it the acceptance of their unique personality as a whole. I am not talking about passive acceptance here, we must accept the child the way he expresses himself "in the moment" while still empowering him with skills.

Liane Holliday Willey, author of four books on Asperger's syndrome including the international bestseller, *Pretending to be Normal: Living with Asperger's Syndrome* says: "While I don't think there's a cure for anything related to autism, I think there is a very real and wondrous place for autism in our world. I like the world cherishing all sorts of individuals. All I ask for is a chance to be me, in any shape and form I come in. If I want to work on becoming more neurotypical, then good for me. If I want to be left alone and allowed to be more autistic, then that should be okay, too."

In this book, I speak from the viewpoint of a therapist and a parent. To be honest, it would be wrong if I say that I enjoyed every single bit of my parenting journey. Sometimes, it is really exhausting, messy, and tiring. Even after knowing the principles of therapy and understanding the theory of respecting the child, I sometimes lose it and things go wrong. At times, I even scream and shout, my kid has seen my worst side as well. Not just that, I have also pleaded, threatened, and rewarded my child without understanding his true needs. Regardless of these facts, I am my most authentic self with my child and he has also seen the best in me. When my son surfaced some so-called socially inappropriate behaviors, I took him to a developmental pediatrician so that he can get a medical label. I thought a label would help me prove that he is the one who needs to be fixed and I am absolutely doing my level best. But, I did not get any label and was told that I need to parent without getting stressed or anxious, which by far was the most difficult thing for me to do. This is because I was teaching the same thing as a therapist to others and I realized how difficult it is to practice in real life. What I am trying to emphasize is, parenting is not an easy job. It is difficult to stay calm and centered in the midst of tantrums, meltdowns, and other stresses.

So, don't let those bad days overshadow your parenting journey. Remember, you are not alone in this, parents of neurotypical and neurodiverse kids across the world are battling it every day.

Compassion towards yourself is a great fuel that will keep you going on this path.

However, a medical label brings judgment from other parents about your parenting style. People often frame a decision on the basis of your kids' behavior; behavior on the other hand is just the tip of the iceberg.

I strongly feel that there are emotional roots to every behavior and there is meaning beneath every single behavior of the child.

So, working on the behavior does not help until we work at the root level. I would like to share a viewpoint, take opinions from the experts about your child, but also know that no one understands your child better than you. So, let your "inner voice" take the decisions for your child. Anchoring this strategy to your parenting compass would ease the hassles of your journey.

There is ALWAYS room for hope in any adverse situation. It is necessary to acknowledge that your child is not a mini version of you. That being said, you cannot know every aspect of your child. As parents, therapists, or teachers, the onus lies on us to provide a secure environment that is free from judgments and expectations for the child to grow and blossom. The relationship of a child and a parent is a sacred one- of a guru and a student - where the roles keep reversing dynamically to promote personal and spiritual growth.

I would like to conclude here by emphasizing and reiterating that I love to see individuals with invisible disabilities as just being "different" and work with them to help them evolve. I embrace this viewpoint to not see them from a "deficit" model. Hereby, I do not deny the fact that deficits exist or understate or downplay the challenges that they go through. I just want to focus on the strengths while working on the deficits. I just want to grow and evolve with them instead of trying to "fix" them.

CHAPTER 2

ACCEPTING AND RECEIVING A DIAGNOSIS...

"Pessimism is a luxury that i can't afford."

- Anonymous

"Is my child neurodiverse?"

"Is he neurologically different? Why did he get the label of ADHD/ ADD/ ASD/ SPD?"

"Does my child have Autism?"

"What is Sensory processing disorder?"

"What are sensory issues?"

"Do we need a second opinion?"

"You know what, he did not sleep well when we went to the developmental pediatrician."

"I am a bad mother, I don't keep a watch on my child's screen time. I am sorry to admit but maybe he spends around 4-5 hours watching the screen each day."

"It was all my fault..."

"It is a new place and so my child did not comply, otherwise he always listened to me."

"I was in a foreign country while I was pregnant. I was all lonely and depressed throughout my pregnancy, is that the reason why my child has received a diagnosis?"

"Reena, I was not in India, and all he had was me. I did not know how to raise a small baby all by myself. Is it my fault?"

"I opted for a babysitter to resume my career, I put my work ahead of my child, and it is all my fault."

"You know people are over-diagnosed and over-treated these days. "

These are a few of the many statements that I always hear from my clients daily.

Once a parent told me, "Reena, I love my child, but still when he was diagnosed with Autism, the torrent of depression made me see him as an alien. It took me a lot of time to accept his eccentricity and love him for who he truly is. I can never forgive myself for depriving him of my love for days I took to accept him".

Another parent said, "I felt so relieved to know that my instincts were right. I always knew that things were not going as per the developmental curve. I am so happy that I got the diagnosis, at least now I know how to help him out".

Each parent reacts differently when a diagnosis is shared.

Once a parent told me, "I don't believe in anything like these "syndromes". I will work with him and you shall see how in a year or two, he will be ABSOLUTELY fine."

I can completely relate to each one of them.

Initially, I used to JUDGE them. I was new in the field and was unaware of the power of positive intention that a yearning parent beholds. I always thought books know us better. Such that, if the books and the doctors say that a child will improve by the age of six, then I used to go by those rules.

I was rigid, but I soon witnessed the universe responding to the words and intentions of those parents. I was bewildered and cried many times in awe of those miracles.

Thereafter, every child that walked into my office humbly contributed to converting my rigidity to resilience.

Initially, I used to work only with the child in isolation - just me and the child- as I was indifferent towards the emotional ties that a child shares with his parents. These emotional chords have immense power to transform each one of them. Just working with the child did not make me feel fulfilled as a professional. I did not know that these chords let the emotions run in both directions, simultaneously teaching the players to co-regulate. I knew it theoretically but did not apply it to my clinical practice.

Right from birth, a child is equipped to read the facial expressions and body language of their care-givers. These little creatures internalize and personalize those cues to turn on the "mirror neurons" in their brains. These mirror neurons mimic the state of the parent or the caregiver. A consistently and emotionally available caregiver during the formative years is an important and fundamental need for human infants.

In the paper presented by the Center on the Developing Brain at Harvard University, the authors emphasized that the relationships children have with their caregivers play a critical role in regulating stress hormone production during the early years of life. Research has shown that the presence of a sensitive and responsive caregiver can prevent elevations in cortisol among toddlers, even in children who tend to be temperamentally fearful or anxious. Another paper mentioned, "The emotional health of young children is closely tied to the social and emotional characteristics of the environments in which they live"

If the parents are happy, the baby is happy, if the parent is sad, the baby feels sad and so on. When parents are emotionally unavailable for whatever reasons, the baby feels rejected and unloved. This feeling is stored in their implicit memory to eclipse all other relations that they form in the future.

Negative triggers can come from implicit memories of early developmental trauma, such as chaos, neglect, and abuse. All infants develop ways to interact with their caregivers to ensure survival. These are called "attachment strategies."

According to the family physician, Dr. Gabor Mate, 'The right hemisphere of the mother's brain which is the location of the unconscious emotions programs the infants' right hemisphere. Since the infant is too small who does not understand spoken words, he receives messages from his mom which are purely emotional. The infant picks this up from the mother's gaze, tone of voice, and body language which represents the emotional environment of the mother. Anything that threatens the emotional security in the mother can disrupt the electrical wiring and the chemical supplies in the infant's brain emotional regulation and attention allocating systems. So, it is important to note that the emotional states of the mother programs the neurological activity of the child's brain for a lifetime.

Children learn to gauge their feelings while developing their inner compass, during this process, they rely on their parents or guardian to check which feelings to ignore, surface, or hide. Hence, parents need to find their inner compass and ensure it works well. Feelings like excessive fears, stress, inadequacy, low self-esteem, etc, should be balanced with love to assure proper functioning of the compass. Despite your efforts to hide it, kids can pick up on your immature coping strategies, feelings of low self-worth, and distress.

These little babies are constantly attuning to the mental states of their parents or care-givers. Emotional stress in mothers interferes with the brain development of their kids because it meddles with the attunement. The attunement process is not something that can be done at will. Infants, particularly, sensitive infants know the difference between a parent's real psychological state and a feigned emotional expression. These little kids have their emotional sensory radars working all the time. They are capable of reading the feelings and emotions of their parents with accuracy.

Brain scientists term the first three months after birth as the "fourth trimester". A lot of brain growth happens during that time. Babies spend a majority of their time with their parents and rely on them for almost everything. This emotional connection is hardwired into their brain to become a part of their implicit memory.

A study at the University of Washington compared the brain waves of two groups of six-month-old infants. EEG is the printout of the electrical activity of the brain. One group of mothers was suffering from postpartum depression and the other group had happy mothers. The results were alarming. The EEG of infants with depressed mothers depicted asymmetry. Parental mood affects the biology of the child.

Hence, I realized that unless I involve the parents, my efforts will fall short in some ways. I started undergoing courses on the same. I stayed with Merry Barooah and learned to work with kids and adults with ASD at Action for Autism. The training taught me a lot of things, but I still was not fully equipped to help the parents. There was still a lot to learn and explore for me."

Then I pursued a course in personal counseling, thinking this will finally equip me to get what is needed. While both these courses further polished my skills in the more complex aspects of counseling, they weren't just enough to get the results I desired.

And then came the time, when I was pushed in the ocean to see if I can swim through the rough waters of hard times - I call it the "birthing process"- into a new me. My dad was diagnosed with cancer and I was shaken to the core and broken.

I was in complete denial, I thought the results of the biopsy were incorrect. I prayed every single day, wishing for the reports to be wrong, wishing for the tumor not to be a malignant one. I remember feeling helpless, incapable, and powerless those days. My noxious feelings were contagious enough for the parents who visited my clinic during those days. They too were in denial of their child's diagnosis, our helplessness echoed and re-echoed in contradiction of our ignorance. I could relate myself to those feelings now.

Days passed by and I received the new reports. The diagnosis had left me emotionally numb and disgusted. I screamed to ask, "Why my dad? He was so good and led a good life. He never smoked or drank in his life, he never did anything wrong...Why him?" While still coping with the catastrophe, I carefully picked the pieces of my shattered soul to pose a strong face at the adversity, not forgetting my duties being the eldest of the siblings.

I shared my experience to harmonize with my readers and to remind them that adversities propel us to move ahead. I want to remind them to give access to the feelings they are afraid to experience. I want to remind them that it's okay to shout and cry. .We need to befriend fear and anxiety and allow them to wash over us. This will help us to process these emotions. It is important to be strong and face the situation, but it is also important to PAUSE. STOP, AND BREATHE to feel our inner fears. Parental fears and anxiety have a transactional relationship with the child, hence, it's an important aspect to consider.

Learning to deal with our fears is the biggest untold challenge of parenting. Children mimic their parents' actions, beliefs, and emotions. Signs like hyperactivity, impulsiveness, reserved personality, indifference, lack of eye contact, and self-stimulation might seem to curtail their attentiveness, but like sponges, they keep absorbing everything from us. We are their earliest environment. To provide richness, breadth, and depth to their world, we need to be fully ourselves.

Elisabeth Kubler Ross talks about the stages of Denial, Anger, Bargaining, Depression, and Acceptance which we all go through when there is a big loss in our life. It can be a loss of the role that we desired, a loved one, a dream, our fantasy child. It is important to permit yourself to go through these stages at your pace. Nothing can be forced. At the same time, the therapies and other things must start so that you start helping your child and yourself.

A parent named Vini, told me, "Reena, No matter how much I love and accept my son, there are days when I experience very real, excruciating and brutal emotions which have the power to burst me into tears." I could completely relate to what she mentioned and applauded and appreciated her because it requires immense courage to speak and express yourself when you feel vulnerable. I now started to feel that I am working with the family and not just the child. Any relationship is a two-way process, in this case, between the child and the parent. So, both need to be involved in the therapy process and both need to feel peaceful.

Talking about my dad again, those reports finally confirmed the diagnosis of Non-Hodgkin's Lymphoma. The acceptance was distasteful, but essential to put our derailed lives back on tracks. We all pretended to return to our routine lives. But, inside I was full of anger towards cancer, doctors, nurses, and the pharmaceutical industry. I didn't spare a chance to put a blame on everything else but my dad. That was my way of justifying and protecting my dad. People expressed their concerns about his health but I became a ferocious lioness ready to pounce on anyone who speaks about cancer or his health. The "anger" of cancer was projected on everyone else who was not even responsible for my dad's cancer. Others were only concerned about our family but I did not see that because I was busy processing my emotions.

Soon, I witnessed the same scenario at my clinic. Vani, a parent, came to me and said, "Reena, just because my child was making sounds and flapping in the garden, people were looking at me. I felt so angry and shouted at them!" I kept listening to her and realized, others might be looking to understand or help what was happening, but Vani's surging emotions obfuscated her perspective.

Another parent, Uma, told me, "I have stopped going to my relatives because they do not understand my child. They stare at him and leave hurtful remarks when he cannot sit in one place. We know he finds it difficult to sit and focus. But my relatives do not understand. I feel so angry". I just listened as Uma vented her feelings. She was unaware, just like her, even her relatives' needed time to understand her kid's diagnosis.

Most parents ask me, "Will Occupational therapy make my kid completely "normal," like the other kids?"

The therapy isn't done to make the child "normal". No, I am not saying that the therapy has no goal and we just work blindly?

For every kid that steps into my office, I set him a goal. We review changes and improvements monthly or every two months. So, what does it mean to "not work on making the child normal?" Unknowingly, we as parents, not just micromanage every action of our kids, but impose our decision on what they think too. I also feel that when we are attached to outcomes, the fear of failure plagues our senses. If we are not attached to outcomes, the need to control also disappears from the picture leaving us to be peacefully present at the moment.

The parent gets so desperate that they put their kids in therapy at a very early age. Children are made to go through intensive therapy on an everyday basis for years to come. I have seen little ones -as young as 18 months - start intensive therapy for sitting tolerance. If you look at my yardstick of the "occupational role of a child," no child at 18 months will sit and learn to match and imitate.

Please understand, I am not against intensive therapy, but it is very important to ensure what other children of that age-group are doing developmentally. It is unrealistic or illogical to expect a 2-year-old to start scribbling and writing, even if a child does so then that's not a role for his age. A 2-year-old is supposed to play, move, run, and explore; these activities are necessary for his brain development. Just because a child can learn, it does not mean we teach him anything that we feel should be taught!!

So, why do I say," Do not join the race of making the child normal?"

Bipasha, a parent of a thirty-year-old autistic girl once mentioned, "I did not realize that my daughter has such thick and long lashes, she is so pretty. All these years, I just looked at her autism. All these years, the barrier of autism restrained me from connecting with her. My anxiousness for her future ripped away from my daughter Mishti's happiness." Imagine, if your husband says that you must lose weight for him to love you, or your wife says that she will love you only when you have a certain amount of money, would you call that love?

You just want to feel loved the way you are.

Khushi, another parent came to me and mentioned, "Reena, I have taken admission for junior KG and I have only 6 months. I want you to ensure that your goals are set in such a way that writing and sitting tolerance comes first and then communication. I want to see to it that he goes to a regular school and I will push him as much as possible." I refuse to take such cases and tell them that I sense a lot of pressure and stress in such statements. We will work but Mother Nature has a way to develop skills. I cannot build a house if I aim to set the ceiling first and not the foundation.

I am also shocked to see some parents who are also doctors, take more time to accept and start therapies. One such parent, Suru, once said, "When I told my husband and in-laws that our child seems to have some delays and doesn't seem to follow the developmental curve, they scolded me and asked me to use my medical knowledge outside this house." Their criticism pulled me into self-doubt. They were in denial and so was I, thus, I wasted a good one year despite being a doctor."

It takes time to "accept" the diagnosis. It is ok to take time and it's ok to feel angry, sad, or deny the diagnosis. All these feelings are like the "inner compass" of our soul. We need to allow ourselves to feel and process them. It is important to ask ourselves questions like:

- What am I feeling right now?
- What is triggering me to feel what I feel?
- What is stopping me from feeling that feeling?
- How am I dealing with this situation?

You can sit with the feelings and allow your reactions to rise and fall within you. That will stop you from being driven by them. It's like watching a movie. Research shows that the best way to deal with any negative emotion is to observe it with mindfulness. Try to notice your thoughts and feelings without reacting or judging them. This kind of self-observation distances you from your feelings. You can name the feelings that you are experiencing to acknowledge them. For example, you can simply categorize your feelings with questions like, I feel sad that I am stuck in this situation or I feel scared of the future.

Just acknowledging the feeling also helps to defuse that feeling to an extent. Sitting with emotion is like pressing the pause button, it helps us to slow down. It gives us time to think and discover, it can be done when our kids are asleep while taking a bath, or while traveling for therapies.

I also feel that trying to use your mind to calm yourself down is okay, but the fastest way to self-soothe is physical activities like running, swimming, or cleaning your house.

Taking a couple of deep breaths helps too. Sometimes I ask the parents to lie down with a few heavy books on their bellies and observe them go up and down. Just do anything that works for you, but make sure you allow yourself to ACKNOWLEDGE those feelings, to process and transform them - for better.

Please also allow me to share this with you —If you are seriously depressed and have not been able to find ways to overcome the overwhelming sadness and lethargy, there is no shame in seeking help. Remember, when we fly in an airplane, we first put on our oxygen mask before helping our fellow passengers.

This is important to learn to ask for help. I would love to share two experiences that jolted me. Audrey used to come with her son, Alson who was 5-years-old then. She was struggling and trying hard to accept the diagnosis and she was not getting any emotional support at home. Her husband believed that she was just creating drama and was an attention seeker and that Alson was absolutely fine. This is because he was in denial and she was in a state of anger -both were on their way to accept the diagnosis but at different stages. The strife between them was widening and that was affecting the therapies and the child. One day, while I was at a party with my friends, Audrey called me. I ignored her calls a couple of times but as she kept calling me, I answered. Audrey was crying, she said, "Reena! I am sick, tired, and fed-up of this life. No one is supporting me. I don't want to live." I was shocked to listen to her words. In a blink of a second, I forgot about the party, the lovely music, and the scrumptious sizzler just being served. I was terrified. I was too young to manage such situations. It was just a year of working as an Occupational therapist and I didn't know what to do. So, I decided to just listen to her and understand what she has to say.

Audrey continued, "I am on the terrace and drunk. I cannot walk, I am losing balance. I do not see any hope for me and my child. I want to end my life. I am planning to jump!!" I asked her where she was and where was Alson. She told me and I just went on saying "Yes Audrey, I am listening... tell me more... yes...I understand you." This went on for 15 minutes. Meanwhile, I wrote down her husband's number and asked one of my friends to contact him. Thankfully, her husband went to get her and everything was fine.

This incident was a big "wake-up" call for me to work with the parent and the child together. Both need support in such trying times as they feel **emotionally fragile.** I ensured that she met a counselor and worked on herself.

Audrey is now doing very well and the couple is in harmony. Alson is now twenty-three years old and is doing very well for himself. He is completely independent. He has finished his graduation and is working as a data entry professional.

Another parent, Vinalee comes to my mind. She and her husband kept blaming each other for their child's diagnosis. One day, fed-up with daily fights and criticism, Vinalee took her 5-year-old son Harsh to the terrace of their fourteen-floor building. She was on the edge of losing her mind and jumping off with her son when these thoughts struck her. What if I die and Harsh lives? What if Harsh dies and I live? What if, we both don't die and become handicapped?"

When Vinalee shared this with me, I had goosebumps. I wanted to react but I somehow controlled myself and took a deep breath.

I realized how important it is for the parents to feel and express themselves.

At such a time, a therapist needs to LISTEN and provide space for the parent to open up. When a parent shares a traumatic situation with someone, it helps them to rewire their brain. The assurance that they get from sharing their deepest emotions with a friend, relative or a therapist works like magic to change their lives. It helps them to organize the chaotic and maladaptive state to a new state of being.

As time passes by, acceptance comes and denial, anger, sadness, and bargaining gets processed. Acceptance brings with it that peace of mind which makes your child feel accepted. Different persons have different levels of acceptance and it takes years to fully immerse yourself into it. … Acceptance brings with it that peace of mind which makes your child feel accepted and loved, for your peace makes them peaceful and complete.

CHAPTER 3

BEGINNING YEARS.....UNDERSTANDING THE DIVERSE BEHAVIORS!!!

"All I ever wanted was to reach out and touch another human being not just with my hands but with my heart."

- Tahereh Mafi

I always knew that I loved kids and wanted to make a career working and playing with them.

But when I completed the occupational therapy curriculum, the subject was so vast that I really didn't know where to start.

I started observing a senior Occupational therapist, Medini Padhye. She worked with kids who had delayed motor milestones. Every single day, in the month of May 2000, I would carry my tiffin and go to Grant Road, Mumbai, a place in the town side, to observe her work with the kids all day long. After a month, Medini Madam mentioned that I was ready to see some kids and work with them, but I was shocked at my reply.

I told her, "I will not be happy doing this – just making the kids exercise for my entire life... no, I want to do something else!"

I bless myself for speaking my heart out that day because she then referred me to another occupational therapist called Priti Butti. I started my training with Priti Madam, I felt happy to see what she was doing. She gave me the reference of a boy, Satyajit Modak, aka, "Satyu," and I started working with him. He was my first client. I was 21 years old then and he was 11-years-old. He had a diagnosis of Autism.

I had read about Autism, but have never actually worked with a kid with

Autism. I just loved working with Satyu and his mom, Beena, was adorable and extremely supportive.

That began my journey working with neurodiverse kids.

Child after child, several children were referred to me and soon, I had my session slots full for the entire day.

I used all the skill sets that I learned as an Occupational therapist but learning about Autism, ADHD, and other neurodiversity was something that I had to really dive deep into to learn and explore each day.

I got to know that a parent support group ran a library for kids with Autism. I went every week to that library. Like a voracious caterpillar, I wanted to devour the knowledge of Autism to help those kids and their parents. I wanted to understand more about DSM (the diagnostic and the statistical manual of mental disorders) and how the professionals diagnose it. I worked mainly in the role of an Occupational therapist. The philosophy of its practice included the ideas that people are Occupational beings and that engagement in Occupations is the milieu through which adaptation occurs.

You must be wondering what these Occupations are? Let me explain- Occupations are the daily activities people engage in, which include everyday life activities with individuals, groups, populations, or organizations to support participation, performance, and function in roles and situations in home, school, workplace, community, and other settings.

The sensory difficulties affect a child's participation in daily-life activities to fulfill his/her role at home, school, or at play. This is what I saw in Satyu. Even with his intermittent eye contact, he was able to listen and follow my instructions. He kept self-stimulating himself and that affected his participation in tasks. He would keep making sounds or flap his hands or play with his fingers – more on some days and less on others, a phenomenon that was difficult for me to understand.

As an Occupational therapist, I knew that there were difficulties in social communication and he would not reciprocate to my appreciation. I used to feel really sad about not being able to help him as much as I wanted to. And Satyu being my teacher kept pushing me to learn more about him.

By the time I thought I understood Satyu and Autism, my short-lived mastery of the subject was busted by another Autistic child who was completely different from the previous one.

There was a kid named Siddhant, he could speak and talk and express himself well, but whenever I asked him about his school and friends, he got stuck and sometimes repeated what I asked. To help him, I used to share some funny anecdotes, but Siddhant's blank face towards my efforts used to break my heart.

I knew Siddhant wanted to relish the gift of sharing emotions but it was really difficult for him to do so.

The more I thought, I know about Autism and other conditions, the more I explored it to learn and educate myself.

Kids or adults with ASD or ADHD or any so-called "label" are like us. I am different from you and you are different from your friend and so on.

When I realized that kids with ASD do not make friends because they find it difficult to interact with peers I started conducting group therapy sessions. Being an Occupational therapist, I thought, the occupation to participate and function in roles and situations in school and community is essential. By giving opportunities to be in group therapy sessions, I wanted to promote their participation. The kids in my group were so different that I had to club up the kids according to their functional levels. I had five such groups. This is because kids with ASD are inadequate at nonverbal communicative behaviors of social interactions. These deficits may range from poorly integrated verbal and nonverbal communication skills to abnormalities in or a total lack of eye contact, body language, and facial expressions. Some of the kids in that group didn't know how to play or transition to a new situation.

Kids with ASD have deficits in developing, maintaining, and understanding relationships. The "hidden rules" that we can easily understand takes time to develop in kids with ASD. The most basic group that I conducted had kids who were not even interested in each other and used to simply run around or flap or engage in self-stimulatory behaviors. While the most advanced group had difficulties initiating and maintaining conversations. Such vast is the range of Autism and even so bigger were the expectations on me to understand those kids and their problems.

But as I said earlier- my focus is to improve the child's participation that every work in play activities, family outings, and everyday living skills such as eating, dressing, grooming, bathing, toilet, and functional mobility. I do everything to ensure that the participation challenges could be minimized as much as possible.

Some kids with ASD also experience language difficulties which are not my area of expertise. I remember working with a boy named Harsh. He used to sing songs and repeat sentences, but upon asking what he wanted, he used to just repeat the question and didn't answer. He used to repeat it back and did not answer.

Then I would answer on his behalf, saying, "I want water," and he would repeat the same.

Another child, Som, has a habit of singing while being upset, sad, or angry. Som very creatively picks up a song that matches his feelings to deliver his message instead of saying it directly.

Another boy, Tanay, used songs to tell what he wants, like a chocolate song to get a chocolate or a papa song whenever he missed his dad and never a direct conversation.

A boy named Dylan came to me during my initial years of practice and handed me a bottle of water and said, "You want water?".

I answered- "No, I don't want water."

His mom realized that I did not understand him, she might have thought that I am a novice at understanding kids with ASD. She very politely explained to me that kids with ASD have difficulties with pronouns. Like they use "You" in place of "I". So when the kid said "You want water," he meant, "I want water". Later, I saw many many kids who had the same pronoun reversal issue while communicating.

Not just that, I have worked with many kids who wanted similarity in their routines.

Bipasha used to come for therapy always holding an empty deodorant bottle or comb.

Arya always had a leaf in her hand that she sometimes held close to her heart, like a piece of gold. Another boy, Agneev, kept twirling strings, at times those strings were the ones pulled.

Mauli always entered the therapy room with her first step on the doormat and second on the tile on its right. She also repeated this act quite often. If not allowed to do so, she would get overwhelmed. A classic trait of obsessive-compulsive behavior.

Another boy Aryan, was the same as Mauli when it comes to familiarity and predictability. Such that, when allowed to follow their bizarre rituals, all goes well, but any shift in their familiarity brought with it some tricky repercussions.

I am not saying here that all stereotypical behaviors should be welcomed and encouraged, not at all times at least.

NO!

Wait till you read this entire book to understand each of these behaviors with a new light and perspective. I assure you will be empowered to manage and understand these behaviors and you will end up becoming a behavioral detective!!! So stay with me.

Rishabh, another boy, always wanted the fan and lights in each room to be on. If turned off, he would have a meltdown. It was difficult for his parents to visit anyone because of Rishabh's obsession with switches.

Geet, a boy, was obsessed with toilets. He loved to explore the toilets of every house he visited. Again, hindering him from doing so turned him restless.

Many kids that I have worked with had hyper or hypo-reactivity to sensory inputs. Hence, this is the area I am trying to focus on my initial segment.

I can go on and on with illustrations to explain this because I saw so many kids with sensory processing challenges.

Sometimes kids have highly sensitive senses and their inabilities to perform a task or their frequent weird behavior is a direct manifestation of that heightened sensory input. Let me explain it to you in a better way. My old clinic was near the airport. There I was working on a boy named Tanish. Tanish frequently used to cover his ears with his hands and shout, "plane...plane." I initially thought he was doing so on purpose to avoid the tasks, but after a few times, I realized that his auditory senses were sensitive towards a passing plane.

Another child, Vihaan, was unable to write in the class. I was called to his school to check why the behavioral strategies weren't working. He told me that the toilet flush bothered him. His classroom was 4 rooms away from the toilet, yet the flush sound bothered him.

I wasn't convinced initially, but I was shocked to find him close his ears to the actual sound. He was speaking the truth. I realized his state of why he was unable to focus in the class because he was always in a state of a fight-flight in anticipation of that sound.

Likewise, some kids like Dhairya, find it difficult to register the sensation of pain. Dhairya's mother once told me, while she was busy in another room, Dhairya accidentally put his hand in a ceiling fan. Dhairya's mother was shocked to see his fingers bleed, a big chunk of flesh hanging down his little finger. It is really difficult to raise kids who have Sensory processing challenges as parents are always on their toes and on high alert at all times. Unfortunately, Dhairya was oblivious of the pain. He simply couldn't register that sensation.

There are many other factors that a Child Psychologist or Developmental Pediatrician will look out for to make a diagnosis, but that is their domain. I was only trying to make sense of the areas where I could help and understand the symptoms to make a difference in their lives.

As I evolved and grew as a therapist, one thing got clear in my mind that these kids are sensitive and have their emotional radars hooked onto their care-givers. The state-of-mind of these little kids was completely dependent on the state-of-mind of their care-givers. The feelings that the caregivers' experiences are written all over their faces. Children are all the time internalizing and personalizing all of these nonverbal cues, within a fraction of a second. The mirror neurons in the child's brain were essentially copying the state of their parents' brains all the time.

This sensitivity gift that they possess can be transformed from suffering to a blessing. Transmutation of these deficits into gifts can help children to explore their abilities as artisans, poets, musicians, and so on, according to their potential.

Doctors use the Diagnostic and Statistical Manual or DSM, scriptures, and encyclopedia of the American Psychiatric Association for diagnosing kids and adults. Dr. Gabor Mate in his book, *Scattered Minds* says, "DSM speaks the language of signs because the worldview of conventional medicine is unfamiliar with the language of the heart".

UCLA Child Psychiatrist Daniel J. Siegel says, "The DSM is concerned with categories, not with pain."

I am not criticizing the system but only trying to make it clear that if your child has received some kind of a diagnosis, then that does not define your child. Your child is much more than the diagnosis and every single child responds to therapy and intervention.

CHAPTER 4

LAYING THE FOUNDATIONS FOR THERAPY .....SLEEP!!!

"Sleep is the power source that keeps your mind alert and calm. Every night and at every nap, sleep recharges the brain's battery. Sleeping well increases brain power just as weight lifting builds stronger muscles, because sleeping well increases your attention span and allows you to be physically relaxed and mentally alert at the same time. Then you are at your personal best."

- MARC WEISSBLUTH, MD

Before a parent enrolls a child for therapy sessions, there are a few prerequisites that should be fulfilled. This is my viewpoint.

In the present day and age, usually, both parents work and the working hours are longer, not to mention the role of traffic in pushing it further. In some families, moms have the privilege and opportunity to be full-time moms and invest quality time with their little ones. In most of the homes, the child is waiting for their dads to reach back home and so the sleep time is all gone for a toss. Not just that, our affinity for screens to relax and comfort ourselves further disrupts our sleep schedule and quality.

I am not judging anyone, but this lifestyle of sleeping late, exposing ourselves to screen for long, and late dinners, does not seem like a healthy and conscious choice for our families as a whole.

Many kids sleep in the afternoons because they want to stay awake till late at night to spend quality time with their fathers. Research suggests that the night sleep is more restorative and a child does not really benefit from the afternoon naps after 3 years of age.

Sleep is very important for all of us and so also for our kids. Children who consistently sleep fewer than ten hours at night, -before the age of 3 - are three times more likely to have hyperactivity and impulsivity problems by the age of 6.

The symptoms of sleep-deprivation and ADHD, including impulsivity and distractibility, are very similar. We do not know whether the child has ADHD or is hyperactive because of sleeping less, hence, ruling out sleep issues is an important part of the diagnosis. For school-going kids, 30 minutes of extra sleep per night helps them to regulate their moods and impulses to focus well in school.

In some kids who have ASD, they also have sleep-related challenges. This is the difficulty in initiating or maintaining sleep or suffering from non-restorative sleep, accompanied by daytime functional impairment.

In occupational therapy theories, sleep is conceptualized as a restorative occupation with the goal of rest and recuperation. Good sleep and rest could support the formation of the occupation mix of self-care, work, and leisure during the day. Thus, sleep and daytime functioning are closely interrelated, and excessive or insufficient sleep contributes to occupational imbalances.

Occupational therapists evaluate clients in areas that contribute to sleep dysfunction (Including difficulties in sleep preparation and sleep participation), Sleep latency (how long it takes to fall asleep—typically fewer than 30 minutes for someone without a sleep disorder), Sleep duration (the number of hours of sleep, which varies by age), Sleep maintenance (the ability to stay asleep), or daytime sleepiness; the impact of work, school, and life events, such as shift work or care giving responsibilities.

A special mention needs to be made of snoring here. Keep in mind that snoring can be due to many different reasons like impacted tonsils or adenoids, conditions such as sleep apnea or asthma, etc. If your child snores, you should consult a clinician as soon as possible to determine the best physiological supports for sleep.
Some tips for promoting sleep:-

1. Creating and maintaining bedtime routines is one of the best ways to help support your child's sleep. Completing a routine before bed is a great way to prepare the mind and body for sleeping. Carrying out a bedtime routine signals

the body that it is about to go to bed. You decide what works for your child- it is customized. Once you have figured out a routine that works for you and your child, stick to it!

2. Being consistent is very important. The routine can be simple and short. It could be as simple as brushing teeth, wearing the nightdress, and using the washroom.

Some other things that can be added to this routine may include using weighted blankets, warm water baths, and deep pressure massage, all of which help promote sleep. Bear hugs, gentle caresses, and deep pressure hugs also help. Lycra covers on the mattress are also good.

3. It is a good idea to use lava lamps as a night light. Close the door to the bedroom to reduce light and sound. Yellow light is preferred instead of white light.

Sleep with a body pillow, pet, or stuffed animal in the bed – it can provide deep pressure or a sense of boundaries in a large bed. Wrapping in a Lycra sheet before bed also helps as it provides a lot of deep pressure input.

4. Use cotton bed sheets and cotton pillow covers which are soft and washed 2-3 times and are not new. The kind of clothes that the child wears to sleep and their comfort is another important factor which needs to be taken into consideration. Ensure that if the nightdress is new, wash it 2-3 times before the child wears it.

5. Keep the room cool. A decrease in body temperature signals the transition to sleep.

6. Use the bedroom only for sleeping so that the bed is associated with only sleep.

A screen of any kind- TV, Mobile, laptop, or desktop - should be discouraged at least 90 minutes before bedtime to promote restful sleep. , as and when, also make sure you keep all the gadgets out of the bedroom while you prepare the child for bedtime.

7. It is generally believed that calming or mindful activity helps to promote quality sleep. Using the same music on an everyday basis before sleeping helps to set-up the ambiance for sleeping. Instrumental music or slow music is generally calming, chanting mantras or singing a lullaby is another great way to calm down the child and to also build predictability.

8. There are also studies on how positioning could promote sleep in preterm babies. Jarus and colleagues found that the prone position showed more sleep patterns and less awake patterns than the supine position.

9. The lifestyle intervention emphasizes the promotion of healthy sleep habits with activity rescheduling. This means that everyone in the house prepares the child to sleep. If there is a lot of activity in the house with late dinners and excessive screen-time just before sleep, then we cannot expect a child to fall asleep quickly and have quality sleep. We, as parents, need to change our lifestyle to create conditions to facilitate sleep. Lifestyle modification is a great medicine in the present day and age!

9. Have a fixed waking time every day, and even on the weekends. Skip the afternoon naps and chuck the habit of waking up late.

10. Avoid tea, coffee, cola, chocolates, and cold drinks before sleeping. Avoid very tough exercises 2-3 hours just before bedtime.

11. Expose your child to natural light as much as possible. Daylight is the key to regulating daily sleep patterns. Try to go outside in natural sunlight for at least 30 minutes each day. If possible, try to wake your child up with the sun or use very bright lights in the morning. Sleep experts recommend that if you have problems falling asleep, you should get an hour of exposure to morning sunlight and turn down the lights before bedtime. Light helps the body produce melatonin which is a sleep-promoting hormone. Sunlight early in the day is especially helpful in getting your natural clock "in sync" with natural daytime and nighttime (that is, feeling alert during the day and sleepy at night).

12. Engaging the child in heavyweight proprioceptive activities which I will be discussing in the coming chapters, is an amazing way to promote sleep.

13. Epsom salt baths help, but it is still not proven. The research supporting magnesium supplements for sleep is fairly robust. In fact, it's now widely accepted in the medical community that sustaining healthy magnesium levels often leads to better sleep. All thanks to magnesium's vital role in maintaining appropriate GABA levels. GABA is a neurotransmitter that promotes unwinding and slowing down. In my anecdotal studies, I have found magnesium oil foot massages helpful at promoting better sleep.

Some parents allow their kids to make up for the sleep lost during the week with sleeping more on weekends. Although this sleeping pattern helps them to feel more rested, it will not completely make up for the lack of sleep or correct the sleep debt. This pattern also will not necessarily make-up for impaired performance during the week or the physical problems that can result from not sleeping enough. Furthermore, sleeping later on the weekends can affect their biological clock, making it much harder to go to sleep at the right time on Sunday nights and to get up early on Monday mornings.

Children who don't get enough sleep at night will show signs of sleepiness during the day. Unlike adults, children who don't get enough sleep at night typically become hyperactive, irritable, and inattentive during the day. They also have an increased risk of injury and more behavior problems, and their growth rate might be impaired. Sleep debt appears to be quite common during childhood and may be misdiagnosed as attention-deficit hyperactivity disorder.

14. Earthing is the simplest and easiest way to promote sleep. Earthing restores and maintains the human body's natural electrical state. It simply means being in touch with the earth's surface or being grounded.

15. Tracing the triple warmer meridian backward - 5 to 10 times - also calms down a person and helps them to relax.

16. Surrogate tapping – Tapping for the child using Emotional Freedom techniques - helps a lot. This can be done by the parent on behalf of the child. In my experience, I have seen this to be a very useful and powerful tool.

Start small – pick up one or two strategies and then implement-not to try all at one go!

How do we do earthing?

Walking barefoot in moist grass or soil for 30 to 40 minutes is an excellent way to do earthing. Walking, wading, or swimming in the ocean are other great ways to practice earthing. Ocean's salty water rich in minerals is a hundred times more conductive than freshwater. Conductivity depends on the concentration of minerals in the water and lake water is less conductive than saltwater and pool water is less conductive than lake water. Holding a leaf or a plant firmly between the fingers also helps to get grounded.

Earthing really helps kids and in general, all of us to become calmer and regulate our sleep patterns. Earth is like a huge battery that is continuously replenished by solar radiation, lightning, and heat from its molten core. The rhythm of the earth and its pulsations attunes the biological machinery of life to rhythm and balance.

Activities such as camping, gardening, hiking, trekking, or nature walks should be included in your kid's routine. Going to the beach and building sandcastles should also be included.

Now comes the most important point related to a child's sleep; many times, parents are so deeply engrossed in following their kid's sleeping schedule that their anxiety levels go up if their kid doesn't sleep on time.

Kids have super-sensitive emotional barometers through which they pick up on our vibrations and emotional states. So, even if our words are calmer, they pick up on our underlying stress. Remember, we spoke about co-regulation. Children learn that sleeping is a big task and is stressful too. That said, I feel it's important to manage and prepare the child for sleeping rather than suddenly acting on the moment and reacting. It's also important that we find time to make for that time.

Time management is the key to patience. We often get stressed about being late or falling short of expectations. Time management makes us more kind, understanding, and conscious as parents. Regulating ourselves and not slipping into reactivity is an important parenting aspect to raise great kids. It's also important to be mindful that we do not have a tantrum while our child is experiencing one. It's very crucial to be calm in the face of a child's tantrum.

And even if we sometimes react, it's ok. We are all a work in progress and it's important that we are AWARE and MINDFUL of our state of mind when our children have a tantrum. All of us land somewhere on a scale of good to bad, best to worst, perfect to imperfect, terrified to calm and our concern is just to be a better parent and a better person each day.

Hence, it is important to be "aware" and "mindful" of the atmosphere inside you. Such that when stress hits, you know it's better not to instruct your child or better to disconnect from them for a while. It's important to connect with the peace and the calm within you and then implement the sleep routines.

While you disconnect from your child to connect with yourself and ground yourself, it's ok if the child gets deprived of his sleep for those few minutes. I feel it is important that our kids get the "best" version of ourselves as mothers or fathers.

Broken sleep or too little sleep affects a child's behavior, learning, and mood. The inability to sleep on their own can lead older kids to have anxiety around sleep. Children have enough challenges to deal with; we need to at least give them the foundation of good sleep to get them through those struggles.

Create an environment to promote sleep
Create a bedtime routine
Ensure that the child does not nap in the afternoons

But, if the child is still awake and has difficulty initiating or maintaining sleep, I would suggest meeting a developmental pediatrician who can prescribe medications to ensure that your child sleeps well. Sleep is extremely important and children need to sleep well to function at their level best and to learn and regulate their behaviors.

Many parents are concerned and do not wish to start medications for sleep. The concerns are very valid, but usually, doctors prescribe Melocid which is a natural hormone to promote sleep.

The reason I am emphasizing on sleep so much is that having worked with countless kids, I have seen that the kids who sleep well learn well. Their brains are ready to learn. It is very difficult to learn skills with an exhausted, tired, and sleepy brain.

Rushil comes to my mind. He had difficulties falling asleep. His parents used to be awake with him until 2:30 or 3 am every night. Rushil's parents were always tired and Rushil was never fresh whenever they came for therapies. I remember that the best of my therapists worked with him and Rushil would be either cranky or sleepy or restless or hungry. It was all so chaotic and nothing seemed to be work. I kept meeting the parents and suggesting that sleep needs to be worked on, but precious two years slipped by and we did not achieve any measurable growth with him.

Then, we implemented all the above strategies and observed that his sleep improved. I still remember closing my eyes and dropping tears of gratitude when we achieved this milestone. Some kids take a lot of time and teach us to develop "patience". It finally happened. And then, everything was achievable. Rushil showed improvements at a very rapid pace post that. I felt he was a rocket waiting to get launched and then the sky was the limit. He attended a regular school and was very bright in academics. I lost touch with the family once he was independent. This was in 2003 when he was 5-years-old.

I am not trying to convey that sleep is the only factor to work on, but it is an important and very critical factor. Not all kids are like Rushil, every child is different and improves at their own unique pace, but good sleep definitely promotes developmental gains and also helps kids to regulate their behaviors.

Sleep is a powerful contributor to what Dr. Perlmutter in his book *Brain*

Wash: Detox Your Mind for Clearer Thinking, Deeper Relationships, and Lasting Happiness- calls it the "disconnection syndrome." It means that by disconnecting with the prefrontal cortex we lock ourselves into the amygdala. The prefrontal cortex is the part of the brain behind the forehead that helps us with future planning, impulse control, decision making, developing empathy, and compassion. Amygdala is an almond-shaped structure that is present somewhere between the ears. It plays a role in short-sighted impulsive decisions to foster narcissistic thinking to make us live our lives in fear. So, when parents do not get good sleep because of the poor sleep patterns of their kids, they too are locked up in the amygdala. Studies on fMRI scans show and suggest that even one night of non-restorative sleep (depth of sleep -whether sound sleep or not and the duration of the sleep) also lights up the amygdala which is associated with significantly increased anxiety-related responses in the face of stressful situations. Not just that, sleep is strongly associated with higher levels of markers of inflammation too. Thus, it becomes a vicious cycle where parents' anxiety is picked up by their child, and hence, it is very essential to break this pattern and get restorative sleep.

CHAPTER 5

WHICH THERAPY TO DO WITH MY CHILD

"Our first teacher is our own heart"

- Cheyenne proverb

A lot of parents come to me, who are so confused with the plethora of the treatment options available for neurodiverse children today.

When I started working as an occupational therapist in 2000, I was in the same situation. I contrast, the options that were available for me to help these kids and families, were much lesser.

I, however, explored a lot. So for the first two years, I only used occupational therapy and sensory integration approach. As time passed by, I realized that I needed to equip myself further and that's when I went to 'Action for Autism' (a Delhi-based organization providing support and services to autistic individuals and persons working with them). There I learned a lot about structured teaching principles and the exact behavioral approach to learning.

I feel so indebted because during those days I was gifted with many books, from various parents who saw and felt that I was trying to understand their families. They gave me a lot of material to read. I still remember learning and understanding everything from a behavioral perspective, while blending my knowledge as an occupational therapist, and working on the skills as well.

On one hand, I was trying to understand a lot about behavior, using approaches by B.F. Skinner and on the other hand, I was trying to learn about sensory integration. To achieve so, I read numerous books authored by Jean Ayers, who is the pioneer of sensory integration.

Somewhere, I was convinced that the greatly trending Applied Behavioral Analysis (ABA) or Verbal Behavioral Analysis (VBA), was the only thing that would help a child with Autism. During those days, I met several parents who had returned from the USA and were providing their children with 40 hours of ABA/VBA training per week.

I also attended many training and workshops with ABA teachers, instructors, parents, and professionals, to understand the ABA and VBA perspective of helping kids.

In a way, I was working to weave the learning of ABA and VBA into my Occupational Therapy practice. In an effort to bring together the principles from multiple disciplines to formulate my own theory. But, for me, that knowledge wasn't yet enough.

Dr. Skinner was famous for his book, *Beyond Freedom and Dignity*. According to him, all we need to study is behavior. He did not believe in what was inside a person's head because that is something that cannot be measured. He only analyzed and evaluated behaviors. He saw everyone as stimulus-response machines.

B.F. Skinner saw the mind as a "black box". He did not care what was going on in the mind, all he cared about was external behavior. He believed that children are like blank slates and you can train them into anything with the right environment. This is what makes up 80% of the parenting advice, given by most professionals. However, when we train an animal in a lab, we are least concerned about what's going inside its mind, we are only concerned about its behavior. If we measure the stress hormone levels in a lab rat, they are really high. So, in a behavior model, we do get the desired behaviors, but the results are short-lived.

Dr. Gordon Neufeld says, "Stressing a child has a long-term impact on the development." A child's mind is not a black box, it has human needs and certain dynamics. The question is, do we respect those needs and dynamics or our focus is to just work on the behavior.

We need to be clear about whether we want just the behavior gains or the actual developmental gains in the child. The question is not about how to deal with a particular behavior, but to understand what is going on in the child's mind. I feel it is important to blend these two and follow a holistic approach rather than relying on the external sources of reinforcements and rewards.
Dr. Skinner changed his mind when he became old. A psychiatrist at Harvard University, named John Ratey - also the author of *Shadow syndromes and A user's*

Guide to the Brain - while having lunch with Dr. Skinner asked him, "Don't you think it's time we got inside the black box?"

To this, Dr. Skinner replied, "Ever since my stroke, I have thought so."

So, it is important to respect the child's needs and understand the dynamics of a child as a whole rather than just looking at the behavior. I believe there are emotional roots to every behavior that needs to be identified, understood, and spoken about.

Temple Grandin - an adult with Autism - in her book *Animals in translation* says, "The brain is pretty powerful, and a person whose brain isn't working right knows just how powerful. Dr. Skinner had to learn the hard way. His stroke showed him not everything is controlled by the environment."

Behaviorists believe that any animal or person can learn just about anything if the rewards are right, which led Ivar Lovaas to his work with autistic children. In his most famous study, he took a group of very young autistic kids and gave intensive behavior therapy to half of the children and much less intensive treatment to the other half. Behavior therapy just meant classical operant conditioning and making kids repeat the same behavior over and over again. There has been a controversy over whether Dr. Lovaas did or did not cure anybody. But, I feel, his intentions were to help kids and he did his best with what he knew back then.

I feel we need to see kids holistically rather than only behaviorally. Dr. Gabor Mate mentions, "What conditions are needed for human physiological and psychological maturation? What conditions would inhibit or interfere with that growth process? Instead of asking why a disorder or illness develops, we ask why a fully self-motivated and self-regulated human personality does not."

Stanley Greenspan, a leading American child psychiatrist wrote, "We have no idea of what the parameters of development really are."

I shall elaborate more on this topic in the coming chapters.

I also think that using only behavioral approaches while working with neurodiverse kids does not seem like a comprehensive solution. Kids are not just stimulus-response machines and seeing them holistically is important.

Coming back to my journey, I continued teaching and training parents with blended disciplines. I continued equipping myself with more knowledge about behavior and occupational therapy. I kept adding more to my bank of knowledge and checked my techniques using intuitions. My intuitions kept saying that something was still lacking.

And so, I learned more about sensory integration, therapeutic listening, primitive reflexes, Emotional Freedom Techniques, Neuro-Linguistic Programming, and so on.

Now, I am able to blend these approaches beautifully. I believe that nature (genes which are passed to us from our parents, epigenetic as well as our unique expression of our intrinsic nature) and nurture (the environment) go hand in hand.

When a parent comes to me today and talks about the various treatment options available, I feel it is important for them to understand and analyze where and how therapy can help their child.

Hence, parents must check where the intended therapy aims to work- on nature or the nurture aspect. When I say nature, it means helping the child to manage things at a level that is intrinsic or inherent. Approaches like the Masgutova Neurosensorimotor Reflex Integration (MNRI), Rhythmic Movement Training (RMT), Sensory Integration, and Therapeutic Listening (TL) are skill-based approaches to equip children with skills. The natural aspect works on their bodies and helps them to effectively interact and communicate with people and the environment, leading to optimal functioning.

While discussing skill development, it is important to emphasize that the fastest development happens during the first three to five years of life. If a child misses a particular stimulation during this sensitive period then many repetitions are required to achieve it. Brain being "plastic" is capable of changing throughout life, but under or over-stimulation during sensitive periods - mainly for language and emotional development- can reduce its abilities profoundly.

Nurturing on the other hand involves exposing the child to important environments and managing their behaviors in the context of those environments.

I love the way behavioral therapy approaches work, I love how Skinner broke it down into parts and verbal operants. I appreciate many other detailed behavioral principles that are used to bring about changes in behaviors.
Having said that, there is so much more to us than just behaviors. Things like intelligence, emotions, temperament, and strengths - which all kids possess - cannot be controlled by any behavioral interventions.

Seeing things only with the behavior perspective would mean that only the environment can bring about changes in an individual, which according to me, is not a complete truth.

Humans are full of unique and essential qualities and traits. Human instincts, intelligence, emotions, and tendencies are peculiar and cannot always be linked to their behaviors. I am not against behaviorism, what I am trying to say is, if our approach while working with the child is only about nurture, it won't help. The nature part has to be taken care of as well.

The biggest challenge is to discover the hidden abilities and strengths of a child in the midst of his challenges. Our aim should be to patiently, optimistically, and lovingly strengthen and nurture those abilities.

Behaviorists believe that the laws of behavior are universal and all the creatures follow them. So, a lot of what they learned came from the laboratory. I do not agree with this approach because a person who is in a laboratory and a person who is in a natural environment behaves differently. Fortunately, while I was learning about ABA, the concept of natural environment training (NET), came into existence. NET is motivational driven, natural environment training that utilizes the principles of behavior therapy.

As a therapist, I feel it is important to educate parents on the various therapy options. So that they understand the aspect of nature and nurture. If the focus of therapy is just behavior then a lot of work goes into skill-building as well. Even if it's just one skill, there are many levels to it that need to be worked upon.

A holistic approach takes care of all the areas of child development. Empowering parents with information regarding the strengths and challenges of neurodiverse kids enhance their parental instincts.

Many families that I have worked with have sidelined the importance of skills to just work on behavioral therapy for years. Sadly, this approach didn't help them much. Similarly, many families just focused on skills and avoided the behavioral aspect to face a similar unfavorable outcome. Therefore, a combination of the two forms of therapy is important.

During the first seven years of my work, I tried teaching and empowering parents to follow the home program. Though I saw some results, still I was not fully convinced. Then I started offering intensive therapy sessions at my center. The sessions gave amazing results. Still, after a few years, I discontinued this 10-hours-a-week training model, because I realized that providing a nurturing environment to the child was the key to its success.

In simple terms, a 3-year-old child should get a similar environment like any other neurotypical child of his/her age. No child would sit and remain engaged in a therapy session for hours unless he feels that is the need of the hour. Therapy can be done in all those countless hours that a child spends at home with his parents or at the school. With support, engagement, and participation in daily life tasks and activities, you can easily turn those hours into therapy.

There are many kids who experience severe symptoms and almost always require help, I am not contradicting that fact. All I'm saying is, only therapy or no therapy is not helpful, a balance is essential. If therapy takes away the time of playing outdoors, interacting with relatives, meeting for festivals, going out as a family, or going on a vacation, the bank of episodic memories will be filled only with memories of therapy.

I feel we need to re-think whether the child is being provided with adequate opportunities or not. When I share my experiences, I am not regretting what I did in my initial years, neither was any of it wrong. I think I was doing my best and you as parents are trying to do your best to help your child.

Another important thing to remember while engaging in therapy sessions is, not to get stuck in teaching academic concepts of reading and writing. Remember, developing skills to help the child does not mean to help him 'fit' into the school system. A child needs time to learn skills pertaining to emotional regulation and impulse control and all this is developed in the context of the play. Here again, it is important to ensure that we are balancing the time spent on teaching academics (if the child is developmentally ready) and also giving enough opportunities to be in an unstructured but supervised set-up.

Recently, I had a 10-minute appointment with a parent, Radha, who expressed that her child Abheer has no motivation to sit and study or to interact with other kids. He just wants to be in his own shell. Radha is based in the USA. She has been trying various therapies for her kid ever since he was diagnosed with Autism. She felt stuck and wanted my help. I explained to her that I would require a lot more than just ten minutes to be able to help her with these issues.

I am in no way judging her or any other parent. My purpose is to help you reestablish a connection with your inner voice. In the process of trying to help the child, we get caught up in a web of therapies, jumping from one mode of therapy to another. Expecting some magic pill to help the child instantly.

I see that a lot of times. All that I do for those parents is, I ask them some questions. Questions to help them introspect and find their own answers. Believe me, usually, parents already know what is to be done. I have always found all the answers from the parents. They just need some time to introspect. Their gut feeling is always right.

I have worked with a lot of parents who have been told by the "experts" that their child will not improve and might not have a good future. As I have witnessed so, such callous advice ought to be ignored. Those strong-willed parents listened to their hearts and with optimism, indefatigable patience, inspiration, and unconditional love proved those "experts" wrong.

Often, it is the parent who needs to work on themselves. The parent mostly tends to project their own anxieties, fears, and insecurities on their child as behavioral issues. A parent, a caregiver, or any other person who the child spends the majority of his/her time with, is accountable for what the child learns.

Of all the environments, the one that most profoundly shapes the personality of a growing individual is the emotional atmosphere. This atmosphere is very strongly dependent on the kind of relationship that the child shares with other kids.

Margaret Mahler, a child psychiatrist, and researcher mentions for the newborn, "The parent is the principal representative of the world. To the infant and the toddler, the world reveals itself in the image of the parent: in eye contact, the intensity of glance, body language, tone of voice, and above all in the day to day joy or emotional fatigue, exhibited in the presence of the child."

Sometimes, it is not our children's behavior but our inability to tolerate their negative responses that create difficulties. We also need to work on ourselves so that the child does not "trigger" us into having a meltdown.

If we learn to anticipate the children's tantrums and negative emotions and are not threatened by them and do not react to them, the cycle of getting sucked into the zone of reacting can be broken. We can stay firm but loving and learn to gain victory not over the child's behavior problems but on our own anxiety, fear, and lack of self-control.

I have realized that there are three main pieces in helping and supporting our kids. One is taking care of the nature of the child, which would mean checking for the deficit and recognizing the skills that need to be worked upon.

Then comes nurture, that is, what is it that I want to reinforce/remove from the child's environment, from a behavioral perspective.

The third and most important piece is, as a parent/caregiver, what is it that I am contributing? Am I passing my fears, anxiety, and insecurities to the child? If yes, how can I become more mindful and remove those triggers from myself so that the child cannot trigger me into such a situation? Am I able to respond to my child, not from a place of desperation or urgency, but by accepting my child, the way he is?

When I say nature and talk about skills, I do not feel that they are only deficits. Most kids that I have worked with have inherent abilities to be their best, in at least one particular area. Tapping into this area motivates the child to excel and brings out the genius in them.

We all know about Temple Grandin, she was diagnosed with autism in 1947. Four years after Kanner published in the journal *Nervous Child, Autistic Disturbances of Affective Contact,* Kanner took the term "autism" and labeled eleven children in his study as having "infantile autism" in 1943.

When Temple Grandin was diagnosed with Autism, nobody knew much about it. It was a new diagnosis. The reason why Temple Grandin is doing so well today is her mother, who worked with her and ensured Temple stayed engaged for 20 to 40 hours a week. She did not believe in any particular therapeutic approach, she just made sure that her child was always engaged with some activity or the other.

The same principle applies even today. I do not mean that we should make the child's life very structured without giving them any time to do what they like. All I am trying to convey is, engagement and connection really matter.

I have interviewed and met hundreds of experts and thousands of parents in my 20 years of career as a therapist. I have come to realize that any expert - a behavior therapist, a developmental pediatrician, a neurologist, a child psychiatrist, or a special educator – would agree to the fact that children who received the diagnosis of being neurodiverse did amazingly well when they were connected and it a blend of nature and nurture along with the mindfulness of the parent/therapist works wonders.

The child has to be involved, this is the core aspect of any therapy. Some parents come to me saying their child is not improving. When I further quantify the time their child actually spends with them, it amounts to half an hour a day, which is too less. How can we expect any child to improve if we do not give them our quality time? The child spends hours and hours in therapy sitting across a table or engaging in physical activities, but there is no time for him to spare on his own, to just do what he wants to do. In this way, we are teaching the child to become a robot, which is not what our strength as human beings is.

It is very important to identify what our child's strength is and how and when to develop that strength.

Kristine Barnett's son, Jacob was diagnosed with autism when he was two-years-old. Doctors claimed that he would never speak and recommended special education programs and therapy. Then teachers told, there was no hope, but Kristine continued to follow her inner guidance. She used her home daycare facility's philosophy of nurturing the uniqueness of each child and child's natural passion for learning. It took time, but her son responded in miraculous ways. Instead of seeing the deficits highlighted by most people, she chose to focus on Jacob's strengths. Eventually, her son, Jacob, at the age of fifteen, was considered for a Nobel Prize in theoretical physics.

"He liked repetitive behaviors. He would play with glass and observe the light twisting in it for hours on end. Instead of taking it away, I would give him fifty glasses, fill them with water at different levels, and let him explore," Kristine says, "I surrounded him with whatever he loved." Jacob is now a student of theoretical physics at the Perimeter Institute in Ontario, Canada with an IQ measured to be higher than that of Einstein. Kristin shares her story in her book, *The Spark: A Mother's Story of Nurturing, Genius.*

I still remember working with a 4-year-old girl called Bhavna. I used to discuss the concerns with her parents in front of Bhavna, she would flap away and make odd faces and pace around. I thought she was doing this to self-stimulate, but I later realized how uncomfortable I made her feel by discussing her concerns in front of her mother. She was definitely unhappy and had no other way of expressing that to me. By the age of 7, she started speaking and I got my feedback from my greatest teacher. Slowly, her words turned into sentences, and then she could finally communicate to tell me, "Aunty, I was never happy. I did not like the way you spoke to my mom about my weaknesses. You never spoke about how well I drew, you never spoke about how well I wrote, you never spoke about how well I was trying to help myself. My efforts were never appreciated. I was just seen as someone with a disability. I really felt bad. I would really appreciate it if you never do so to anyone. It is okay for me now, but not okay for everybody else.

CHAPTER 6

CARRYING LIMITING BELIEFS FROM CHILDHOOD TO ADULTHOOD

"Trauma is not just personal. It is also historical and cultural and also trans-generational. We can't just help passing it on. If I carry trauma, I can be sure to pass it on to my kids unless I resolve it or work it out and to the extent that I resolve it, I won't pass it on and to the extent that I haven't resolved it, we do pass it on."

- Dr. Gabor Mate

When I was a little child, I remember how my dad expressed his anger by shouting and how my mom would get scared. I loved my parents immensely and I know they were doing the best out of what they knew at that time. They were stressed too because we were experiencing some financial issues. My memory of those days is still vivid. The anger, vigor, and subsequent upheaval of emotions made me so scared of it. Despite the fact that I hated anger, unconsciously I retained that there is nothing wrong with expressing anger with vigor and animation. I was young and wasn't really bothered by right or wrong, neither was I really aware of it, but I inherited it from my dad.

Thus, my anger brought with it a lot of yelling and that yelling was soon taken over by impulsivity. Somewhere I knew, it was not right, but I was following my father, someone whose advice and suggestions I had always sought. We do not choose how to respond in a stressful situation, our default response is that we learn from our parents and caregivers.

Anger or any such self-sabotaging behavior is a result of emotional pain. Our behavior is a mask for our "emotional baggage". Embrace this baggage and your shadowed self with compassion and self-love, to avoid its negative manifestations. Unfortunately, my dad didn't do so, also, he wasn't guided by

41

anyone to do the right thing. Having said that, the family atmosphere has a major impact on a child's brain development.

Then there were days where I realized that I was doing really well academically, scoring great marks. Whenever I would come back home and show my marks to my dad, I would get all the praise and appreciation and I felt great about myself. Somewhere, I started to relate good marks with a good sense of self-worth and self-image. I started competing with others, just to try and prove to myself that I was good. Not because I wanted anyone else to score lesser but just because I wanted that kind of appreciation from my dad, which I would get only when I was the best in my class. It is just a human and emotional need to be cared for and to be appreciated by our caregivers.

Here, I would like to share an example of a boy named Rushil. He had a diagnosis of a learning disability. He underwent my therapies for 3 years as a kid. He again came to me at the age of 18 for EFT (Emotional Freedom Techniques). He was experiencing difficulties in managing his space, time, relationships, etc. He was going through a lot and he believed that in order to get a normal life he needed a cocktail of medications. When I started working with him, we worked a lot on his primitive reflex integration (explained in future chapters). I also gave him exercises to help him organize his time and space and to engage him in physical activities. But it wasn't working for him, so I started to work on his emotional system instead; that's when I realized what a mess he was in.

His unpleasant childhood memories were still fresh and intact to cripple his self-worth. At that time, Rushil was in his 1st year of engineering college. He was doing fairly well for himself, except that, a few of his classmates bullied him saying he got admission not on his merit but for his learning disability. He was not included in any of the groups he wished to be a part of. He was very sad and depressed because everyone else had a girlfriend and he did not have one. He attributed it to his learning disability.

He told me, "Maybe that's how I am supposed to be."

In the EFT sessions, he mentioned that when he was in kindergarten and could not speak, he was accused of lifting a girl's skirt in the class, which he claimed was not true. Since that day, he was always labeled and so were his behaviors. His personality was termed disruptive, challenging, and with frequent meltdowns. The sad part is, at that young age, he started believing that he was unworthy of love and care. As he grew and started speaking, he had difficulties in academics as he wasn't able to cope well and hence, was given concessions in academics. His mom helped him to fight all that, standing by his side, but somewhere, her frustration also labeled him as being stubborn, useless, lazy, and disorganized.

I strongly believe, if you label a child, he/she will grow up to prove that true. As Dr. Bernie Siegel says "You are your child's hypnotherapist".

Rushil too, all through his schooling years, ended up believing what others thought of him. He never made any friends, was bullied and verbally abused by parents at home, and sometimes physically abused too. But now, he wants to mend his broken self-image to prosper in life. He wants to go abroad, to stay away from his parents and all those who have made his life miserable and start a new life, free from judgments, free from notions.

His story shook me deeply. I knew, to help him, I must change the environment around him. So, I decided to start with his parents. That was the first time I worked with any parent, to make them more mindful and more aware of their fears, beliefs, frustrations so that they don't pass it to their children. Rushil made me realize that I need to work with a person's mind, body, soul, and the environment too, to bring about healing.

Having worked with so many parents, I have realized that there are two kinds of parents. One, who overindulges, thinking, unlike them, their child must receive the best in the world. The child, of course, does not understand what is right or wrong at such a young age. The children start measuring their self-worth and co-regulating their behaviors on the basis of whatever the parent feels about them.

Getting too many things for your child thinking that would make him happy is the wrong way to show love. A child does not need a lot of things, but time and a connection with his parents.

I still remember meeting Rowan's parents. Rowan was a hyperactive 5-year-old, but a very intelligent and gifted boy. His reading and writing skills were advanced for his age. The parents were very proud of this fact but were also concerned that he was hyperactive, impulsive, and didn't follow his teacher's instructions. To help him out, they bought him a big screen TV and gave him access to as much screen he wanted. Of course, he only had access to educational programs but nonetheless, television is a passive way of input which also hampers our movement and locks our visual system.

Children benefit when the input is bidirectional. By this I mean, when a child says something he should get a response from the other end, like a conversation, with the sharing of ideas and views. Of course, television provides responses in the form of feedback, but children need that response from another human. We all have this immense need to share, care, and to feel cared for.

Hence, Rowan didn't improve at all. His dad thought, maybe a phone screen would help him, but that deteriorated things further. Moreover, both the parents were working and Rowan was with a nanny. The nanny was instructed to give him whatever he wants. Rowan's hyperactivity and impulsivity kept on increasing. On another end, his bank of academic knowledge and education grew immensely. There was an imbalance between the two levels that he exhibited. To fill this up, the parents bought a lot of educational toys for him. Then again, there was no one except the nanny to play with him because of which Rowan didn't learn sharing and taking turns. He wanted things his way. When they were unable to channel his hyperactivity and impulsivity any further, his parents brought him to me.

When we started working with Rowan, I asked them about his sensory diet and the time he spends amidst nature. They told me, he goes out to play for just 30 minutes per day. He certainly wasn't getting enough time to channel his physical energy. Also, there were no rules or consequences to his behavior. So, if he asked for something, he used to get it for sure. If the parents disagreed, he would throw a tantrum. Since the child was doing so well academically, the parents thought that they should give him whatever he wanted.

Rowan learned that throwing a tantrum was an easy way to get what he wants. That in fact stimulated and consolidated this behavior further. In addition to the hyperactivity and impulsivity, his parents had difficulties in managing his tantrums.

I started his therapy with his parents. Upon working on their emotional levels, I realized that the parents did not get all that they wanted as a child, so, to compensate, they ensured that no such thing ever happens to their kid. I knew I hit the raw nerve, their over-indulgence was the reason behind Rowan's inappropriate behavior patterns. We then worked upon Rowan's parents to make sure that he gets a good balance between indoor and outdoor activities. We also worked on integrating Rowan's primitive reflexes and also did sensory integration. Soon, his impulsivity and hyperactivity started settling down. Not just that, his parents became more aware of how to react or respond to his tantrums.

Reactivity comes when we mix our past conditioning to the present moment. When we respond to the present moment the way it is, we respond to the particular event only. I feel that it is important to integrate all the approaches, where the focus is on both the child as well as the parents. Parents must become more mindful to know whether they are responding from emotions or their intellect; whether they are mixing their past with the present of their child and how they are responding to the situations.

I also very strongly feel that kids do not need a lot of toys. They are very happy playing with the boxes, vessels, twigs, leaves, shells, and pebbles, as long as they are able to interact and get feedback from an adult, who can direct them and help them evolve and grow.

Kids are a mirror to what you put out into the world. Be conscious of your emotions and how your children might see them, feel them, absorb them, or take them on as their own.

CHAPTER 7

UNDERSTANDING OUR PATTERNS...

"Words are, of course, the most powerful drug used by mankind."

-Rudyard Kipling

I would like to share the story of a woman named Saumya. Her 5-year-old son was diagnosed with Autism. Her son was undergoing numerous therapies and sessions as he was still learning to speak. The diagnosis, therapies, and an autistic son- things were not that easy for Saumya, still, she always tried her best to remain calm and collected.

It is very difficult for all of us to stay in that mode. We are ought to slip back with ongoing judgments and notions coming from people around us. Thus, staying aware and conscious becomes all the more important. Saumya did exactly the same, whenever she felt the need to react, she made sure not to interact with her son. Thus, giving herself time to work on her emotions.

Not just that, she also made sure her son, Advait, gets a sufficient amount of outdoor time, playing with kids of his age. On the contrary, Advait was not very social. He didn't even acknowledge the presence of other kids around him. But she knew what she wanted. So she took a break from his school and went to her native place. She kept following the therapy program and also provided him the sensory diet activities of proprioception and vestibular inputs. Saumya's native place was a village and there, Advait was always surrounded by people as hers was a joint family. If we go back a few generations, we will see that kids were usually raised around a lot of people and most of us lived in joint families. But now because of various reasons, our families are shrinking. Being close to different people provides innumerable opportunities to learn social nuances. It also helps us to learn empathy. Thus, having a strong emotional network with our extended families or friends can make children more resilient.

Coming back to Saumya, She took Advait to the farm. She allowed him to walk in the soil. She ensured that he was around the other kids. She let the other kids tease him, she made Advait stay with his aunties and uncles and gave him an atmosphere to nourish and nurture his mind, body, and soul. She reduced his screen time considerably. Those 6 months of her son's school break, wasn't much of a concern for her, instead, she invested that time to connect him with people and nature.

I loved her statement when she said, **"Academics are a small little part of this big, big life. Academics are important to be in a mainstream school, so is to learn how to live in mainstream life."**

I loved that aspect of Saumya. I wish all the parents gain that insight to listen to their emotions. It is important to set our fears aside and understand what our child needs, to nurture their talent, strengths, and the spirit that they were born with.

I am not suggesting that we all should do what Saumya did. It is not possible for some of us to go and stay in a village, but we can meet up with friends and our extended families more often. We can ensure that the child gets the opportunity to be with people of different age groups. It is important that we actively work towards strengthening their emotional bonds and also provide them sensory and "social diets". Advait benefited from this approach and is improving at a fast pace.

We have to teach children to own their spirits and not be someone else. A lot of parents who come to me, want the so-called 'normal' tag for their kids, so as to make their kid live a 'normal life'. Talking about other important things with these parents is difficult and futile as they keep coming back to that same question, "Will he be fine? Will he be normal?"

I tell them, their child is absolutely fine at the moment, all that we need to do is just help him find himself. And to do so, we must find his strengths. Some of them do not like that reply, because all they want is... "normal". I on the contrary believe normal is a very relative concept. I also feel it's very important to accept the child and where he is. Just like "normal," Autism, ADD, ADHD, or any other special need is also a relative state. Having worked with thousands of kids in the last two decades, I haven't come across even a single neurodiverse kid who was exactly like the previous one, irrespective of their similar conditions. They all are unique and neurodiverse, and that's how they express themselves. I feel they're fine the way they are at the moment, while we work to enhance and evolve them and ourselves.

Let me share the story of another such parent, Supriya. When I first met her autistic son, he was just 2 1/2-year-old. The benefit of starting at such a young age is, we get a big window to work on the child and so, the improvement is fast. We gave him all that we could. The parents and grandparents did their best at home and they kept working with Adi. However, he could not improve at the level to which they desired, but they did not push him any further.

Not merely that, when they realized that regular schooling wasn't helping him learn and interact with other kids, they decided to opt him out. They realized that teaching him with self-help skills was more important. Today, Adi is 19-years-old. He is quite independent and also struggling a bit with academics, but his parents are absolutely okay with it. It takes a lot of time to come to this kind of acceptance. When we come into a space of acceptance, children feel loved and accepted for who they are. It's easier said than done, but I have seen many parents who are real-life examples of how it should be done. Believe me, when this happens, the children's behaviors and a lot of other issues start to settle down and they slowly become fast learners.

Many neurodiverse kids improve at a great pace. Regardless of their pace of learning, our aim should be to just lovingly embrace them wherever they are and to keep moving forward. But like everywhere else, here also the life comes in shades of grey. The greyscale here has another shade of parents, one's who always justify and believe that their child knows everything.

My motive here is not to judge anyone, but to help you identify these traits in you - if they exist - and make peace with them to help your child.

A 7-year-old girl, Kirti, who attended a regular school, visited us for therapy. She had been diagnosed with autism. She was unable to sit in one place. Her behavior ranged from moving and bumping around to even being clumsy at certain points of time. So, at school, she often bumped into the desks or accidentally hurt other kids with her maladroitness. Because of this, kids often complained about her to their teachers.

So, when I met Kirti's parents to discuss her issues, they were in complete denial. They said, "No, Kirti has no problem sitting for longer duration. She always listens to us. She never moves around clumsily. I think the school is just trying to make up excuses, they don't want my child to be there."

I tried to get them through and discuss it further, but their response didn't change. There is a difference between accepting your child and denying their issues. Acceptance should always be preceded by awareness- being aware of your child's shortfalls. Kirti's case is a perfect example of how parents take their child's shortfall as a personal attack. Kids come with their own spirits and even when they're doing what they are supposed to do, we must help them out, to help them get better. Also, we must stop criticizing ourselves for being responsible for their undesirable behaviors.

I met another parent who came to me for his son Arjit. Arjit was a lovely five-year-old child who was diagnosed with ADHD. Now, this case was at the other extreme, where the parent felt that the child was not listening to what he had been asked. When I examined Arjit, to my surprise, my findings were exactly the opposite of what I have been told about him. Arjit always followed instructions and was an amazing, beautiful child with good abilities. His parents were oblivious of his qualities as their senses were seized with super expectations.

On one hand, you have parents denying or hiding their child's deficits and on the other, you have parents denying their child's abilities. What we want here is a balance of perspectives, keeping your feelings, emotions, and judgments at the bay.

This greyscale of parents has another set, ones who do not like to give opportunities to their children. I would like to give an example of a boy named Tuhin. He was nine-year-old and he had a diagnosis of PDD NOS. His parents were concerned with his lack of self-help skills. Tuhin wasn't independent enough for his age, he needed someone for dressing, feeding, bathing, and even using a toilet. His parents told me that a maid was taking care of Tuhin, all the time. Whenever Tuhin was asked to do something on his own, he threw a tantrum. According to Tuhin's parents, he had poor motor skills, poor motivation, poor motor planning, and many such "labels". When I evaluated the child, I did not see any significant challenges. His motor skills and balancing was fine. His motor planning was also very good because he was undergoing therapy for it for a few years. His skills were developed, just that, he was not given opportunities to participate in those simple tasks.

The parents were afraid of Tuhin's tantrums for which they avoided any tantrum whatsoever.

I asked them, "What if he throws a tantrum and is not given food, he would be very hungry, but then, he would eat on his own." But they said, "We never let that situation arise." It reached a point where this boy would not take a bath and he would come out without any clothes because he realized that my dad, mom, or maids would do so for him. Tuhin never learned that there is something called private behavior that nobody is allowed to touch his private parts. Not just that, to my surprise, I found out, he was coping very well with the academics because his entire time was just diverged towards that particular skill.

I feel it's important to have a balance between self-help skills and academics. Even in the school, there was a help, who would take him and wash him if in case he pooped. His parents made a big mistake by not teaching him the importance of being independent. As a result of this, Tuhin learned that cleaning his own body was an inferior skill, all he was focused on was his studies. Hence, it is the duty of every parent to first provide self-help opportunities to their kids, as they are more important than any other skill.

Surrendering to your child's tantrums gives them an easy escape from tasks they ought to be doing. I feel your preferences about what skills to master should be clearly mentioned to your child.

There was this child called Amito. He was an eight-year-old boy with a diagnosis of autism. His parents were concerned because he always needed instructions to do simple tasks. According to his parents, he never did anything all by himself. So, when I asked them if there were situations when they did not instruct him. The parent told me, they never waited to observe what happens when an instruction is not given. Again, if parents will keep giving instructions and constantly expect the child to follow them then how would they even assess or know whether the child can do things by himself or not?

In the case of Amito and Tuhin, their parents believed that their children were incapable of doing certain things on their own. Also, in both these cases, the parents' stress came out in the form of blaming, shouting, and criticizing their kids.

Let's talk about another variation of parenting here. A wonderful 9-year-old boy, Joel had ODD & LD. Whenever his mother, Reesha, came to me for assessment, I remember her saying the same thing, "I hope I had something better to tell, but there's absolutely no progress in my son. He is just the same. I don't think my child will do anything in his life. He is a difficult child. I feel so depressed and sad. You know, I was even hospitalized for this. I don't think my son will ever do well in his life."

My effort to discuss anything was thwarted as she displayed her victim card and blamed her son. When I talked to Joel's therapist and other members of his family, they all were coherent with the fact that he is improving. Everyone else was appreciating his progress, however so, but his mother was busy blaming, criticizing, and shouting at her child. Alas, more than Joel, his mother needed help for her depression.

The reason I'm sharing this is, don't see behaviors as just a sensory problem, there is a lot more to it. The sensory strategies - that I will be describing in the next chapter - are important, but it is also important to understand how we work on ourselves as parents. Start noticing the differences, start observing the little things your child is doing. Above all, stop victimizing yourself, stop being judgmental. All your child needs is your unconditional love and support, trust me, it is an important part of the therapy to manage even the most challenging behaviors I have ever come across.

The scale of parenting is vivid and its variations move through various shades of aspects. There is another set of parents who are very controlling- the ones who control everything that their child. This way of micro-managing a child is referred to as "helicopter parenting". Such parents are constantly on their child's head. As a result of which, children learn to ignore and not respond to their parents' comments.

There are some kids that I have come across, who are over-medicated from a very young age. Again, I would like to emphasize that everyone is doing their best with resources that they have, but most of the kids who are diagnosed with Autism are too little to know and discern what they are being subjected to.

I am not against medications but I feel that it should be the last resort. I have in fact suggested a lot of parents to consider medications, because sometimes it gets necessary.

But it should never precede parental awareness, mindfulness, and their efforts to implement the ideal ways of therapy in their child's routine life. Only when these efforts are implemented and you are still not getting results then medications come into the picture. Medications help children to stay alert and learn from the environment which is the main focus of everything. On the contrary, over medication from an early age makes children lose their spirits.

So is the case with micro-managing the kids. One of my relatives who often visits us is an expert at commenting on kids at whatever they do. Like, if my son touches the drawer he asks him not to do so, if he jumps down the sofa or table he asks him not to jump that way or he might get hurt, thus he manages to contradict my son on whatever he does. Whenever he is around, there is a constant flood of instructions for my son and not to mention, during those few days, my son is at his worst. Annoyed with his unfading criticism, my son makes sure he does exactly the opposite of what he has been told. I think such would be our reaction if subjected to such criticism. I am not doubting my relative's intentions, but he must understand that a child too needs his space.

I see this happening with most of the parents who come with their kids for therapy. Sometimes we lose touch with our inner self and forget why we want our child to go for therapy. So when a child comes to me and sits on a chair or swing, the parent would say, "Sit properly, hold the rope, move in the front or see what aunty is doing." Such constant instructions keep coming. I am definitely not against instructing a child, but I am certainly in favor of parallel talking (talking on behalf of the child or speaking for their feelings or needs as parents know and can guess what the child really wants).

Too many instructions usually overwhelm a child to the point that they soon turn rebellious. Hence before delivering your instructions, think, if it is really necessary.

Some kids who come to me are quite independent. They can open the door, dress themselves up, and are very adroit. Still, their parents give them prompts like, "Wear your shoes, now put the right foot in, put the Velcro on, now pull up the strap," "Now open the door, pull it hard, use both your hands, go out. Okay, wait there!"

Kids get really irritated when they are instructed for things they already know how to do. They do not like it at all. This is one aspect where parents need to become really mindful of when and how to communicate with their kids.

Just because some kids have special needs that do not mean they should follow your instruction. Somewhere we project our fears on our kids. I think it's our responsibility to be aware of our fears and provide that much-needed space to our child. If the child is not given an opportunity to do things on his own then how can you expect him to learn?

As kids, when we were taught alphabets and numbers, we were given time and liberty to learn that our way. Nobody ever prompted us. Getting to learn things on our own gives us a feeling that we are good enough to master our surroundings and hence, to feel confident. Therefore, I suggest, please be careful while instructing a child.

However, some kids need instructions, there I suggest giving indirect instructions. For example, if a child has forgotten what he came for and he is just standing in front of the shoe rack and not wearing his shoes, then I would suggest you give him time and if you feel he has forgotten – you can prompt – "What do you have to do?" Instead of 'wear your shoes". Instructing a child immediately without letting him come back to the task would not help the child learn it. Doing so often makes a child question his skills.

Therapies help a child to implement self-regulation, but depriving them of opportunities would hamper their efforts of mastering skills.

Is it our need or is it the child's need? Is it our anxiety that we are pushing on our child?

All we need is clarity, mindfulness, and care. Learn to isolate the present moment from your past or future. Learn to just live and be physically, mentally, and emotionally present at the moment itself.

In the last 20 years, I have realized, it's easy to work with children, but it is very difficult to work with adults. Adults are defensive and they are full of reasons and judgments. Adults have emotional armors around them to cover them up when they feel vulnerable.

I remember conducting group sessions with kids. Every single child in those sessions managed to open up. Most of the kids in these groups were neurodiverse, even so, they were in touch with their feelings. They embraced their feelings and I loved the way they were pure and so open to opinions and changes. Their barriers were few and they had no emotional armors at all. And since they were ready to transform, that transformation came to them with a snap. Those little kids haven't yet made their identities, their souls weren't guarded by their egos. So, they were thrilled and free, free from beliefs, and free to change. All they needed to be taught was to honor their feelings and download the messages that their feelings have been trying to deliver. Also, not to cover their feelings and emotions and never to mask who they really are.

A girl named Raina comes to my mind. She's an amazing nine-year-old girl autistic girl. She only does need-based communications. She is so transparent; whatever she feels, she conveys through colors. When she's very sad or upset, she only picks up dark colors like black or dark-blue for coloring. When she is happy, she picks up bright colors like red and yellow. I love the way kids are so open. It's just us adults who need to understand what they want to convey to us.

I just pray and hope kids to become the truest expression of their inner essence, so they don't have to deal with emotional baggage. For our kids to do so, we must implement that in our lives.

Here, I would like to share the story of the coffee in the cup. I'm sure you all must have read that story. It goes like, "I have a cup of coffee in my hand, which is filled to the brim. Somebody pushed me and the coffee spilled." Now, the question is, why the coffee spilled? I'm sure most of us would say, "It is because somebody pushed." The answer in fact is, the coffee spilled because there was coffee in the cup. If it were lemon juice then that would have got spilled.

This little story very beautifully explains that if I'm angry with my child, then that anger is within me, it didn't come from anywhere else. If I'm okay with my child spilling something, it means I'm okay with myself. How I react to what my child does depends on how I feel at that point.

Just PAUSE for a moment and BREATHE... Give yourself permission to transform into your greatest expression. You deserve it. It's your and your child's birth-right to shine. Your child learns from you.

CHAPTER 8

EMOTIONAL TRAUMA AND CO-REGULATION...

Before self-regulation comes co-regulation. Let's connect instead of punish.

-Suzanne Tucker

Every emotion and thought that you take to your heart gets precipitated into chemical reactions to alter the biochemistry of your body. Even when I write an intense emotion or read one, those negative emotions are capable of causing physiological changes in our bodies. Emotional stress causes the release of cortisol and adrenaline from the adrenal glands which in turn causes constriction of abdominal blood vessels. On the other hand, blood circulation increases in the legs in response to the fight and escape scenario. Our amygdala (emotional center in the brain) starts making a noise like an alarm. The digestion stops, the heart starts to beat faster and many such cascade effects happen JUST with negative emotional stimuli. This happens all the time, just that we stay UNAWARE of it.

When I enrolled in the Emotional Freedom Technique class to become a practitioner, we conducted a lot of sessions on each other. That was done to teach us different techniques to help us identify our behaviors or the problems we wanted to work upon. I was really surprised to learn that every exercise they introduced us to uncover the deep-rooted issues that I had with my mother. Issues that I was myself unaware of, as per me, I had a great relationship with my mom. I was unaware that within those layers of love that I hold for my mom, there were many emotional wounds.

It was not my mom's fault, she was born and raised in an era where every mother wished to raise a baby boy, but I was that unwanted girl child because of who my mom was cursed for. Even while I was protected from the outside world in her womb, I picked those curses. So all through my childhood, I was stabbed with labels. I was young enough to understand the harsh words used against me, it was my mother's feelings that translated those emotions to me. As a result, my emotional radars turned sensitive enough to pick those feelings and internalize them.

We all have two types of memory: explicit or recall memory and implicit memory. Recall memory is the one we can recall like what we ate, whom we spoke to, etc. The part of our brain that remembers explicit memory that encodes this memory develops by the second or the third year of our life. So, we do not remember how we crawled, or we started walking or where we were born and so on. Our brain is not ready to recall those memories before the age of 2. Implicit memory, on the other hand, is the emotional memory of what happened to us before that age, but it is not available for recall. So, the emotional experiences are imprinted in our brains but we cannot recall what caused those impressions. I definitely could not recall what happened with my mom but my body had the emotional memory of those events.

As a result of her frustration, I internalized her pain and suffering and considered myself responsible for her woes. "I am not good enough and being a girl is not a great thing," is what I started believing. In an act to protect my wounded inner child, I turned stubborn and rebellious.

When a parent is emotionally unavailable for whatever reason, the child feels abandoned, rejected, and unloved. This gets embedded in their unconscious implicit memory and the feeling of abandonment shadows their future relationships.

You must be wondering why I am sharing this here.

This is to emphasize the point that children share deepest relationships with their parents and the effect of these relationships stays with the child forever. Dr. Gabor Mate, a Canadian physician who has a background in family practice and a special interest in childhood development and trauma, and in their potential lifelong impacts on physical and mental health conditions talks about trauma. He says that we see trauma as a physical trauma always- like sexual abuse, tsunami, war, physical abuse or death of a loved one. Society has never considered what emotional trauma can do to people.

Trauma comes from the Greek word "wound" and trauma is an unhealed wound. We protect our wounds and constrict around them. While these protections help us in a way, they also constrict us and limit us in the long run. We develop self-limiting physical behaviors, mental patterns, beliefs, and emotional dynamics. Trauma is a limitation of self and disconnection from the self. Just like scar tissue is hard, lacks feelings and growth, trauma is similar to an unhealed wound. Trauma constricts you in your capacity to respond to the world.

In the same way, if such psychic wounds are inflicted upon a child, it results in them harboring fear and acting accordingly. Children act against those fears by being aggressive, non-compliant, or by shutting down and going into their zones.

As the child grows up, he will know that he is good, capable, and worthy of being loved, all thanks to his explicit memory. But the implicit memory which is available in the child's brain right from or even before birth holds the emotional memory of experiences. This implicit memory stores new emotional memories all the time to influence how we think and act. We always make new strategies to deal with situations as we mature, but the implicit memory of childhood is like a default program. This default program opens up every time a child feels stressed. We keep reverting to the early pattern automatically without a conscious choice and without even being aware of its occurrence.

So we grow up as adults who are not in control, connection, or communication with their inner feelings. When we disconnect with our inner feelings just to fit in the environment or just to be accepted, we unconsciously suppress those feelings only to uncover their bigger versions later.

I am sharing this because if we understand the power of what our relationship does to the child then we will stop setting unrealistic or too many expectations from a child. When I say all of this, I am in no way trying to justify a child's non-compliant or aggressive behavior.

We can be firm while still being grounded. When the parents get angry or when the child sees a sudden shift in their parent's tone - from being supportive to hostile- then the child feels threatened, unsafe, and he anticipates punishment. The child gets engulfed with fear and does not have access to the logical centers in his brain to understand how to deal with such a situation. All that he needs at that time is emotional support. When parents put "relationship" first and "behavior goals" later, a child learns that his parents care for his well-being and that is what gets stored in the implicit memory.

What I am only trying to say is, it is important to understand what is precipitating such feelings or behaviors. Understanding the reasons behind it helps us become more mindful and to take appropriate actions.

We all want to feel connected and accepted. Not getting opportunities to express ourselves and with constant labels being imposed on us, after a certain time, we start believing in what others think of us. In my case, I started believing everything that my mom told me. She told me, I was bad, stubborn, non-compliant, and a difficult child; I believed her as I did not have the access to my feelings. I suppressed myself for the sake of fitting in and that is something that every child goes through.

If parents are disconnected from their own feelings, how will you expect them to tolerate their child's expressions? They see that as a trigger because their own psychic wounds are still intact.

I thus see kids as teachers who come to us as healers and spiritual gurus to heal the psychic wounds we have been harboring since ages.

Most often, it is not the child's behavior that triggers us or makes us feel uncomfortable, it is our inability to tolerate their negative responses. It is our job to fix that fault within us.

There is a lot of research coming out now, where they say warmth is needed and the best warmth you get is through human relationships. To feel that warmth a lot of connection and communication are needed. The Internet is cold; there is nothing there but only information.

What kids need from us is that constant connection. It is important to know that a calm mind is required to instill calm.

We need to know that children are constantly co-regulating. They are like sponges, constantly picking up on our vibrations. So the message here again is to consciously come out of our triggers.

When we see our kids having a tantrum or a meltdown, it's our responsibility to select where we come from, from a place of reacting or from a place of understanding?

Are we living in the present moment or in the present moment triggering us out of our past to react?

And you know what, just as the negative words, positive words too have the power to affect our physiology. They help to activate the parasympathetic nervous system to order the body to "rest and digest". As a result of which, our heart rate and blood pressure go down. Appreciation, non-judgment, and unconditional love helps us to relax and use the bonding chemical oxytocin which helps us to bond socially.

Words have the power to bring about chemical changes in our bodies, tissues, organs, and cells...

CHAPTER 9

CONNECTING WITH NATURE AND PLAY...

"Let the children be free; encourage them; let them run outside when it is raining; let them remove their shoes when they find a puddle of water; and when the grass of the meadows is wet with dew, let them run on it and trample it with their bare feet; let them rest peacefully when a tree invites them to sleep beneath its shade; let them shout and laugh when the sun wakes them in the morning."

- Maria Montessori

Kids need to play in natural surroundings with emotionally available adults. Outdoor play is often underrated and is all the more important during preschool age. It is important to introduce different playing opportunities into your kid's schedule. More physically unstructured time is essential to give way to their creative expressions.

It is easy for kids to play, but for kids with sensory processing challenges, playing does not come easily. Their parents feel that the child is not interested in play.

Kids with motor planning difficulties have trouble in planning new games and so, they stick to familiar games and tasks. Many other kids get overwhelmed and anxious with difficulties in modulating vestibular inputs and also because of poor postural responses. Many kids who have tactile issues and challenges avoid being with other kids for the fear of being touched unpredictably. Many kids are keen to play but are embarrassed by their clumsiness. Many other kids cannot organize their play effectively, which is more of a behavior issue. Many times, kids cover their ears at the sight of other kids playing. Hence, kids deal with a lot and the best we can do is empathize and understand them to help them come out of their challenges.

Most parents guide their kids on how and what to play. Play is an expression of a child's inner drive towards fulfillment. It is important that the child "actively" participates and explores the environment rather than being prompted for the same.

I have elaborated on this concept in the chapters covering sensory integration. A child needs to follow his inner drive and participate in physical activities to master his environment and body. Through play, a child gets sensory inputs that are essential for motor and emotional development. Sensory inputs help a child immensely and that is one of the reasons why play is an essential part of a child's development.

The more a child plays, the more his senses are stimulated and the more control he develops over his environment. Play helps a child to feel competent and capable. This way, he also learns to relate his body to space he is in.

Emotional availability is even more important for the child to feel safe while playing. It's ok if the child bumps, falls, or gets hurt; these are ways to learn, develop, and gain more control of the body and the environment. Coming from a place of calm, we can offer our much needed emotional support to the child whenever they get hurt and are sad. Allow the child to process the emotions rather than trying to calm them down prematurely.

If we are calm, the child feels its okay to fall and he focuses to try again. If we are concerned, he picks up the signal that falling is risky and unsafe and develops reluctance to try that activity again. These are small and simple steps but are significant enough to shape the personality and attitudes of your child. Your reactions to such situations help them to either master the environment or to create setbacks in their minds.

Our presence should motivate them to try things on their own. They shouldn't keep looking at us about what needs to be done next. If the child is pushed to play and he is not playing with his inner drive, the opportunities to learn and master the environment are lost. Your feedback matters a lot. Creating the right challenge is important to ensure we do not push the child to do things that he cannot do. Help the child to sandwich difficult activities between the easier ones.

A thing that needs to be considered is, sometimes kids want to play with toys or do tasks that may seem too simple and easy to us as parents. But participating in such tasks helps them to feel more confident about their abilities.

Be aware of the fact that the challenges of sensory processing coupled with other diagnosed difficulties that the child has, may result in non-uniformity in the child's performances. Which means, some days might be better than the others. Your patience, calmness, and compassion are important for your child to believe in himself and his abilities. Your child doesn't have to reach somewhere, it isn't important for him to climb that monkey bar, but it is important for him to enjoy himself while he participates in such challenging activities. These opportunities and activities are like "building blocks" for your child's brain and overall development and hence, are important.

Most parents get trampolines and therapy balls to create a therapy center at home. This is a nice effort, but it cannot dominate the benefits of playing outdoors. There is no denying the fact that physical activities like jumping on a trampoline help to lessen hyperactivity. But the volcanic amount of pent up kinetic energy finds its greatest expression and channelization in the context of playing outdoors. Kids are wired to play!

As mentioned earlier, it is most important to focus more on your child's efforts than to seek results.

Another point that needs to be emphasized is, be vigilant regarding the safety of your child. Sensory processing issues make some kids accident-prone. Children may be overcautious while playing if they know they are unable to manage their environment. Some kids are clumsy and keep bumping around, they need more care while handling. Kids with tactile issues might react strongly to even smaller cuts or bruises while some kids might easily ignore bigger cuts and wounds. Hence, monitoring kids' safety is important.

Children need to be taught that the human body is resilient enough to heal such wounds. Once they know and understand the capacity of their bodies to heal on their own, their reaction towards injuries would be subdued.

Nowadays, kids as young as 3 years of age attend school not just that, they are also expected to develop sitting tolerance from that young age. We must understand that even a healthy and normally developing 5-year-old child will have an attention span of just around nine minutes. Sitting idle is against their nature, they are meant to move, explore, and learn. Disciplining these little ones and telling them not to be fidgety or move is not just futile, but also wrong.

It is important to have a lot of moving opportunities in school so that kids can get ready to pay attention again. When their tired bodies need movement and they do not get it, they slouch and lean. When kids can no longer pay attention, they turn fidgety but are asked to sit straight and focus. Kids need movement! Their bodies need constant and frequent breaks from sitting, but if they do so, they are labeled uncooperative and daydreamers.

The human brain develops at a faster rate during infancy. To develop their brains, kids need to move and explore. Exposing them to screens at a young age restricts their movement. Exposure to smartphones and the various learning apps is detrimental to a child's language development, says a study done by Frederick Zimmerman at the University of Washington. Playing and moving in the presence of emotionally nurturing adults helps their brains to grow and learn better.

Let us understand what the stages of play are:

Early social play: This kind of play which is mostly initiated by adults in the form of silly sounds like peek-a-boo. Through such plays, infants - as young as 6-weeks-old - start learning and setting the base for language development. Infants learn to pay attention, understand the use of language, and learn to read the intentions of their caregivers. There is a lot of base being set in these plays for future development.

Exploratory play: Children learn to explore the environment through the sensorimotor play of banging, mouthing, throwing, smelling, and feeling their toys and surroundings. These little scientists-in-the-making need inquisitiveness and intrinsic motivation to sustain their fun-filled exploration. They are developing a large repertoire of sensory experiences and are also laying foundations for body schemes which will be needed for motor planning or praxis. This and a lot more learning happens from 6 to 15 months of age.

Constructive play: Children learn about cause and effect, simple fixing, pulling, and stacking from around 12 months of age. In doing so, they train their postural muscles, attention skills, and also gross and fine motor skills. They learn to effectively use their bodies while playing. Their plays soon become more goal-oriented. They learn to expect results from making a tower of cups or blocks or stacking rings. Their little brains also develop social connections of getting praised for their attempts. A lot of language development also happens during this phase.

Pretend play: This kind of play starts as early as one year of age. For example, an infant holding a remote to his ear and pretending to talk on the phone or he is trying to eat from an empty bowl with a spoon or drink from an empty cup. First words emerge with pretend play, where they learn the names of objects that they play with. When a sequence of play is done, they learn to understand two-word sentences and even understand "first-then" relationships.

Parallel play: Children play next to each other and not with each other. They learn by observing their peers. A lot of imitation skills develop at this stage. Their basic level of pretend play is expanded and extended by observing other kids. Their language skills also expand and they learn to coordinate their actions with other kids. They also learn to manage their stuff and toys.

Socio-dramatic play: This play emerges at around 30 months of age. Simple plays like doctor-doctor, fireman, lift man, or assuming the role of parents or whatever environments that they are exposed to. So, these kinds of plays develop language skills. Kids also learn to read and understand other children's interest in their activities and games. They start developing preferences for those who listen to understand them. Interpersonal relationships start developing by now and the whole big world of social development now opens for them to learn and explore. They learn to incorporate their friends' ideas in their plays and thus learn what to and what not to imitate. They also learn to express their fears; adults help them to understand how to express and manage fears and anxieties. They also get to learn the critical skill of self-regulation. They learn to manage their own toys and maneuver within space, without wandering around too much. They also learn to organize their behaviors through self-regulation.

Games: This starts from 48 months of age to then stay with us throughout our lives. Here is where the abstract language starts to develop. Games such as hide and seek and stone, paper scissors start coming in. Reading storybooks and fairy tales helps kids to create and experience emotions. Some children love to tell stories that have been mixed with their imagination over and over again.

I have spoken about the defiant stage or the assertive age in the future chapters. But it is important to note that all kids pass through this stage by the age of 2. They start expressing their individuality and learn to say "no" most of the time. However, if a child has a sensory processing challenge, unintegrated primitive reflexes, severe motor handicaps, or autism, they do not pass through this stage and remain in symbiosis with their parents. Such kids display extreme shyness and a lifelong inability to assert themselves. They may lack curiosity about the world and will disturb the play of other children as they have difficulty understanding social nuances. They may lack emotional responsiveness or be impulsive and may exhibit bouts of depression or anger.

Play trains us to become more flexible and resilient. Play is actually the preparation for life. Lack of play combined with retained primitive reflexes is resulting in more and more children with anxiousness, depression, and suicidal tendencies. Such kids are not creative and have rigid behaviors. They see mistakes as the end of the world. There is no negotiation, no sharing, and no flexibility in their personalities which is often coupled with a low sense of self. If there is a lot of structured play and kids are over scheduled, we are unknowingly robbing them of their opportunities to play. Childhood is becoming stressed because adults are tightening their control over childhood. An adult's role is to allow the child to play and support the child's expression through the play. Sadly, in the present age, we are controlling the way a child should play and also with what he should play.

Most parents tell me that their child is "JUST" playing all day. I feel amazed because as per them, their kids must become mini-adults to sit in one place and to learn. Also, we often overlook a child's preferences on what they want to learn and play, instead, we impose them with our liking and preferences. Peter O Grey in his book Free to Learn: *Why Unleashing the Instinct to Play Will Make Our Children Happier, More Self-Reliant, and Better Students for Life* says, "We have forgotten that children are designed by nature to learn through self-directed play and exploration, and so, more and more, we deprive them of freedom to learn, subjecting them instead to the tedious and painfully slow learning methods devised by those who run the schools."

Opportunities to play and self-educate require a lot of unscheduled time and the freedom to choose what the kid wants to do. The child needs time to make friends, maintain friendships, make mistakes, and learn from them. They need time to get bored and develop their passions. ***Play is an important area and providing opportunities for unstructured time and outdoor playtime is the responsibility of the authority figures in the child's life.*** Children learn skills by playing and just as we allow them to develop motor milestones of crawling, kneeling, standing, and walking, we must allow them to play and unfold their tremendous learning potential.

Naturally, kids are meant to push their boundaries. They jump from various heights and learn to climb to constantly explore their potential. They learn to reach places they could not. It fuels their "curiosity" and drives learning for a lifetime. The scope and vividness of their imaginations and creativity are astounding. Remember the story of Jacob's mother and how he was allowed to play the way he wanted to by his mom, Kristine. Such unrestricted and natural playing exercises develop skills that are beyond anyone's imagination. Parents must allow their children to play and not see them as projects with deadlines.

You might have noticed that children often talk to themselves or repeat instructions. By the age of six or seven, our inner voice develops to make us capable of thinking, then the self-talk and repetitions appear to fade. That is the reason why a five-year-old talks continuously, because they have not yet learned to process information in their minds.

Our lifestyle has changed and we live in small tiny compartments with constant access to screens. Our technology is evolving at a much faster pace making it tough for our physiology to adapt to those changes. So, just as we need sleep hygiene, we need to develop screen hygiene for ourselves and our kids. Our brain reflects the world in which we grow and, nowadays, our kids are having "relationship deficiency". Humans love being around other humans, most of us do. We need rich social stimulation from people of various age groups.

Dr. Gordon Neufeld says, "All the attachment instincts are to arrange us in a way to either care for or to be taken care of. It will evoke a set of alpha instincts in one and a set of dependent instincts in the other. Ideally, it will be reciprocated and any one given time, one takes care of the other but over time both take care of each other so that there is a lead, dance, and a follow. And the outcome is equality which develops when the natural dance has been practiced enough."

This is lacking these days, we need to get that stimulation to stimulate the parts of our brains that are involved in forming and maintaining healthy relationships. We cannot teach our kids to care and share until we introduce them to socially enriched environments where they feel safe to enjoy and play.

We need to plant the seeds for a resilient brain in their childhood so that they can emerge as resilient adults. It is our responsibility and all that we need to do is, ALLOW THEM TO PLAY!

CHAPTER 10

PROMPTING OUR CHILDREN

A 5-year-old boy with a diagnosis of Autism, Nihal, visited my office with his parents and grandparents for follow-up evaluation. The last I saw him - almost 2 months back - his disinterest was clear and constant throughout the session, but this time his eyes chimed as he wished me good morning. Curious to learn what has changed, I started talking to him. As I spoke to him, he kept answering my questions, without any eye contact. He was constantly moving from one end of the room to the other, his fingers constantly fidgeted the blinds and the toys around. He was all over the place. He appeared to be not paying attention, but the more he moved around the more it became easier for him to answer my questions.

His parents tried to redirect him by asking him to sit at one place and focus, something which really slowed down his processing ability. I feel it is important to allow children to process things their way. I don't mean that we shouldn't teach the child to sit at one place and maintain eye contact, but if doing so affects the child, it is a good idea to let him do what he wants.

It isn't mandatory to focus if the child can respond accurately. Many times, asking a child to focus stresses him out. The sensory overload overwhelms their senses and pushes them into fight-flight or freeze mode. In such a state, repetitive behavior may seem like an attempt to soothe the stress, manage the overload, and reduce the exposure to more such stimuli.

Hence, think of how to facilitate your child to answer better, it wouldn't matter if he moves around or is sitting and is still.

It is very easy for me to comment on this as a therapist, but when I see my son move around or be fidgety at home, my first response is to advise him not to do so. This default response is so strongly ingrained in my system, the more I do it, the more I realize I am pushing my son to do something that he is uncomfortable with. I later realized that the more he sat still, the more distracted he became and lost his motivation to study.

As a therapist, all of this is easy to say but as a parent it is really difficult to follow. But believe me, the day I allowed my son to move around, fidget, walk around or do whatever he needs to enhance his processing, his motivation to learn went up. I love this blended experience everyday where half of my day is spent with kids, working as a therapist and the other half at home, as a parent. The latter aspect helps me to actually understand and implement my strategies as a parent. I see my son giving me ample opportunities in a day, to learn how to be a parent and how to give lesser instructions in the lab of parenting.

So, coming back to Nihal, at the end of the follow-up, his grandparents asked me if they can do anything at home to help him improve faster. One of the important things that parents do not take into consideration is that they keep instructing their child. I do the same with my son and I constantly need to remind myself that I don't need to instruct him so much.

If the verbal prompts that we usually bombard our kids with are reduced, we give our kids the opportunity to do things on their own and the way they want.

What I do is, after instructing my son, I count till 30 and wait. Waiting is something that we need to learn as parents, it is difficult, but important. When we go on and on with our instructions, the child bears a verbal overload. When so much information is being given at once, children get confused.

As a parent, I feel it is important to ascertain who is instructing the child and how. By "who" I do not mean the child's mother, grandparents, or anyone else, but the state of our minds at that time. When a child does not follow instructions, instead of giving them time, parents and grandparents choose to prompt further instructions, pushing the child as well as themselves into a mode of anxiety. This anxiety forms the roots of future fears that if he does not listen then things might get worse. An anxious parent is similar to a child having tantrums or the one lacking self-regulation. Anxiety brings with it rage, impulsiveness, and even helplessness. This kind of approach as well as our anxiety is picked up by the child propelling them more into non-compliance. Their non-compliance further fuels our anxiety and thus goes the vicious cycle.

What if we just stay in the "present" moment, "self-regulate" ourselves, and give our kids "time" to respond?

Another point to remember, we need to teach new skills to our children, but once they learn that skill then it's time for us to learn to wait. Allow the child to process and follow through on a particular task, rather than repeatedly bombarding them with information. **Constant prompting robs the opportunity and satisfaction of doing things on our own.**

As a child moves ahead of the learning curve for a particular skill, it's time for his parents to move ahead too. Getting stuck in the same pattern with repeated prompting and breaking each step of your child would hamper their abilities to do things independently. Therefore, it is advisable to give kids the time they require and if instructions are still needed, let them be the indirect ones.

For example, if the child looks at the blocks, ask him to do whatever he plans with the blocks. He might just fix them, make a tower or copy your patterns, it is entirely up to him. Only if you feel that he is stuck or if he asks for your help then you intervene.

When parents go back home, I see them saying things like, "Okay, now get your shoes. Put the right foot in first. Say bye to aunty. Open the door," and so on. As I mentioned, their life is full of instructions. If a child is already independent in wearing his shoes, I would probably tell him something like, "Okay, it is time to go home, what shall we do next?" That's an indirect way of prompting a child.

So, there are two main things that you can do: do not bombard the child with instructions and wait for the child to respond.

Many parents argue with me and say that their children do understand what they are asked, but still take time to follow through.

Just as we take time to do certain things, kids need time to complete what they are already doing and then follow subsequent instructions. Grace time can be easily provided sometimes. A child is not a robot and wouldn't always follow everything that he has been told; maybe, he needs time or has another thing in mind to be completed before pursuing a new one or maybe, he does not want to do it immediately.

So we need to sit down and ask the child about his preferences and to do so, we must be aware of how we speak to the child.

Are the instructions too many or too little?
Are the prompts direct or indirect?
Are the prompts enough?
Does the child need a verbal and gestural prompt?

Does the child need a physical prompt or even shadowing?
Am I giving prompts that are too advanced for his developmental level?

These are a few things we need to be aware of, because with therapy the child will improve and acquire the skills needed. If the instructions do not match to the speed with which the child acquires skills then we will deprive him of enough opportunities to practice that skill.

We need to know that when a child doesn't follow instructions or is not responding to his name, it could be because of poor motivation where he is not interested in doing that task.

Then we need to check on how to make that activity interesting or do things that he likes. However, if his reluctance is because of inability or a difficulty, then we use prompts. Let me explain more about prompts here:

Verbal prompt: I give an instruction and the child follows. For instance, I ask for a mobile and the child gives it to me.

Gestural prompt: The instruction that follows a verbal prompt. It can be in the form of pointing or looking at what is needed.

Physical prompt: This instruction follows verbal and gestural prompts. So, I will physically hold the child's hand and make him give me the mobile. The physical prompt can be gradually relaxed by holding the hand at first and then holding the elbow and finally the shoulder.

Many books talk about behavior modification principles in detail and you may refer to those to understand more about them.

Coming back to Nihal, I met him for the second time after two months. Now, he had access to the resources in his body which helped him to make eye contact, sit, and interact. This time, because he was allowed to move around and talk, he started getting into the habit of talking while moving and without making eye contact. Somewhere, that gentle nudge to look and speak is needed. Nihal's understanding improved considerably, but his parents still thought that he did not understand a lot of things. He was still prompted and was not pushed to his potential.

We must be clear on what prompts are needed and what not. This helps immensely as our job is to mentor the child and not do the things for them. They have to learn to become independent and that is the greatest gift we can give to our kids.

So, to conclude, I would like to suggest parents to be vigilant and mindful while giving instructions and prompting their children. Too many instructions from too many people, do not help. Also, our instructions and language need to change with the pace our kids improve and develop.

CHAPTER 11

ACCEPTING THE CHILD WHERE HE IS .... AT THE MOMENT!

Accepting Autism, learning disability, or sensory processing issues in any child needs to be done simultaneously as we focus on their development. It is important to see children as separate individuals and to put our roles and identities parked on to one side. When we see our children as separate individuals, we do not project our roles or emotions on them and work with them with "awareness" and "mindfulness".

Mitiksha, a meritorious student throughout her academic life and now a successful professional and also a mother to a 2-year-old autistic child, Ahaan, decided to wage a fight against her son's diagnosis, comes to my mind who has been a topper all through her school and college. Her quest to prove herself right meant a lot of therapies and no unstructured play for her son. Everything was prompted, planned and organized by Mitiksha to ensure that Ahaan gets the right kind of therapies. She did all the courses that were needed to help Ahaan and started working with him at home.

She saw Ahaan as a project in which she had to excel. When Ahaan failed to make significant progress, she saw that as her failure as a mother. It was difficult for her to accept failure, she had never failed before or compromised for anything in her life. Her efforts with Ahaan were mixed with her personal fight against "Autism". When I worked with Mitiksha, I made her aware of how her agendas are getting mixed up. Ahaan had no choice over his routine, no say in anything and was expected to follow the strict discipline set by Mitiksha. He was never allowed to fail or come out of his comfort zone.

Therapies and academics stole away a lot of Ahaan's childhood. I am not trying to say that therapies are not important, the only point that I wish to convey is that BALANCE is essential. When I met Ahaan, he was seven-years-old. He was not independent in eating, dressing, grooming, bathing, toilet needs, functional mobility and many other self-care tasks because that was done for him by someone else. Because therapy had to fit in his tight schedule of classes and school, everything was done for him.

We all know that most animals like horses can walk immediately after birth, but human babies are born with a "premature brain" and need adults to help them till they turn three years of age. During this time, the brain undergoes intense changes. 90% of our brain growth happens in these early years. Human brain develops from down to up. As the brain matures, the infant learns to crawl, walk, run, talk, and achieves many more skills. The sequential mastery of motor, emotional, and cognitive functions continue throughout our childhood as the brain areas mature. And all of these brain areas need to be interconnected so that everything coordinates well. One of the vital systems to achieve these connections in the neurotransmitter systems. It originates in the lower areas of the brain, the neurotransmitters send projections to every part of the brain and down to the body through the autonomic nervous system. The wide distribution and central location allow these systems to regulate and influence the rest of the brain and body. It also forms one of the most important components of the stress response system.

Patterned, repetitive activity is necessary for all kinds of learning- whether we want to train our systems to manage stress or to build muscles in our body. Stress regulation can also be taught by moderate manageable experiences to prepare our system for large stressors. I cannot pick up heavy weight on the first day of my weight training, but I can do that with regular training.

Now, let's implement this point in the context of parenting. If I allow a child to eat on his own, dress on his own and participate in the daily self-care tasks, it will eventually teach and train his body to do those tasks independently. It also teaches his brain that some things that he was unable to do earlier can now be done, this helps to build the concept of 'self'. Such small daily doses of stressful situations helps the child to develop a well-modulated self-regulation system. Help should be provided when the child has tried but feels that he is failing, at such times, their stress is relieved by the help of their caregiver or parent. This helps their system to mature and their brain apparatus to develop a healthy stress response system. Start with your child's participation in self-care and then into planning and organizing the day by themselves.

I asked Mitiksha about her son's schedule. She told me that she sets the schedule for him and he just follows it with prompts. This does not allow the child to develop decision making skills. Sooner, he will develop a feeling that he cannot make good decisions and will get dependent on prompts. The point is, parents need to be aware of their child's needs before they start working on them. Mitiksha wanted to be a perfect mom and did what she thought was right,

I am not blaming her. But while fulfilling her unmet emotional need and to prove that she is a good mother, she robbed all the opportunities that she could provide to her son.

When a child plays, he fails, makes wrong decisions and experiences a lot of setbacks, which in turn trains his stress response system and helps him to develop self-regulation. Parents' role in this case will be of a mentor and not of a teacher because children naturally and instinctively want to explore all the time. Sometimes, labels shadow our abilities to think naturally and instinctively. We all become parents the day our child is born; the child gives birth to us as parents! We have to trust our gut feeling also and not just the experts. Like a teacher, the child teaches us what he wants through his behavior, only if we learn to listen and nurture him like a gardener.

The diagnosis or the label sometimes fogs the way we see our child. Often, the child is seen with the label and our agenda becomes to erase or undo that diagnosis and turn the child normal. We forget about the child's development, give up on our instincts and blindly follow the expert even when we feel that something is not right.

It is also important to know that the formation of the child's brain circuits is influenced by their mother's emotional states. Babies are like radios constantly attuning to their mother's frequencies. In the early months, the communication between the mother and the child is purely unconscious. The infant is receiving messages from his mom only through emotions. Baby is constantly filtering and understanding the tone of voice, facial gaze, and body language of the mother, which also reflects the mother's internal emotions and environment. Anything that threatens a mother's security affects the electrical wiring and chemical supplies of the infant brain's emotion regulation and attention allocating systems.

Infants know intuitively whether the parent is genuinely smiling or just trying to soothe the baby. Dr. Gabor Mate says, "Attunement is the quintessential component of a larger process called attachment. Attachment is simply our need to be close to somebody. It represents the absolute need of the utterly and helpless vulnerable human infant for secure closeness with at least one nourishing, protective and constantly available parenting figure".

I meet a lot of parents who follow therapies, but stay emotionally unavailable to their kids. When we see a child beyond his label and accept him for who he is, when we attune with them at an emotional level and provide them with opportunities to participate in stressful tasks then we partner the child in their development. It is necessary to follow the advice and tips of experts, but it is also necessary to follow your intuitions and understand what your child needs.

It is also crucial to work on our triggers and emotions so that they do not get spilled on the child. While we develop our child's skills, we must develop the skill of mindfulness within us.

CHAPTER 12

COMMUNICATION IN AUTISM

Throughout my career, I have worked with a lot of autistic kids and almost all of them have communicated with me at an instinctual level. They do so with everyone who interacts with them, we just need to learn how to tune with them. I did not believe in all this until I actually started working with them.

There is this 13-year-old boy called Harsh, who used to come to me for therapy. He had severe autism and mental retardation, along with frequent seizure episodes. Every time we worked with him, he had a seizure, the skill that he had newly acquired would get partially lost and we had to start over again. Imagine a kid having 20-25 seizures every day, hats off to his mother, who worked so hard to help him cope with it every single time. During my one hour session with him, he used to get around 10-15 seizures. While I worked with him, I used to enter into a state where time stands still. I wanted him to learn how to communicate and his mom wanted him to learn to sign.

We did activities to work on his gross and fine motor skills. Whenever he did well, I made him sign a chip as it was his favorite. When I made him sign so frequently, each time holding his fingers, I was really zapped by how he used to look into my eyes. His eyes were naive at making contact, but expert at communicating his feelings. He was completely attuned to me and gave his 100%, even if it was for just a fraction of second.

It took us 2 to 3 months to introduce and embed just one gesture of how to communicate whenever he wanted something as it was difficult for Harsh to learn new things. I did not work on a specific sign language with him and just introduced that one gesture without worrying about where it would take us as his mother believed in me and so did the child. After 4 long months, on one fine day, he took his index finger to the palm of his other hand and signed for what he wanted. That day, my eyes shed tears of gratitude and so was the case with his mom. That moment has left an imprint on my memory. Even as I write, my heart fills with gratitude for that moment. I have been truly blessed to be with and to help such lovely individuals in my life. As a matter of fact, they are the ones who helped me evolve. Harsh was 13-year-old when we managed to teach him just 5 signs. His eyes on the other hand were way ahead of any of us in their ability to express feelings. Harsh was finding it hard to settle with any other therapists, even after multiple attempts. His case was severe and I feel grateful to be able to be a part of his story and progress.

Quantum physics is now trying to prove the science behind what our mystics have taught us thousands of years ago. We are now understanding that everything is made of energy and that we are all interconnected. Our thoughts are also a part of this energy. The quantum field connects all life and matter with energy and suggests that there exists just one single system.

Sessions with Harsh were stressful and sometimes disappointing as well, his progress was much slower than I anticipated. There were days when Harsh would not look into my eyes or give any sign, I could sense that during those days, he wasn't calm. I had to instill that calmness and belief within me to reverberate the same energies within him. I strongly believe that kids with autism or severe needs, understand and communicate at a much deeper level than what we can fathom.

In his book, *Autism: A New Perspective: Inside the Heart and Mind of a Non-Verbal Man*, Joao Carlos mentions how his body needed a holistic approach to heal. He communicated by writing while his mom supported him. He described how his energy levels vary according to the kind of food he eats like when his diet is not wholesome, he experiences bloating and teeth grinding. He also adds that it is not just important to clean the diet but also to clean the toxic mind formations. He says that as an autistic individual, he is highly sensitive and has to deal with a burdened body and mind through exposure to toxic thoughts and that most of the time, being around people increases his pain. The point that I am trying to convey is, no matter how severely Autistic or disabled you might feel they are, the fact is, people with such diagnosis are more sensitive than any one of us. So, it is really important to be vigilant and mindful of the internal atmosphere within us.

For 2 years, I worked with a 5-year-old boy, Sanket. He was diagnosed with severe autism along with cerebral palsy. During our training, he displayed significant improvements and slowly progressed towards achieving his milestones. He learned to walk, stand, sit up and stand, and more. He achieved most of his milestones, but the sensory issues were still present. Unfortunately, for some personal reasons, his parents discontinued the therapy.

They came back to me, when Sanket turned 19. I was really shocked to find that he couldn't walk or get up from the floor from a sitting position. He could only manage to get up from the chair and stand; his regression was evident. He kept tapping his fingers on his face and constantly moved his head from left to right. His knees arched upon standing, his shoulders were tight and abnormally positioned to touch his ears, leaving his neck locked. His elbows, fingers and wrists were bent and he was always in a posture of protecting himself from something. He was only on semi-solid food which can be put directly into his throat, not even his mouth or else he would gag and throw up.

My heart broke to see him so, because he had already achieved these skills when he was young. I did not ask what went wrong because I was sure his parents did the best they could, but something definitely did not go well. I remember Sanket was overtly sensitive even those days when he was young, he didn't allow his mother to brush his teeth, feed him, or help him drink water as a result of which his teeth decayed and he also experienced constipation. Sanket was perpetually stuck in a fight-flight response and that was his brain's way of protecting him. This kind of response isn't just limited to such kids, all of us experience it at some points of our lives. I remember the day one of my friends was driving me back home, she was about to take a turn when she saw a truck approaching us and she froze with terror. She thought she was screaming and trying to turn the steering while in reality she just froze. These fear, fight, or flight responses strike automatically whenever we get exposed to traumatic situations, while some of us settle into a primarily hyper-aroused state, many experience a primary dissociative state with it. I have elaborated on this subject in the chapter of primitive reflex integration. For some persons, even a little stress can put them into an extreme end from where they find it difficult to return as they have issues modulating their stress response system.

Similarly, anything I did with Sanket used to put him into a hyper aroused state, in response to which he recklessly moved and shook his body, hit his face, and acted hysterical. I spoke to Sanket heart-to-heart, believing he would understand me, I told him, "Sanket, I am going to work on your mouth. I will not push you. I'll only do as much as you can take. Please allow me to help you, let me do this for you." I then gently tapped his face. As I worked with him, his guards relaxed. I always trust my instincts, whenever I plan a technique or treatment, I always check and make sure how it feels to my own body. Only when I am sure it's relaxing then I move ahead to implement it on others. So, as I calmly tapped Sanket's face, I sensed the shift in his energies towards a calmer side. I work with kids all the time and sensing their energies now comes inherent to me.

Apart from this, I also consciously work upon attuning myself with the person I am working upon. I mindfully track a kid's body language, expressions, and posture to get an idea of what he is feeling right now.

Even though the experts labeled Sanket 'severely autistic' and non-verbal, in my opinion he was communicating all that while, probably in his own way, he just needed someone to understand his idea of communication. When I worked on Sanket, I was able to perform all the exercises and the oral motor desensitization program. After a week of which, his mother reported improvement in his eating and chewing skills.

When I worked with Sanket, he passed very subtle energy vibrations and all that decoding happened at the level of the heart. When I would push my finger to his gums, he sometimes tightened his body. That was a clue for me that he is uncomfortable and I should stop. I do not know what relationship I share with these kids and individuals who come to me, but it is very sacred. I feel blessed to be able to help them out.

The body conveys things all the time only if we are willing to pick that up. Pushing such kids or adults beyond their levels would make them feel stressed. If we learn to pick up these little cues that their bodies give in the form of frowning, tightening, closing or blinking the eyes, and many more - which I have described in my chapters of primitive reflexes - we can know if they are being pushed too much. Our bodies never lie! As the body relaxes, the frowning eases and the eyes relax as well. There are many signs to know if the child or the individual is relaxed.

I once met a 2-year-old boy named Kanha. His big, bright eyes shone with sparkles every time his thick lashes uncovered them. He came to me for an evaluation and was all over the place. I thought I should give him some deep pressure so that he could feel calmer and more grounded. So, I held him close to myself to apply pressure on his hands and feet, Kanha looked into my eyes. His look was similar to Sanket's and Harsh's look. Kanha was communicating non-verbally, that my efforts are helping him to settle down. I felt the same calmness with him.

His parents were surprised because he sat with me for a long time, allowing me to do what I was doing. He calmed down in just 15 minutes. He traveled from another country and was jet-lagged, hungry, and had an upset stomach. Despite all this, he was pretty settled and at his best. It is just because he wanted to communicate at a deeper, instinctual level. We do not always need to speak to communicate.

You know I am married to a Maharashtrian and my mother-in-law can speak and understand only Marathi whereas my parents speak Punjabi. Once my grandma - who can speak and understand only Punjabi - was unwell, my mother-in-law wanted to speak to her and inquire about her health. So, I called her and my mother-in-law spoke in Marathi and my grandma answered in Punjabi. I thought it was really mad and that they probably did not understand each other. I laughed and asked my grandma if she understood anything that they spoke, to my surprise, she told me that she understood everything that my mom-in-law and mentioned. She said, "You don't need a language to talk. I understood all that she spoke energetically!" I was shocked.

There is another boy, Veer, who came to me at the age of 9. His mother was extremely unmotivated; everyone in his family had almost given up on him. He was given a diagnosis of autism coupled with severe self-injurious behaviors like hitting himself. He was going through a lot of stress at that time. His mother started to feel that nothing could be done about it. Veer never listened to anything or anyone, on the contrary, he made everyone else listen to him. I still remember my first session with him, where he was trying to gauge me, just like all the other kids. **It's not that I try to evaluate them, they evaluate me. They check, whether I come from a place of judgment, anxiety, desperation, urgency or a space of connection, wanting to just connect at a heart-to-heart level and trying to meet them where they are...**

So, when I worked with him that day, I asked Veer to keep all the things back in the cupboard and he picked it all up. It was the best of the sessions according to his mother, because Veer listened. Somewhere through the session she was sure that her child won't listen to me, but she also wanted to understand her child better and so, she didn't interrupt us with her thoughts and opinions. When I worked with Veer, I aligned myself to understand if he wanted to comply or not. If I sense non-compliance, I focus to understand the emotion behind it and start my work from there. I am sharing so many examples because I want you to understand the importance of connecting at a heart-to-heart level; a place free from judgment, bias, and expectations. When that happens, you will see a transformation in the child and yourself, which is beautiful.

Once I was conducting my group therapy sessions in a huge playground with a group of autistic kids along with their mothers. Other kids who were not a part of my group were also playing there. My group had kids in the age of 6 to 9 years and the schedule of the session was visually explained to all the kids to make them feel comfortable and safe with the session. As we all know how unpredictable the world is, the playground's watchman came and told us to vacate the playground. With the sudden change in plan, we explained the new set of steps to the kids. While other kids were unaffected with that change, a boy named Jatin didn't seem happy with it. He started to flap around and made sounds and covered his ears, he was obviously uncomfortable. I tried explaining to him, but his sounds turned even louder. He communicated that he wasn't happy with that change, his rocking and flapping was only to ease his anxiety. I understood what he was going through and the situation distressed me for three reasons. Firstly, because Jatin was taking longer than usual to deal with the change and that being a group of other kids of his age and condition, his restlessness felt contagious. Secondly, it was a 2-hour-long session and we were just halfway into it. And lastly, because we were surrounded by spectators and their curiosities. This incidence was in 2004 and people did not know much about Autism. Some of them started to suggest, advise, and even shout and scold him to check if he was doing that on purpose. All that made Jatin all the more restless. I tried to convince people to leave, but the crowd's curiosity just kept increasing. Now Jatin lost it and was really overwhelmed, he ran towards the gate which was right next to a busy lane. Jatin was only expressing his anger and his inability to settle himself with the situation, but even while we understood his point, it was important for us to ensure his safety and hence his mother took him along to leave the session.

As Jatin left, the crowd dispersed, but everyone in my group, including I, were shaken. Nevertheless, I continued my session with the rest of the kids and upon reaching home I called up Jatin's mother. She told me that he turned fine as soon as he got the space he needed. After 3 days, Jatin came back to me for a consultation session, he was a non-vocal child and hence, was like a mystery to me. The research around 2004 suggested that kids with autism spectrum disorders could not feel emotions or empathy, still, I always tried to connect with those kids at an emotional level. That day, I tried to convey my feelings to Jatin, through my thoughts, without saying a thing my mind told him that I can understand why he was unhappy with what happened at the playground that day. I told him that I also know he did his best to manage himself that day and I too wish things to be better in the future. I felt better after doing so and then Jatin asked for a pencil. He slowly wrote down something. He seldom wrote anything because it took a lot of effort for him to do so. He wrote the following words for me: "Reena aunty, I was really bothered by the change. I know it was not right to have a tantrum but things are not in my control. My inner self tells me to stay calm but my outer self is not in my control. It is very difficult for me. I am sorry but this is how I am!!!" I was in tears and so was his mom. I and his mom were left all agog with emotions.

CHAPTER 13

SELF-STIMULATORY BEHAVIORS ...

"It is not what you look at that matters, it's what you see."

- Henry David Thoreau.

A parent came to me with her four-year-old son, Vehan, for Occupational therapy evaluation. I tried interacting with that chubby, curly-haired boy, but he was busy kicking football. I greeted him and he just repeated it softly, a phenomenon commonly known as echolalia. Vehan's mom opened her small book which had the list of her concerns and she started reading it. She told me that her son has been undergoing therapies for over three years, but his progress is not significant. She wanted him to stop flapping, fidgeting, pacing, looking from the corner of his eyes and to start sitting, focusing, and listening. That is all she wanted. When I asked her why these behaviors concern her, she told me that these behaviors are a part of her son's Autism and if she lets him do all that, he will go into his own world. So, she was constantly on her toes to ensure that he does not engage in any of those behaviors.

She also mentioned that when she engages with him, he focuses and learns, but when left alone he starts self-stimulating. She told me that therapists have told her to follow a sensory diet and give him exercises at home. But if she misses that for even a single day, then those behaviors return. She has tried using positive reinforcement (rewards) when he does not do "stimming". I loved how clear she as a parent was and how she managed to gather all the information.

In my opinion, "nature" and "nurture" both maintain behavior. So "just" working on the environment using rewards alone does not help. I feel we have to see, feel, and experience what the child is feeling. Sometimes, rather most of the time, kids with Autism have sensory processing issues and thus they engage in such self-stimulatory behaviors. In my experience, it is also maintained by the presence of certain primitive reflexes. If you imagine the world from an autistic individual's perspective, there is an overload of sensory information almost flooding them and they have no way to express their challenge or describe the problem that they are going through. It's like being in an overcrowded mall where there is a lot of sound and numerous other sensory inputs which overwhelms them and they are trying hard to listen to the instructions which are whispered by someone.

It is difficult for them to filter out the unnecessary information. To escape from this confusion and overwhelm, they withdraw into a world of repetitive behaviors as they want predictability. These repetitive patterns help the autistic individual to shut out the chaos and overwhelm. And they slip into an invisible bubble and appear locked! Repetitive behaviors are an attempt to self-soothe the stress that comes from not being able to take comfort in relationships. Because of bombardment of sensory input, the individual goes into overwhelm by sensations, he starts self-stimulating because of which he misses out many of the repetitions and opportunities that children get to learn language and understand that people have different perspectives, thoughts and feelings.

Unfortunately, if an individual misses these experiences during the early years, many many more repetitions are needed if stimulation has been missed at the right time. **Our brains are resilient and we can spring back but being over or under stimulated during sensitive periods, particularly for language and emotional development, can reduce abilities profoundly.**

I feel that it is important to start where the child is and not where we want him to be. It is easier for me to say that we need to accept him as he is "in this moment" and work with him to help him to access the resources within his brain. As mentioned in the earlier chapters, the parent's ability to self-regulate is the most important ingredient to help children learn the art of self-regulation. Children are constantly reading their parents' facial, postural, and vocal cues, so we must be aware of what our body language is conveying to them.

Tito Mukhopadhyay, an adult who is non-verbal and has ASD, communicates by typing. In his book *How can I talk if my lips don't move*, he speaks about "pacing" as a child. Whenever there was a change in the environment, he used to pace around. Simple things like power cuts used to make him anxious. He tried calming himself down, but he could not. So, he started pacing around to manage his anxiety. But when the anxiety was too much to contain, he would pace two rooms. He says that his body felt like a prison which trapped all the heat and anxiety. He could help himself only by pacing and when that did not help, he would scream. He knew what is expected behavior and what is non-desirable behavior, but he was simply not in control of his body. It was too much for him to handle. He talks about how he experiences reality in two parts - "thinking self" and the "acting self".

Not everyone is like Tito, many are different and thus the only thing to do is to "understand" the reason for everything that the child is doing. Same applies to any individual who has different styles of learning and this may include ADHD, learning disability, cerebral palsy, and children with sensory processing disorders.

That is the way that they regulate themselves in the present moment with the resources that they can access in their brain. Things get better as they undergo therapy and connections start developing.

Temple Grandin is another adult who has published over 300 scientific papers on Autism. She says that, "Non-verbal individuals with ASD might be far more engaged in the world than they seem to be. They just happen to be living in such an extraordinary jumble of sensations that they have no way of productively experiencing the outside world, let alone expressing their relationships."

The first step is to work on ourselves and check which of the child's behavior is triggering us. If the behavior is triggering us, then we need to first learn to identify our triggers and defuse them. One little five year old Bhavya (diagnosed with moderate Autism) used to always flap while doing facial movements which looked odd. Every time I asked a question, she started to flap. I did not understand anything at that time. When she started coming to me, she was non-verbal. I still remember discussing challenging behaviors in front of her and that made her flap even more and tensed her body.

She started speaking at 7-years-of-age and when she started speaking clearly, she told me, "Aunty, you told my mom that I do not listen to her but I always wanted to listen. I just couldn't get myself together to do the task and I really wanted to." She remembered the date, time of the day, the clothes I wore, and the place where I sat when I spoke to the mom.

Recently, I met a 7-year-old boy, Tanav. He is a cute little boy with a diagnosis of Autism. He has been undergoing therapies since the age of 2.6 years and had a lot of bumps in his development. One by one, with the perseverance of his family, he crossed those barriers and began to talk. He would sing a song when he wanted something like if he wanted chocolate, he would sing a "chocolate" song. But he never asked for what he wanted. Now he is 7 and he can express beautifully what he wants. During one of our sessions, he was playing and looking out of the window as I talked to his parents. His mom praised and spoke great things about him and she was happy with his progress. His dad agreed, but he also wanted to discuss something. His father lowered his tone to discuss one of Tanav's challenging behaviors. Before his dad could start, Tanav came running and sat on his father's lap, "let's go home," he said. His dad was smart and he changed the topic.

Then, again, Tanav ran back to the window and started jumping and playing. His dad again thought of sharing his concern and Tanav again came running to sit on his lap. Tanav again said and this time even louder, "Let's go home." This process happened 4 to 5 times and he made sure not to allow us to discuss his issues. Tanav's behavior left my eyes wet, he was with us through our entire conversation and hence, wasn't happy whenever we tried to discuss the negative aspects of his behaviors. To someone else, it might seem that he was playing and lost in his own world, but he was completely attuned with us.

Tito mentions this so well, "Many times, I am sure neurotypical people ask whether any understanding is going on in the minds of people with autism. That is because the learning of the required skill is not demonstrated in the way a typical person expects. I get very embarrassed when I cannot perform a task, even though I have performed a related task".

I still remember when I was in Delhi and learning more about Autism at the Action for Autism, I was staying with Merry Barua and her son Neeraj who has a diagnosis of Autism. During dinner or breakfast time, Neeraj sat next to me at the dinner table. He wanted me to repeat the same statements over and over again and when I didn't, he used to dig his nails into my arms. This was not to hurt me, but he would get disturbed if things don't go his way. I used to ask Merry what to do and she suggested to explain to him not to repeat the same things over and over again. Neeraj and I were of the same age, but he was much bigger than me. Keeping my apprehensions at bay I tried to say no, but that made him even angrier and in response he rocked and flapped his body. The thought of saying no and making him angry didn't seem like a great idea to me. Eventually, I got scared of spending time with him.

He is an amazing person and I love him for the way he is, but I wanted to give him time to regulate his behaviors. Often, an underlying medical issue is the reason behind such self-stimulatory behaviors. I have worked with numerous kids who shout and display various self-stimulatory behaviors because of the acid reflux or other gastric issues. Many kids get cranky with inadequate sleep or when they are constipated. Other such issues include urinary tract infections, ear infections, or dental issues.

I remember a 17-year-old autistic girl, Shivangi, who developed self-abusive behaviors like hitting her head and jumping while screaming. Her parents tried behavior modification or sensory diet, but realized that she also had a swollen throat and was experiencing severe headaches. Such issues along with the existing difficulties with poor interoceptive awareness makes a difficult combination for individuals with Autism or sensory processing disorder to handle.

Remember, if your child or an individual who is neurodiverse is doing fairly and consistently well and suddenly behaves terribly, then a painful medical issue must be ruled out.

I have worked with a lot of kids who engage in self-injurious behaviors. Devinder, a 12 year old boy, used to hit his face every time he experienced stress. Once, he hit his temple so hard that one of his eyes got damaged and he had to undergo surgery.

I was going through a book named, *Soon Will Come the Light: A view from inside the Autism Puzzle,* by Thomas McKean. Thomas Mckean mentioned in the book that he experiences low intensity pain throughout his body which is relieved by pressure. People like Thomas convey to us exactly about how they feel. The spectrum of Autism is so broad that every individual experiences different and at times unique symptoms. So, when I saw Birender hitting himself, I knew that he was unable to convey what problems he was facing that time.

In her book *Nobody Nowhere,* Donna Williams tells that she rhythmically tapped and sometimes even slapped herself to determine where her body boundaries were. She described how she once unknowingly bit herself in response to an overload of painful stimulus.

There are some kids and adults who are trying their level best to cope with these self-stimulatory behaviors. They need help to desensitize or integrate those senses. Devinder always felt bad after hitting himself, he even asked his mom to tie his hands because the consequences of his behaviors were quite painful. Now he is 25 years old and still, he wants his hands tied up behind his back. When Devinder was 8-year-old, he used to tell me, "Aunty my hands are melting!". I couldn't understand him back then, I was new in the field and lacked those skills, but now, having seen so many kids and adults with Autism, I realize how they struggle to maintain calmness with their chaotic emotional state and constant fight-flight mode.

The purpose of sharing so many examples is to emphasize that these self-stimulatory behaviors are for a reason. If we come from a place of understanding the child or the adult, they feel accepted. Only using a behavior model to reward or punish the behavior does not help.

In his book How Can I Speak If My Lips Don't Move, Tito mentions that whenever he had a fall and got hurt, he couldn't locate or point to the area where he experienced pain or discomfort. Such was the pain perception and threshold capacity of his body. Reading these books helps me to understand more about kids and adults who have sensory issues.

Sometimes, the body boundaries are not clearly established. As a result of which, it gets difficult for neurodiverse individuals to understand and secure their personal space.

During my initial years as a therapist, a neurodiverse kid standing very close to my face used to make me uncomfortable. I failed to understand why they did so, but as I worked I understood them.

If they can't understand their body boundaries, how is it possible for them to understand anyone else's space or boundaries?

I also want to talk about visual stress sometimes referred to as Scotopic sensitivity syndrome or Irlen Syndrome. Many kids who have a diagnosis of autism, learning disability, sensory processing disorder and ADHD, also have visual stress. They find it difficult to look at certain things and prefer looking from the corner of the eye. They also have difficulties with reading and writing. Some kids tell me that the text is jumping and they cannot understand how to read it. Some say that the text gets distorted or blurred or burnt. Bright light produces visual stress. You can refer to the literature on Irlen Syndrome but this needs to be mentioned here because some parents do not allow their kids to look from the corner of the eyes or force them to read even when the kids say that it is difficult for them. I have seen so many kids cover their eyes with hair or palm or cap, sometimes they partially open their eyes to reduce the visual stresses. For such cases, Irlen glasses and overlays help a lot.

Let me explain how I realized this phenomenon. While I was just 15, I used to feel giddy in certain spaces and I did not understand why that was happening. My parents took me to doctors and got the blood tests and EEG scans done. Everything was normal and doctors told me that I was stressed because of exams. My parents believed the doctors and asked me to take a break from studies. I did what I was told to, but still felt giddy. Nobody understood why it was happening and I was kept on anti-vertigo medications. I used the medication symptomatically, but that didn't seem to solve my problem. I was labeled as an anxious Type-A personality who doesn't know how to handle stress.

Many years later, when I started learning about rhythmic movement training which is an approach to integrate primitive reflexes, I learned that I had a few unintegrated primitive reflexes: the Moro reflex, the spinal galant reflex, and the tonic labyrinthine reflex.

The tonic labyrinthine reflex was the reason why I felt giddy whenever my head position changed. We worked on so many things to help me out of it, but the basic reflex got missed all that while. I started working on the TLR reflex and it helped me to some extent. Still, at times when I read or when I would go to a place with a lot of light, I feel disoriented or overwhelmed (this is because of the Moro reflex). Gradually and unconsciously, these reflexes affect my thought process and my ability to answer logically.

Visual stress is difficult for me to handle. So, whenever I go to a movie or for conferences, the artificial and bright lights make me uncomfortable. If you watch the video on my YouTube channel by Tehnaz Ragi, she has beautifully explained about Irlen Syndrome. She has also explained about Helen Irlen and how they use overlays to assess and understand what color would be suitable for a particular child.

In my anecdotal evidence, I have realized that when we work on the unintegrated Moro reflex, the visual stress seems to reduce and the children can read, write, and focus well. The peripheral vision that they use also tends to reduce. Along with this, it is also important to work on the vestibular system because it has important connections with the visual system. I have started seeing this association, but I am not a researcher yet. These are my speculations, but I would love whoever is reading, if you are a professional, to research this matter. I have seen that, the more I work with the Moro reflex and the vestibular system, the more the visual stress reduces. For the time the visual stress is causing challenges, overlays can be used to re-mediate the symptoms.

Like whenever I feel the light of my screen is too bright, I use cyan or blue filters to make me feel better. So it depends, you can experiment your preference if you have access to an Irlen specialist who can identify and evaluate what works best for you.

As we work and integrate the unintegrated primitive reflexes, the visual stress starts reducing. Also, not every child will experience visual stress at all times, their occurrence depends on the presence of stressors. So, it is important to understand behaviors and the reasons behind them.

Self-stimulatory behaviors also increase in cases of sensory overload.

This is described in details in further chapters. I feel that when there is a meltdown, we need to take the child or the individual out of that overwhelming situation, some of the examples are a strong smell or sound, crowded place, etc, so that it becomes easier for the person to self- regulate.

CHAPTER 14

BECOMING A BEHAVIORAL DETECTIVE

As I talk about the sensory stimulation or the "stimming" behaviors as we commonly call them, there are a few things that come to my mind right now which I wish to elaborate upon.

Many times, parents feel that the self-stimulatory behavior needs to be stopped. As mentioned earlier, we need to provide the child with opportunities to establish connections and find access to the higher levels of his brain and thus, learn mature ways of self-regulating.

That said, the reason I am sharing so many examples is because when we as parents, educators, and therapists come from a place of understanding then it becomes easier for us to learn how and what to expect from the child. I feel that even if self-stimulatory behavior is present, it does not mean that child should not get the opportunities that any other child of his age is getting. Every child must be given opportunities to participate in self-help skills even if they find it challenging.

Often, self-stimulatory behaviors get replaced by mature ways of self-regulation as connections establish with the higher centers of the brain. But the accommodations or the modifications of the activities stay the way they were.

Let me explain this to you, Adwait is a 9-year-old boy who came to me with a lot of sensory issues. He had difficulties in writing, copying from a board, focusing, sitting at one place in the classroom, paying attention, and learning from group situations. As time passed by, he improved to a great extent and skills emerged and developed. He could then copy from the board, write, sit and focus. Two years after the therapy was over, his parents came to me and mentioned that he is not participating in writing tasks that are expected in the classroom training. I was shocked and wondered why he is not doing so because he had made significant progress in acquisition of skills. So I spoke to Adwait and he said, "Aunty don't you know that I have a sensory issue and kids who have sensory issues have difficulties with all of these things? So, I am not expected to do what everyone else does. I am supposed to get concessions."

This is not acceptable. Even if a child has difficulties, we work on developing those skill deficits. Eventually, as the skills emerge and are acquired, we do not allow the child to use those compensations as an excuse to avoid the behavior or to avoid participation in a task.

This is extremely important. We have to learn to balance our parenting skills so that we are neither over protective nor over strict with our kids. So, we must come from a place of understanding when to help and when to take away the compensations and the concessions that the child gets.

I once counseled a 6-year-old autistic boy, Adhvik. His mother mentioned, "He can sing songs but always repeats when a question is asked. He cannot initiate or maintain a conversation, only repeats what is asked. He understands all that is being told to him and follows instructions very well, but he finds it difficult to label things that I ask him. I am sure he is doing it on purpose."

Now in this case, the parent was not understanding her child and thinking that the behavior was done on purpose. I tell the parent that children who have a diagnosis of Autism have echolalia, which simply means these kids understand a phrase by repeating it. Donna Williams (an adult with Autism) stated that if she didn't repeat the words, she only understood 5 to 10 percent of what was said. Children with echolalia appear to have speech perception problems.

In her book, Somebody Somewhere, Donna writes, "As a child I had been echolalic and had difficulty learning the purpose and significance of language." She had problems with perceiving both words and the intonation or tone of speech. When she was young, she thought that the intonation of a voice was the words. If she listened to the intonation, she could not hear the words.

So in the case of Adhvik, he had difficulty while Adwait who initially had sensory issues (which were resolved successfully) was now using them as an excuse for availing concessions. He was also using it to avoid participating in tasks. In case of Adhvik, he had a skill deficit and thus had difficulty participating in the task and his mother was losing her cool on him and also labeled him lazy which actually wasn't the case.

The aim is to become a behavioral detective and to see how much we need to push.

Is the child really unable to perform a task or he is trying to get away with it by using his past inabilities as a bait. This difference would prove beneficial to strategize our approach. Should we work on developing the skill that is deficit or on shaping the behavior?

Thus, understanding the difference is important. I remember reading Temple Grandin's book where she mentions the squeeze machine. So, in the earlier stages when Temple experienced a lot of anxiety attacks, she would go into the squeeze machine and stay in it for thirty minutes and after that she would feel calmer. A lot of kids who I work with, do respond very well to deep pressure and they do calm down. This strategy is a part of Sensory Integration which was put forth by Jean Ayres who is the pioneer of sensory integration and started working on it in the early 70s.

In those days Autism was thought of as a psychological problem and not as a sensory issue. So, Temple's mother and teacher told her that going inside the squeeze machine isn't acceptable and she must discover other ways to regulate and manage her anxiety attacks. Being an obedient girl, Temple did as she was asked to, but she couldn't deny the fact that deep pressure in the squeeze machine did calm her down.

So, when such a situation occurs the child may feel misunderstood and develop poor self-concept. Child may think, "I'm being a bad girl, I'm not listening to my mom," whereas, in reality, the child has a biological need to seek that pressure. So, when parents, educators, and therapists understand the source or the cause of a particular behavior, then the way we approach that behavior changes.

It is also important to understand the concept of sensory overload. It could be a vestibular overload, tactile overload, or anything too much that the child is not able to handle. I will be discussing overload in the next section of this book.

When we work with young kids - up to 7 years of age - the rate of improvement is much faster.

When Temple Grandin was diagnosed, she was in a severe condition and started speaking at the age of 4. She received a diagnosis of Autism but if we see her now, she has worked a lot on herself and she continues to work. She can live a functionally independent and successful life now. She is a very good example and an inspiration for people to see that with the right kind of therapy anyone has a high chance of getting better and living a functionally independent life.

I still remember a child named Kavir who first came to me when he was 3-

years-old. He was diagnosed with Autism spectrum disorder. He had a lot of sensory issues and his mother Millie really worked hard with Kavir. His sensory issues were so severe that he would keep tripping into overload with outbursts of crying and shouting. He was completely non-verbal and could not express anything when we started with therapies. In the first 2 years of therapy, where we combined occupational therapy, sensory integration and behavioral therapy, Kavir showed significant improvements. His mom ensured that she will follow up the program at home for 20 hours in a week. When I say 20 hours in a week I do not mean that the child has to undergo only ABA or speech therapy, it means engaging with the child in a one-to-one set up and ensuring his participation in age-specific activities and tasks.

Now, for every parent, it is sometimes financially not possible to get someone to come home and do the individual therapy every day. Millie would go to colleges and put stickers to urge students from NCC background and social volunteers to come home and work with Kavir. A lot of time was spent in the therapy and these volunteers would work at home while Millie did her bit too.

Then Millie's husband got a transfer and they moved to a different city after which Kavir was re-evaluated. The diagnosis now stated that he moved from Severe Autism to Mild Autism. His CARS (Childhood Autism Rating Scale) also changed significantly. While she moved to a different city, she continued to follow the home program. After two years, Kavir's father again got transferred to a new city. In this city, to seek admission in school they again sought re-evaluation from a developmental pediatrician. This time, it showed that Kavir has just a few features of Autism. Kavir and Millie are both classic examples of how with the right way and determination even a child with sensory issues can become independent and contribute to society.

Today Kavir is 16-years-old and is doing well. He is mainstreamed and excelling in his academics. He has friends and has no issues socializing and interacting with them. That's the kind of life that every child has a right to live provided, we are clear with what strategies or therapies are needed.

Rudransh is another child who comes to my mind. He was also diagnosed with autism at 3 years of age and his mom, Smita, ensured that she followed the program accurately, even at home. He came to us for therapy for around four years, we used a combination of sensory integration, rhythmic movements (which are primitive reflex integration techniques), and behavioral therapy principles. Today, Rudransh is in 9th grade and is coping very well with his academics. Smita avails concessions for him in the classroom setup. When he was in his 4th grade they made an Autism disability certificate for him. Now in

9th grade she had to get him re-evaluated because kids improve with therapy. In his report it was mentioned that there are no traits of Autism now and that he is not eligible for concessions. Good tidings! Kids improve to that great level.

Rudransh is doing well now and is living a life like any other child of his age and is completely independent and has friends. He is a little introvert though. There are challenges at every age and every stage of our life holds a part in our overall growth and development. Parents of neurotypical kids also work on challenges and we all evolve in the process.

The point that I am trying to convey is, it is important to become a detective to understand where the behavior is coming from and what it expects us to do for the child.

Does it involve a behavioral approach or does it involve teaching a skill to overcome the issue to have access to the higher areas of the brain and have more mature form of self-regulatory behavior in situations that produce stress. Our final aim is to help the child or the individual to stay regulated.

CHAPTER 15

SPECIAL ABILITIES AND SAVANT SKILLS IN AUTISM

As I talk of self-stimulation, you would be amazed to know what kind of magnificence lies in these little ones who just appear to be self-stimulating.

Sia, a little 3-year-old autistic girl came to me for therapy. She was an extremely cute girl with porcelain skin and curly locks. She was unable to communicate effectively as she used to talk in broken sentences. She also had echolalia. I am blessed to have worked with clients who stayed with me for long to follow-up with their improvements. I worked with Sia till she turned 6, after which she didn't need therapy.

Ever Since, I have been in touch with the family and today, Sia is a 17-years-old girl. When she was young, she would self-stimulate, move around, pace and repeat things that made no sense. I also would like to mention the associative process that I have seen in many kids who come to me. So, Sia would repeat certain awkward words like potty, again and again. Her parents used to feel really odd about what she said. I feel this is the case with many kids on the autism spectrum because they associate words with experiences. So, Sia associated the word potty with a pleasant experience and thus was repeating it. This is what her parents as well as many other parents do not understand of their kids. I have seen a lot of kids working on a visual association basis. They would see something and associate it with an object in their life.

I remember reading Temple Grandin's book Thinking in pictures, where she mentions how she would repeat one word over and over, even if it made no sense to her. At the age of 6, she learned the word 'prosecution' and had no idea what it meant. She kept on using that word as an exclamation, every time her kite hit the ground. Everyone would wonder what she meant by it. She now realizes that the reason she would say the word 'prosecution' was because to her, it sounded nice. Sometimes, children on the spectrum use words that are not contextual to us, but it certainly holds some meaning to them because in their memory, that particular word has been linked to something in their mind.

Coming back to Sia, as she grew, we became aware of the inner magnificence that she held. Very gradually, one day, at the age of 4, she started speaking. At that time, the words she spoke actually baffled and amazed us to wits. She came to her mom one day and said, "Teacher wearing pink dress, coffee fell. Teacher wearing brown dress." Her mom didn't understand a word but when she went to drop Sia to school, she saw that her class teacher was wearing a brown dress. Her mom was shocked and asked the teacher if she was planning to wear a pink dress in the morning. The teacher was shocked and asked how she knew that. Sia's mom asked if she had spilled coffee on her pink dress. At this point, the teacher was really shocked as she was the only one who knew about it. Sia's mother was convinced that her daughter wasn't uttering random thoughts. Also, during *Ganesha Chaturthi's* celebrations one year, Sia asked her mother to buy her a pink chaniya-choli (traditional Indian dress worn by girls), but her mother had already bought her a red one. So, she told Sia that she cannot buy another one. Sia insisted, saying her dress colour should match the Ganesha idols', but her mother did not understand. A week later, the Ganesha idol arrived in her society for the festivities and it was decorated with a pink outfit. That incidence shocked Sia's mom again.

Many such bizarre incidences proved that Sia knew a lot more than we could imagine. She is amazing with dates, past, or future. These are called 'savant skills' and are said to be present in some kids on the Autism spectrum. Darold A. Treffert explains in the book *Scholars with Autism Achieving Dreams,* shares that not all persons with autism are savants, and not all savants are autistic. Rather, approximately one in ten persons with Autism Spectrum Disorders has some savant skills and approximately fifty-percent of persons with savant syndrome have autism spectrum disorders as the underlying disability on which the savant skills are superimposed; the other fifty percent have some other developmental disability, brain injury, or brain disease as the underlying disorder.

Savant skills cannot be understood as to how they fit in the working of a human brain because they are rare and do not develop in neurotypicals, even by rote. Individuals on the spectrum have a way of accessing memories in this particular manner, though. Often what they say might not make sense to us, but it definitely makes sense to them and we would probably get it if we try to see things from their perspective.

As a child, Sia enjoyed peeking out of the window and staring out into space. Everyone thought she was getting lost in her own world and tried to pull her out of it, but Sia persisted to do so. No one knew what she was doing, neither did Sia explain to us. I am so grateful about how much these kids have taught me. The more we restrict them from doing something, the more they continue to, if it interests them, despite the judgment. So Sia, kept looking out of the window at all times and would constantly check the climate on google. One day, Sia pointed out and named a constellation, which shocked her parents. I was really happy, because as her mother told me, Sia's knowledge was so deep and boundless, that she was mentored by an expert to pursue astrophysics. I believe she will greatly contribute to the field with her eccentric skills and capabilities.

So, a behavior that seemed self-stimulating or getting lost, turned out to be much more. Why I am sharing this story is, if a behavior indicates so much interest and passion, we need to facilitate its development because you never know how the child can end up contributing to the world, through those very behaviors.

I also feel that it is important to Train the Talent! Train the talent in whatever form, whatever direction, and in whatever quantity it presents itself.

Temple Grandin talks about her childhood and self-stimulatory behaviors in her book Thinking in pictures. She spoke of the tantrums she would throw when she would not get what she wanted or when she was tired or stressed out. She mentions that her behavior was not under her control at that point. She mentions that tantrums occurred like seizures and she had no control over them. She definitely felt bad after the tantrums. There was one incident, where she was really tired and started to throw a tantrum. In that fit of rage she bit her teacher's leg and only once she came out of it did she realize that her teacher's leg was bleeding. She was very upset with what she had done, but when she was right inside her 'emotional storm,' she had absolutely no control over what she did. She also talks how she would space out for hours at the beach, watching the sand fall from her hand. She would almost get hypnotized by the whole process and could sit there forever. It seems like she was getting lost into her own world, but if we see it from her strength perspective, we would believe that she is seeing the sand differently. That is how she is wired neurologically.

That is why it is important to develop and nurture the skill that does exist in any child with any label. I feel every child has his or her strengths and challenges. We almost always help them to navigate through the challenges but seem to overlook the strengths. What I am trying to emphasize is, weaknesses as well as strengths must be given utmost importance. We should provide the child with opportunities to do something he really wants to be intensely occupied with.

I remember this 5-year-old girl, Nivea, who loved all kinds of bottles. As a child, that was the only thing she loved and her mother hated her obsession. If you gave her a big basket of bottles, all she would do is stare at the logos. What we did was, we kept bottles all over the house and used them for identification on a table top set-up. With the help of this, she was able to identify more than 200 objects, which initially, she was unable to do. To take it further, we took print outs of the logos and asked her to match them to the bottles, which she did really well. That's how we taught her alphabets too, using logos of brands. We also asked her to scan the room for bottles while working on her listening skills as well. After that, we started to form sentences out of it like, "I love Cadbury". We used her obsessions to make her start reading, to work on things that she didn't find interesting before.

I would also like to mention that many kids love to rock and spin around a lot. Rocking is the vestibular input that the child seeks to calm down. A child will generally guide the parent or therapist by engaging in behaviors that show what is it that the child really wants. A kid would go and squeeze himself in between the sofa and the wall, indicating that he wants tactile input. A child may rock a lot, indicating that they need vestibular input. So, the way the children engage themselves can hint us what they need and we can provide them that input from a therapeutic perspective so that they can regulate themselves in the form of a sensory diet which can be followed even at home.

While I say so, I have worked on integrating primitive reflexes and have seen magical results. I'm not saying there always is a huge leap in improvement, but sometimes, any small improvement is also magical. These small improvements, over a course of 3-4 months become big gains to help develop skills. What I have seen is, when I help kids to integrate their unintegrated primitive reflexes, provide them a sensory diet, and teach their parents to self-regulate, it really helps.

Working on parents is also very essential. Parents are so defensive because they constantly feel judged. When they finally stop seeing themselves as the target of judgment, they start to realize that some people are trying to help. When I start helping parents and work on their triggers, kids improve too. When I do a combination of these, the self-stimulatory behaviors that the child engages in seems to be less of a need for the child further on. After all, self-stimulation is a way to calm down the stress response system and achieve a state of balance.

A 3-year-old autistic boy, Krish, engaged in similar self-stimulatory behaviors like flapping, pacing, lack of eye contact, and not responding to his name. One day, Krish's mother called me and said that he can point to things that we ask and answer appropriately. Initially, I didn't believe his parents as I feel that sometimes parents could be overly positive or negative towards their kid and the information shared by them cannot be termed objective. But many kids like Krish have proven to me that I should listen to the parents as well, because they know and understand their children the best. These are the parents who use their parental instincts and inner compasses to wade their way through the therapy over the years.

Most of the time, parents underestimate the helping power that their love, belief, optimism, and hope can have on kids. They also tend to underestimate their own ingenuity in discovering and applying what works or doesn't work with challenging behaviors. I try to reinforce this idea in many ways, since parents know their child best, their remedies may be as useful as those of the 'experts.' I am not saying that the special knowledge or expertise of specialists is unimportant, but the combination of the knowledge and expertise with the parent's observations, suggestions, and input from the family helps immensely. So moms and dads should not disqualify themselves as 'experts'.

Coming back to Krish, his mother gave him a very large number (for example 6550/35) and wrote down 3 options, one of which was the correct answer. Within seconds, Krish pointed to the correct answer. Then she asked him, when was his father's and mother's birthday, he again pointed to the correct options. She was really shocked because he knew everything. After answering, he would run, pace, and appear to be lost, but in reality, he was completely engaged and understood everything. His mother asked him to tell the capital cities of various countries, which again he answered correctly. I too was amazed with his abilities.

Then, we decided to use this skill to work on his deficit areas. We started to ask him general things in the form of multiple choice questions like how he came to the therapy center today, what he ate for breakfast and so on. It is really shocking to see that kids have such immense capacities in them. I'm not saying that every child has it, but it is our duty to be Sherlock and find out what they love and use that opportunity to connect with them, improve our rapport and develop them holistically.

Jeevesh comes to my mind, he is based in Europe and takes consultations from me over Skype. Usually, I talk to the parents to explain to them how to work on their child. Jeevesh is a 4-year-old boy, who just wants to learn to communicate his needs, but he seemed to be lost in his own world; singing the same song the entire day and dancing. He seemed disconnected from everyone in his house. One day, his parents sent me a video and asked me to see how we could capitalize on the ability that Jeevesh demonstrated in the video.

I do not encourage parents to send videos generally because otherwise there will be so many videos in my inbox and I will not get a chance to do my consultations. I was not happy and told her that I would not be able to see the video, but they still insisted. It was a 4 minute video. I tried to ask her to wait and discuss this in the session, but she claimed it to be urgent, so I watched the video.

In the video, Jeevesh was sitting on the floor with a huge sheet of paper. He seemed completely engrossed in the act and I was instantly magnetized to his zeal. Soon, Jeevesh's hand moved at super speed following arcs and curves of strokes, the zoom wasn't clear and I couldn't really make out what he drew. By the end of the video, his mother zoomed in to show what he actually drew. I saw an elephant, a zebra, and some other animals. What appeared to be random scribbling was actually figures of animals which he made without thinking at all, it came natural to him. It seemed as if he was downloading those beautiful images from his brain. After seeing his expertise, I didn't waste a minute and spoke to his mother on how we could use this strength to work on him, while working on the deficits side by side. Six months later, his mother shared his comic strip illustrations, with intricate dialogues and details, even of the background. None of this has been taught to him. I was really amazed and I now believe that every child, no matter what they look like, has something in them. We just have to explore and work with them.

Jeevesh reminds me of Stephen Wiltshire, the famous autistic savant from England. He draws detailed pictures of buildings and also has great musical ability. In his book *An Anthropologist on Mars*, Oliver Sacks describes how Wiltshire's ability to improvise in music improved over a period of time. His signs of Autism disappear when he sings and reappears when the music stops. Music just transforms him.

Navin is a little 4 year old boy who was given a diagnosis of Autism. He can play any rhythm on any keyboard. And when I say any keyboard it means, it can be a keyboard on the phone, piano, harmonium, or a toy Casio. He can play the same music and tune. He has not learnt music, but is born with this ability. But Navin has core deficits of Autism and we are working on those deficits while his parents are training him to build on this strength.

I can go on and on talking about the savant skills. Calvin, a 5-year-old boy diagnosed with Autism can play drums on any surface- table, zembe, bongo - with his hands or with sticks and he is not taught how to do so. He can copy any rhythm without even practicing it once.

There is another 9-year-old boy, Ashrut, he has Asperger syndrome. He used to love eating and would only watch TV channels related to food. Every time he came to me for therapy, he always brought along something he cooked. Initially, he would bring sandwiches, lemon juice, or simple food items, but as his passion and experience surged he started cooking complex dishes like *biryani*, pizza, burgers, and so on. He completed his first 6 years of education in a mainstream school and did the rest through NIOS. He is now a certified chef. He works in one of the most reputed hotels in India and enjoys his profession thoroughly, because that was his interest from the beginning. He is contributing to society so constructively.

Sammy, a 9-year-old boy diagnosed with Autism comes to my mind. He is based in Canada and when he came to India, he underwent 1 year of therapy with us. Even now, when I have Skype sessions with him, his mother says that he cooks better than her. He goes to the supermarket and makes his mother buy food items that she has never bought before. He also watches YouTube channels to try various cuisines using those exotic ingredients. 1000 such videos are registered in his memory by watching them just once, such is the fondness of Sammy for cooking.

The reason behind me sharing these experiences is to let you know, there are kids with intense preoccupations, that we often see as behaviors to be gotten rid of, because we want the child to communicate with us. I don't see this as a behavior because if this is developed, it could develop into their vocation itself. I feel that this needs to be nourished, nurtured, and balanced, while working on the challenges.

CHAPTER 16

THE TRIUNE BRAIN

Our brain has networks for "stress" and "reward" in the primitive and essential regulatory systems. We need to know that our brain is not just one organ but has multiple systems that have evolved with us. And we need to understand this so that we can help ourselves and our kids better. Human brain is actually like three different brains with each one built on top of the other. The best part is, each part has its version of intelligence, its sense of time and space, its memory, and its own subjectivity. It's like having three identities in our head!

The oldest part of our brain is called the "reptilian brain" or the lower brain. This is located deeper down in the brain and is responsible for the automatic functions needed for survival like the heart rate, which require monitoring and immediate correction. This primitive part of the brain speaks a **language of sensations**. So, if I go to the mountains to feel the air and watch the beauty, I feel calm and relaxed, but if I see a snake creeping towards me, I will flush with panic, my heart rate will increase, my feet will tremble and my breathing will turn fast. As I mentioned earlier, this part of our brain ensures our survival and homeostasis. This is the way my reptilian brain speaks to me through sensations. This part of the brain does not understand words and we learn its language by becoming aware of our sensations. Since, it is the oldest part of our brain, it is also that wise adult who befriends the deep instinctual layer of our consciousness.

Another part of our brain is called the "mammalian brain". As time passed, the midbrain developed which has the key areas to regulate sleep, appetite, pleasure, motivation, and attention. These regions also operate without conscious control. The stress response systems originate here and send connections down to the reptilian brain and up to the higher areas of the brain. A region called the "limbic system" surrounds the midbrain. It is also known as the "emotional brain" as it processes memories and feelings. This part of our brain also speaks a different language. It speaks the **language of feelings**.

The most advanced and the uniquely human part of the brain is the highest and outermost brain region called the neocortex. This part allows language, abstract thought, and planning. This brain speaks the **language of words**. Paul Maclean, the originator of the three brain theory believes that evolution simply added each newly evolved brain on top of the one that came before, without changing the older brain. The widely distributed architecture of the stress response network allows it to **"take over"** any part of the brain to respond to the threat which means that it can take over the new part of the brain – the cortex too. Another important thing to know is that all the systems work in coordination so it is impossible to separate their languages- sensations from feelings to words. Every sophisticated decision and analysis requires positive or negative emotion. Every idea requires a feeling. So, if I go trekking on a mountain and observe the beauty around and start panting, the reptilian brain will act first and bring my awareness to the discomfort (sensation) that I feel. The stress system gets active and says that something is wrong. Stress system sends signals to the new part of my cortex and my attention shifts from the beauty of the mountains. The stress system says- stop looking at those beautiful mountains, first control the breath or slow down.

So if you see, the stress system has the power to "shut down" the cognitive processes or the thinking part of the brain. Remember, what I am trying to tell you is that safety is rewarding and stress is distressing and painful.

When a child feels stressed because of sensory overload, his stress response system gets triggered and he gets into a zone of fight-flight or freeze response which is a protection response. In such a state, expecting a child to pay attention or focus is impossible. Remember the stress response system has the power to "shut down" the thinking part of the brain. Secondly, if we are angry or shout or yell and ask the child to do something, we are again activating the stress response system in the child. Hence, I would again emphasize that we can learn something when we feel safe and not when we are stressed! If you listen to people who describe shock – words they use are – "I don't have words to describe what I felt" and "My legs were shivering, I felt numb," when we are stressed, we **talk in the language of sensations.**

There is a world of sensations inside us and we can learn that language by being aware of it. To help our kids achieve self-regulation, we need to be aware of our sensations. These sensations can be like pressure or temperature changes, muscle tension, constriction, trembling, or tingling. This is the lower brain's language that gets activated when in danger or when unexpected changes occur. Noticing sensations may seem weird but the more we learn about the ups and downs of our body's moods, the more intuitive and instinctive we become. The sense of wellbeing is based on the body's ability to regulate itself rather than escalating it out of control.

There is a rhythm of contraction and expansion happening in our bodies and nature. Being familiar with this reminds us that no matter how bad we feel in the contraction phase, expansion will happen for sure and bring in a sense of relief. One way to "track" the body's rhythm is to pay attention to your breath and notice the chest or belly rise and go down. Is there a pause between breathing? Do the muscles tense or relax as you breathe? When we experience our sensations consciously, we begin to empower ourselves to move with the flow from one state to another. Any new skill needs practice and as we become more "mindful" of the sensations and "notice" what happens and what we "feel" from moment to moment, especially during or after our child's tantrum or a meltdown, we are then getting ready to help our kids!

Any overwhelm or stress that the child or you feel cannot be always prevented and things will and do go wrong sometimes. However, they will not be traumatic to you or your child or the loved ones around you. Now, coming to a tantrum or a meltdown or a change of routine for your child. Notice first your own level of fear or the concern you feel. If you have practiced mindfulness, you will be able to receive the messages from your sensations. Before attending to your child, take a deep breath and exhale out slowly from your mouth. If you are still upset about the situation, you can repeat this. Breathing can bring you to a state of calm.

Focus on your feet and try to bring your awareness to the **"present moment"** and feel grounded. This time that you invest in calming yourself before attending to your child will do a great deal of good to you and your child! Your composure will greatly reduce the likelihood of frightening or confusing your child further. Children are very **sensitive** to the emotional states of adults, mainly their parents. Your calm and confident voice communicates to your child that you know what's best and it helps the child to feel safe.

It is also very important to allow your child to process his emotion. For that, you have to first contain your own emotions so that you do not spill them out on the child. Resist your impulse to stop your child from crying or shouting. If your child is overwhelmed, take him away from the overwhelming situation. You can do parallel talking where you speak on behalf of the child if that helps. Constantly attune yourself with your child. This helps!

Kids usually move through their feelings very quickly if they are not hurried or inhibited by us because of our tight time schedules. Allowing the child to move through his feelings is very important. Most of us want to stop crying or anger prematurely (if the child is engaging in self-abusive behaviors or throwing things when angry then he can be taken to a place which does not have too many things). Being attuned means we have the patience to allow the child to go through his uncomfortable emotions. We pace at the speed that suits our child. This way we are teaching our child to move from the reptilian brain to have access to the neocortex. We are also allowing the child to process his emotions and integrate them.

Our undivided attention and space of non-judgment and complete acceptance set the conditions for the child to rebound to his healthy sense of well-being. Most of the time, kids are co-regulating and are sensing our emotional atmosphere to take that energy to help themselves. **The point that I am trying to emphasize is that when our kids are vulnerable, they benefit most from feeling a connection with a calm person who can make them feel safe and offer compassion and empathy to contain their feelings rather than overwhelming them!**

Everything in nature is dictated by rhythms and cycles. Seasons come and go, moon waxes and wanes, tides ebb and flow, sun rises and sets. Animals too follow that rhythm. We too resolve overwhelm of our kids or neurodiverse individuals by natural cycles of contraction and expansion. It is important to understand that stress is not bad and such situations are unavoidable and also very important for learning and development of self-regulation in kids. All learning requires some small dose of stress because we are getting exposed to something new and unfamiliar. Through exposure to tiny stresses, our brains learn to deal with large and big stresses in life. When an emotionally available, attuned, and calm caregiver is present, the child learns that the state of overwhelm won't stay forever and that he will be in a state of calm very soon.

Frequent activation of this stress response system is necessary for learning and healthy development. When stress response system networks are activated in small, moderate doses, they become stronger over time. In contrast, large, irregular, and extreme doses of stress interfere with the development. They need the right kind of "exercise" to develop strength and resilience. It is very important to note that problems in the development of the stress response system can interfere with the development of social and emotional functioning and vice versa.

The steps mentioned above help and emphasize on the importance of giving sensory integration and primitive reflex integration. I shall describe more on primitive reflexes in the coming chapters.

CHAPTER 17

UNDERSTANDING SENSORY INTEGRATION AND SENSORY PROCESSING DISORDER

Sensory processing disorder is also known as sensory integration dysfunction. It is a term coined by occupational therapist Jean Ayres. Before we go into the theory of sensory integration, let's read a story on how sensory integration helps in forming beautiful and wonderful memories of childhood.

Ruhie is a little girl who while coming back from school loved to jump in the puddles (tactile input). Sometimes there was a lot of water in the puddle and sometimes it was really mucky. Ruhie would sit in the puddle and dig her hands into the muck. Her soiled hands didn't stop her from caressing her tresses as they tumbled about her face. The gooey muck was alluring to play, but soon her eyes saw the empty swing amid the running and jumping chaos of play. She knew how to zoom the lenses of her eyes (visual input) to overlook the flock of kids and focus only on the swing. Her vision (visual perception and visual discrimination) was sharp like that of an eagle, to grab her swing immediately as someone vacated it. Then she sat on the swing (vestibular input) and enjoyed the movement. Amongst the sounds (auditory input) of birds chirping and the children playing, she heard her mom calling (auditory filtering). So Ruhie ran back home.

As she entered the house the smell (olfactory input) of the yummy food pulled her towards the kitchen. She was asked to wash her dirty hands and face. And then once all clean, she got to relish the delicious meal. She ended her day by finishing her homework.

You must be wondering what Sensory integration has to do with the above example. All that Ruhie did above was sensory integration. Read this along to know as I explain.

Proprioception and jumping in the puddles –

- Ruhie could jump because she has an intact proprioceptive sense that helped her to decide how hard or gently to jump. Proprioceptors are present in all the joints of our body and the muscle bellies. They help us to understand the position of the body in space and also helps to grade the movement.

- Tactile sense and Jumping in the mucky water- Gave Ruhie the tactile input. Tactile sense is the sense of touch which tells us what we are touching or where we are getting touched. It also tells us the pressure of the input. Touch helps us to understand the world.

- Vestibular sense and swinging – Helped Ruhie develop vestibular sense. This is the sense which is present in our inner ears. It tells us about movement of the body in space and also the kind of movement. So, it tells us whether we are on a swing or a car or a roller coaster ride and guess what, it also tells us the speed.

- Vision- While Ruhie played in the muck or the mud, her eyes were glued on the swing. This is the visual system which tells us how to focus on what we want and ignore other distractions.

- Auditory- While Ruhie played amongst the sounds of children shouting and screaming, crow cawing away, she was very clearly aware of her mom calling her. This means that we can separate ambient sounds from focal sounds.

- Olfactory-is the sense of smell which helped Ruhie know what was cooked for dinner.

- Gustatory- is the sense of taste helped her to relish the food.

- Interoception- It is the sense responsible for detecting internal regulation responses, such as breathing, hunger-thirst, bowel bladder and heart rate cycle. What else was happening?

- Attention- as you read all of the things above, it must be clear about how attention is a by-product or fruit of the 8 systems working effectively.

- Motor planning- this was needed for Ruhie to grab her swing whenever someone vacated it- the speed and the coordination of her body to run quickly. Motor planning is needed to wash hands, feet, and face and also to complete her homework. So a lot of motor planning is needed in our day to day tasks.

- State of arousal- Even though Ruhie was very tired after school, playing in the playground was something that she could not never miss out on. She could SELF REGULATE and keep herself active in the playground. But once she was home, she was dull and lazy- she had control over the knobs of arousal which helped her to be dull or active.

All the 8 senses were integrated, Ruhie will grow up challenging her limits and exploring her surroundings. She will want to relive it. It helped her to celebrate life each moment and develop self-competence and self-confidence.

Now, what happens when the senses are not integrated- let's consider Ruhie again. If the sense may work less (hypo), more (hyper) instead of just right (optimal), then what happens

- Jumping in the puddle may not happen because of poor motor planning or there may be a big need to just jump irrespective of anything else.

- Jumping in the puddle may be avoided because of the texture of the mud or water.

- Touching mucky or gooey things may be just impossible because of tactile defensiveness. Or the child seeks just that irrespective of anything else. Because of the tactile sense of being more or less, everything goes into the mouth including non-food items or kids may be picky eaters.

- Swinging may be avoided completely or it may be the only thing that is sought. Because the child gets absorbed into the input, attention suffers.

- Visual attention or looking around and focusing on what is needed may be difficult because of poor filtering.

- Listening to mom's call or any sound directed towards the child may be ignored because the child is again absorbed into one of the senses intensely seeking it or completely avoiding it. Lot of smell seeking is there or the child is completely oblivious about it.

And then I am sure by now, you know what happens to play and forming connections. Everything is broken and shattered because there is no integration of senses.

There is poor self-regulation or regulation of arousal states making it really difficult to fall asleep – children may fall into patterns of no sleeping, difficulty falling asleep, irregular timings of sleep and so on.

And then you can imagine what it will be like to live with an interoceptive system which does not tell you when you are hungry and how hungry you are. How much to eat and when to stop eating? This system also signals when to go to pee and poop.

So, coming back to sensory integration- it is a process by which all the senses work together to make sense of the world – wanting to live and enjoy the world to seek and make connections. When the senses are not integrated, or when an individual has a sensory processing disorder, life gets difficult!

The good news is that Sensory integration can be facilitated by occupational therapists by providing "just the right" opportunities and kids can have a lovely childhood with memories to cherish for lifetime.

CHAPTER 18

UNDERSTANDING BASICS OF SENSORY INTEGRATION

"A recognized fact which goes back to the earliest times is that every living organism is not the sum of a multitude of unitary processes, but is, by virtue of interrelationships and of higher and lower levels of control, an unbroken unity"

- Walter Hess

Sensory integration functions typically occur automatically, fluidly, and subconsciously for most people. Some parents become alarmed to think that there might be a problem in their child's brain. However, sensory integration difficulties are not like the problems usually associated with "brain damage" or trauma. In most cases, the structures of the brain and nervous system are probably intact. It is more likely that the "messages" sent from one part of the brain and nervous system to another are not as clear, fast, or complete as expected.

Sensory integration refers to both a neurological process and a theory of the relationship between the neurological process and behavior. **When I say this, it's important to know that there is a relationship between the processes and the behavior. If these neurological processes are not intact, then it affects the behavior.**

A child's difficulty in processing and integrating sensation affects his participation in play activities, family outings, and daily living skills such as eating, dressing, grooming, bathing, toileting, functional mobility, and functional communication and so on. Further, parents report that these sensory difficulties affect the child's ability to participate in everyday routines too, which include leisure activities of daily chores.

It is also important to understand that behaviors such as anxiety, regulation of activity levels, arousal, and sleep are all linked to difficulties in assessing and integrating the sensation.

Social participation (playing with other kids interacting with outsiders and strangers) and communication, both involve the child to be able to interact with the complex world of sensory and motor demands. It may get affected by the sensory differences because it is really difficult for a child who has a sensory processing disorder to negotiate the unpredictability and the changing variables associated with social activities we involve ourselves in. It may be really challenging for a child who may exhibit anxiety and self-stimulatory behaviors to regulate himself.

Jean Ayers defined sensory integration as 'the neurological process that organizes sensations from one's body and the environment, and makes it possible to use the body effectively in the environment.' It means that adequate processing is very important; that the processing and then the integration of that information are very important. Both of them are important for the foundation of adaptive behavior. If these two are faulty, it becomes difficult for a child to participate.

The main basic systems- vestibular system, proprioceptive system and the tactile system - interact with each other and help at a foundation level for a child to be able to participate in higher level tasks. So for example, the vestibular and proprioceptive systems both are needed for the ability to develop adequate posture, balance, muscle tone, movement of the eyes, and coordination with the head and the body, so forth.

If the child is just leaning all the time, lying down all over the place, has poor muscle tone, does not copy from a board, is not able to read well, then we know that these are somewhere being impacted by the near senses, which have been developed well. When the vestibular and the proprioceptive systems work together, they provide a very important foundation with the tactile system, so that the child develops body awareness and coordination of the two sides of the body and planning. The tactile, vestibular and proprioceptive systems are very important, which work together to be able to develop higher level skills of eye-hand coordination, visual perceptual skills, and engagement in any kind of a perceptual, purposeful activity.

In combination with the auditory system, these basic level sensory systems help the child to contribute to development in speech and language. They also provide a very important foundation for all those behaviors which are needed for a child to perform academically, so that he can learn.

Many times when parents come to me they say, "My child is unable to write. He's not able to hold the pencil. He's not able to copy from a board." I give them activities in therapy and at home to work on the vestibular systems, to work on swinging and giving proprioceptive input; but then they correct me, they feel that I have not understood them well, and say, "You know what, Madam, we told you that our child is not able to do read, write, and copy from the board, but he can swing very well."

It requires a lot of time for me to make them understand how vestibular, proprioceptive, tactile, and interoception foundation systems help in the development of the higher level skills, so that the child can get ready to learn other skills.

I love how Dr. Jean Ayers was so ahead of her time when she originated the theory of sensory integration, and how she was solely responsible for bringing to our consciousness a way of looking at children, which has never been done before. She didn't see them as just someone with behavior problems, but she saw behavior from a neurological standpoint and how its processing gets impacted.

It was in 2013, that the presence of sensory differences was recognized as a part of 'Diagnostic and Statistical Manual of Mental Disorders,' which is the basis for diagnosis of ASD, under the restricted repetitive patterns of behavior/interest/ activities criteria. Sensory processing disorder is not yet identified as a disorder in itself. So, if I go back to Jean Ayers, she was really amazing to see the behavior of kids in a very different way. Ayres' deep understanding of hidden sensory integration disorders shaped her emphatic intervention with kids.

She was not very bossy, she was not always giving instructions. In fact, she was always asking them if they would want to participate, always giving a choice to the child and making the child be in control. She was very clear that her sole aim of providing sensory integration was to ensure that the child feels and discovers his skills which he is not aware of. She never imposed input on her clients. The role of the therapist is to just help guide the child towards discovering his abilities, without being too pushy, while the child is in touch with his inner drive.

Sensory integration ideally is a natural outcome of typical development. Normal sensory integrative abilities provide the foundation on which meaningful and purposeful participation happens in full range of daily occupations. Ayres also emphasized the relationship between adequate sensory integration and the development of self-control, self-confidence and a sense of mastery. In Jean Ayers' words, "Sensory integration is the organization of sensations for use." According to her, sensations flow into the brain like streams flowing into a lake and there's so much sensory information which is entering the brain at every single moment from so many different receptors and parts of our bodies. The main job of the brain is to make sense of all the information that it receives and then to locate, sort, and order sensations-somewhat like a traffic policeman directing the cars. The brain takes care of which information goes where.

When a child develops naturally the early developmental steps determined by the evolutionary history are pre-programmed into the human brain at conception, but the experience of interacting with the environment is also necessary for the full expression of the inherent developmental tendencies.

It is generally held that each developmental step is in some way dependent upon a certain degree of maturation of previous steps. For example, a child at three months learns to hold his head. Then, he starts rolling from his back to his tummy. When he achieves staying on the tummy and holding his head up, that's when he starts getting ready to crawl. So, there is one step which is achieved and then the next step follows. The child must be given a lot of movement.

Jean Piaget has also stressed on the early sensory motor (including reflex stage) stages of the infant. He was the first to recognize that the child's interaction with his environment was a critical factor in his development. It is very important according to him and that there is a lot of reciprocal interweaving. That means, there are a lot of things which are happening together. Piaget stressed that learning does not just happen to us. We create our own learning process by responding to various stimuli.

So, in development there are motor milestones and the reflexes, which go hand in hand. There is a good amount of reciprocal interweaving which happens together for any child. But the main playground for a child is the environment. The more movement the child engages in, the better the development. That's why the first seven years of the life of a child are called the 'sensory motor development'.

When I talk about reflexes, I'm talking about primitive reflexes. So, even the primitive reflexes have a journey, they come to support the development of a particular milestone and when that is achieved, they are at the peak and are then integrated or transformed.

If the sensory motor processes are very well organized in the first seven years of life, then the child has an easier time learning mental and social skills.

When the child experiences challenges, - which he can respond to effectively – he has fun. And according to Jean Ayers, 'fun' is the child's word for sensory integration. If you observe a child, when a child learns to jump, he jumps from one step, then to two steps, and then to three steps; a child constantly challenges himself.

In school usually educators often call reading, writing, and math as the basics for learning academics, but actually this complex foundation is built on sensory integration and the development of the vestibular, proprioceptive, tactile, and interoceptive systems.

When the development of the brain has deviated from the normal range, the resultant behavior that we see in the child would be a little lower on the phyletic scale, with the interference in the sequential expression of these developmental patterns. Sometimes even primitive reflexes are present and the sense of touch is apt to be diffused rather than well differentiated.

Some children are overly ready with a fight-flight reaction in response to some tactile inputs. This is one of the reasons why knowledge of a more primitive function is helpful. It's important to understand that sometimes a child is behaving very well, and at other times, he's not able to modulate because his brain is trying extremely hard to focus, regulate, and to calm down.

Most of the time parents do not realize that the child's learning and behavior problems are because of neurological disorders and the child does not have control over it. They think that the child does sensory stimulation behaviors on purpose. Kids are seen with judgment and parents sometimes feel guilty about it later. The aim is to help the kids to organize the input and help them feel better about themselves.

Dr. Roger Walsh of Stanford University and Robert Cummins of the University of Queensland reviewed a large number of studies on therapeutic environments and found that the critical factor in recovery was active physical interaction with the sensory environment. When the individual merely received the sensory stimulation passively, his brain did not recover.

Jean Ayres believes that learning skills is not the objective of sensory integration. The development of a sense of mastery, meaning, satisfaction, and self-direction were the end products of sensory integration. She saw how the difficulties in participation affected the emotional state of the person. She saw how clumsiness and poor motor planning would lead to feelings of inadequacy and loss of control over the environment.

When we work with kids or adults, our focus is not just on evaluating the components which cause dysfunction but also on understanding the mental phenomena. The interaction of mind-brain-body connection and interrelation needs to be the focus while using sensory integration. As neuroscience evolves and progresses, this connection is emphasized even more and I believe that the mind, body, and brain may appear as different systems that are functionally inseparable and interdependent.

Normal children do not need sensory integration because they receive the sensory stimulation through play. When a child has a sensory processing challenge, he is not able to process the sensations from his play and thus cannot develop adaptive responses. I have explained and elaborated more on this in the chapter of Art of therapy. So, a child with a sensory processing challenge will play, but that does not help him to integrate his brain.

The main aim in sensory integration involves providing and controlling the sensory input, especially the vestibular, proprioceptive, and tactile. Therapy is most effective when the child initiates and directs his actions. It really helps when the child wants the stimulus and he initiates to get the sensation.

It means that I will give opportunity to the child to participate in swinging and not pick the child passively and put him on the swing. I will allow the child to choose what he wants to do- swinging, jumping, or therapy ball. I follow the child and help him feel capable of learning any motor skill or academics or socially acceptable behavior. Most of the time, kids know intuitively what they want; they go in between tight spaces to seek pressure or go in circles when they want vestibular input or jump when they need proprioceptive and vestibular inputs.

We aim to watch, notice, and observe the child and check what the input does to him and report it to your therapist. It is also important to watch and look out for safety and to make the activity more meaningful. When we do sensory integration, it should feel like playing to the child. Play is the most powerful tool in the hands of parents and therapists to bring about changes and improvements in sensory integration.

Sensory integration is a holistic approach and involves the whole body, senses, and the brain. When the child initiates a task and engages in vestibular, proprioceptive, and/or tactile inputs, the muscles work together to get an adaptive response which helps send organized sensations to the brain. It takes a lot of repetitions to develop the neural connections.

It has been studied in both animals and humans that we receive internal signals that cause us to do what is most appropriate at a particular moment. For example, if an animal is deprived of certain vitamins, it will eat foods that contain those vitamins, even if those vitamins are not a part of their normal diet. When the animal has had enough, it will return to its usual diet. The animal does not understand about nutrition, but his body knows and tells how much to eat and what to eat.

Children also follow the internal signals and their actions are always purposeful. It may seem that the child is just playing, but he is following his instincts and building blocks of further development. It is important to create a therapeutic atmosphere where the child feels safe. Many times kids do not want to participate in activities that they aren't good at because they don't want to show their weaknesses. They have learned that people expect too much from them and often criticize them. When they are judged, they are not sure of listening and following their inner drive. If this is noticed in your child, a lot of time needs to be given to work on our self-regulation and our inner triggers before we make them feel safe.

Once the child is encouraged to follow his inner drive, he will realize his dormant abilities and experience self-fulfillment through participation in therapeutic activities at home or school. The spark in the child and his interest to participate is the best guide for us to know that we are allowing the child to shine and giving his brain the opportunities to develop.

I remember working with a 4-year-old girl, Dipi. She had sensory processing challenges. Her inner drive to play and explore the environment was buried under layers of inadequacy and failure. It took us more than 4 months to make her feel safe and feel non-threatened so that she could open up and direct her growth. Once this was done, she improved in leaps and bounds and opened up at school with her friends and teachers. She was a different child in a matter of just 2 years. A lot of cajoling, coaxing, and assisting was needed initially.

I hope this helps you to get an understanding on sensory integration and gives you a different perspective to see your child's behavior from. I will be elaborating more on this in the further chapters.

CHAPTER 19

SAFETY AND PREDICTABILITY

"Showing up, being present in the moment and helping someone feel safe, seen and soothed, that's my North Star. That is always the answer."

- Tina Payne Bryson

I was working with one child, Vedansh, who came to see me from Orissa. He was a 7-year-old boy who was diagnosed with severe autism. His parents were really concerned as he was not making any progress. He was completely dependent on his mom and lacked self-help skills. He had trouble following instructions and was completely in his own bubble. He was undergoing 2-hours therapy every day, six days a week for more than 4 years. They met doctors and checked if there was any medical condition that needs to be ruled out but there were no medical issues and he was fine. Parents were really dejected and came to me hoping for some help.

When I evaluated him, I realized that he was very scared. His mother told me, he has sensory issues and so he was scared. I did not touch him, but he was still scared. I gave him a lot of time to relax and get comfortable. I allowed him to jump on the trampoline or immerse himself in the ball pool and then tried getting closer to him. The trick seemed to work, so I touched his hands and legs. He was comfortable with that, but as I took my hand closer to his face, he got anxious. His mother said that he has a lot of sensory issues and they surface when someone tries to touch his face. I played around his face and his hair to ease his discomfort. And then, he allowed me to touch his face. Clearly, he was just apprehensive and there wasn't any sensory issue. It is really important to identify and evaluate the roots of any behavior. The moment my fingers came closer to his mouth, he again got tensed, his eyebrows curved and slowly his shoulders shrunk to touch his ears. He pulled his knees closer to his stomach, his entire body went into protection.

I inquired his mother to learn more about his heightened anxiety related to that particular region of his face. His mother mentioned that his speech therapist has suggested a few painful exercises to help him speak. So, wherever he visited the speech therapy center, they performed those painful exercises on him and didn't stop even when he cried. So, his apprehension was a consequence of painful experiences. We did a lot of parallel talking to prepare and assure him that I will touch his face only when he allows me and will stop if he feels any discomfort. He allowed me to touch his face and also to massage his gums and cheeks. If it was a sensory issue, he would not allow so soon. Fear was the reason holding him back. It is a very difficult task to separate and analyze roots of the behavior- sometimes it is a combination of sensory processing difficulties combined with fear but in Vedansh's case, it was pure fear.

I explained to the parents that Vedansh doesn't feel safe when those painful exercises are forced upon him. I asked them to communicate the maneuvers and communicate the steps with him before performing any vigorous exercises on him. His discomfort was never noticed and his reluctance to pain was termed a behavior issue and an escape tactic. Those exercises were performed on him for around 2 years, with the promise that he will speak soon. Parents continued taking him to the therapist and the boy withdrew himself as he felt unsafe every day. I am sure the therapist had the best intention to help the child and the same goes with his parents, but safety comes first. We are always taking care of safety -the physical safety of our kids everywhere. "Don't jump...Eat well...Take a bath...Do not cross the road alone," and so many things are beautifully taken care of by us, but most of the time, we only care for PHYSICAL safety. Emotional safety is also important.

It is important that kids feel safe when they are around their therapists. The integration of primitive reflexes are important especially Fear Paralysis Reflex (FPR) and Moro (have explained these in the future chapters) , because they play an important role in the development of connections through the limbic system to the other parts of the brain, especially the prefrontal cortex and the subsequent effect these links have on our emotional and behavioral development.

We all wish to fit into this world and to feel safe while interacting with people or in various situations. If the FPR and the Moro reflex are still active, we can feel overwhelmed by these interactions. And then instead of participating we tend to withdraw and enter into our cocoons. Also, in some cases, we may feel the need to control the environment to feel safe.

We are wired for survival and connection. If we do not feel safe, our system switches gears automatically and moves from thriving to survival. I need to emphasize that it is very important for a child to feel emotionally "safe" with the people or the environment. We want to give them the opportunity to learn – a very gentle coax. If they feel threatened or unsafe, they switch into survival and they don't do so intentionally.

When a child goes into the survival state, the autonomic state shifts from calmness to defensiveness. Child's body slips into fight-flight or freeze state. It also distorts their social awareness and they start seeing things as more negative. It may shut down the system and the child's body takes these cues of threat to immobilize into freeze or to disappear. Being frozen is adapted and the child's body may dissociate or tune out. Shutting down or passing out is potentially lethal to mammals and so the adaptive function is to dissociate.

Dr. Stephen Porges says, "Our body functions like a polygraph. We are continuously responding to people and places…we do this normally. If we do not feel safe, our polygraph is on high, we are in a chronic state of evaluation and defensiveness." This polygraph is switched on high, most of the time with neurodiverse individuals. They are constantly in a scanning mode checking if they are safe.

All of us require constant interaction with others to develop and optimize our potential. We get cues of the social interaction from smiles, eye contact, and laughter to know that we are safe and that the people around us aren't a threat. It is a physical process but also an emotional one. Even babies read parent's faces. They know instantly who is safe and who is not. We implicitly read faces and pick up body language cues. We pick up this important information from the tone of the voice irrespective of the fact whether we understand the language or not. We feel this connection at the level of sensations and in our body states. And when we are unsafe, we register the waves of distress throughout our body.

If we feel secure, our cortisol (stress hormone) level goes down, our dopamine (calm hormone) level goes up and we start to breathe slowly. If we feel unsafe, the opposite occurs. We have an internal pharmacy of chemicals which knows how to balance when we feel balanced emotionally. Every emotion that we feel sends information to the brain with an electrochemical reaction.

When we integrate the primitive reflexes - especially the FPR (intra-uterine reflex) and Moro – and work on sensory processing challenges, it helps individuals to access the resources needed to establish themselves safely in the environment. Developing the ability to feel safe in the world is an important part of growing up. Learning to be safe is linked to our ability to become independent, assert ourselves and our overall well-being. However, if the Moro, FPR, and sensory challenges are present, they do not allow us to truly experience safety which becomes a major roadblock in the process of development. If we struggle with feeling safe, then the brain stem fails to develop a strong neural network with efficient connections to the higher levels of the brain. Without safety, there is limited function and we cannot use our body effectively.

Going back to Vedansh, all that I did with him was to counsel his parents and explain to them the importance of feeling safe emotionally. For a child, parents are the safety anchors with whom they feel most secure. But in Vedansh's case, he felt very unsafe emotionally with those exercises which were performed "on" him rather than "with" him. I only told the parents to respect his fears and enter into his space only when he allows them to. I told them to treat him as a person with emotions and not just as someone who needs exercises to become "normal".

The parents sincerely followed the advice and did not push him but very gradually coaxed and made him cooperate while respecting his fears. We also worked on a sensory diet that his parents followed at home along with primitive reflex integration exercises. In a week, his parents sent me a video of him eating on his own and certain other significant changes in his life. Children are always co-regulating, we anchor ourselves first in the space of feeling calmer before we help our kids. We first self-reflect and check our own states first before we help kids. It is important to connect with our inner compass so that we can help our children.

Feeling emotionally safe and integrating the Moro and FPR allow us to have the resources to be able to calm down after experiencing perceived dangers. It helps us to see the complete and the whole picture to understand real and perceived threats. It is extremely important so that we can navigate the world without being in a constant state of stress and panic.

Jacob Barnett's mom Kristine in her book *The Spark*, gives a beautiful analogy to support this concept. Imagine that you live in a tree house in a beautiful forest, and the only place you feel safe and calm is up in that tree house. But people keep intruding, "Hey, come out of the trees!" They yell up at you. It's crazy to live in a tree. You need to come down here. Then one day somebody comes into the forest, and she doesn't yell or try to make you change, but instead climbs into your tree house and shows you that she loves it as much as you do. Wouldn't you have a completely different relationship with her than you do with anyone else? And when she asks you to come down for a few minutes, because she has something amazing to show you, wouldn't you be more inclined to check it out?

Learning can take place when children are in the "calm" mode. They do not learn when there is a soup of stress hormones in their brain.

CHAPTER 20

TACTILE, VESTIBULAR AND PROPRIOCEPTIVE SYSTEMS

As mentioned earlier, according to Jean Ayres, the fundamental sensory systems include: The tactile sense, the vestibular sense, and the proprioceptive sense (near senses). These sensory systems develop very early in the womb. They interact with vision and hearing. Let's understand each one of them in detail.

Touch is phyletically (on the ladder of evolution) a very old system to receive input. Touch is the biggest and the oldest sense. It is the first sensory system to develop in the womb and can function effectively when the visual and auditory systems are still under development. Touch is the catalyst for healthy development of cognitive, social, emotional, and physical spheres of an infant. It is very strongly related to motor planning.

The following will be seen if there are difficulties with this system.

- Child may want a lot of cuddling or may shrug off hugs and kisses.
- Tickling may be extremely uncomfortable even though he may appear to laugh.
- The natural reaction of the child to any touch input is that of intense fear and he's immediately thrown into a fight flight response.
- Does not like to touch messy gooey things or may seek them often.
- May dislike tags and get uncomfortable with seams or even shoes.
- May prefer a certain type of clothing only.
- Dislikes having a nail cut or a haircut.
- May not notice hurts and wounds and be completely oblivious of the same.
- May have poor peer relationships.
- Will be a picky eater and avoid eating certain foods completely because of the temperature or texture.
- May hurt other people or pets by holding them with a lot of pressure

and not understanding their pain.
- Keeps touching objects and people constantly.
- Chews on finger nails, T-shirts, collars, toys or pencils.
- May have difficulty holding and using tools like scissors, pencil, spoon etc.
- Uses vision to touch body parts.
- May have poor eye hand coordination and poor fine motor skills.

In his book, *How Can I Talk If My Lips Don't Move?: Inside My Autistic Mind*, Tito Rajarshi mentions, "I could not touch anything sticky. The experience of getting sticky rice on my hands made my nerves freeze. Yet I needed to learn how to eat rice with my hands because everyone is supposed to learn the traditional way of eating. I could eat bread and dry food, but I would not touch rice. Someone needed to feed me rice till I was five."

Touch also has strong connections with the emotional and social functions. Dr. Harry Harlow and his associates in their study took the newborn monkeys away from their mothers and raised them with "artificial mothers" which were made of wire and terry cloth. Whenever the little monkeys were stressed, they hugged or clung onto the terry cloth surface as if it was their real mother. They formed an emotional attachment with their artificial mothers and felt secure after hugging them. And the infants that were raised on artificial mothers made of plain wire did not develop that attachment. Harlow concluded that touch sensations are a critical factor in the infant's emotional attachment to the mother.

In her book, *Thinking in Pictures*, Temple Grandin mentions, "Motivated by love, my mother worked with me and kept me out of institutions. Yet sometimes she feels that I don't love her. She is a person for whom emotional relationships are more important than intellect and logic. It pains her that I kicked like a wild animal when I was a baby and that I had to use the squeeze machine to get the feeling of love and kindness. The irony is that if I had given up the machine, I would have been a cold, hard rock. Without the machine, I would have had no kind feelings toward her. I had to feel physical comfort to feel love. Unfortunately, it is difficult for my mother and other highly emotional people to understand that people with autism think differently. For her, it is like dealing with somebody from another planet."

Now let's talk about the vestibular system, this is present in the inner ear and plays a very important role in detecting movement of head in relation to the rest of the body. It works very much in unison with the visual and the auditory system.

So, what does that mean? In simple terms-you may close my eyes and make me sit on a swing, in the car, on the roller coaster ride, on a revolving chair, or on anything that moves, my vestibular system will tell me where I am and in which direction I am moving and the speed at which I am moving. All this complex information with just the vestibular system. Amazing!

Before a child learns to form a relationship with the mother, he learns to form a relationship with gravity. If the child's relationship with mother earth (gravity) is not secure, then all other relationships fail to develop optimally. So, the relationship that we as humans form with our mother Earth is more important for development and it is one of the significant relationships.

So from the example above, it is very clear that the vestibular system will sense movements

1. In a vertical plane like jumping or bouncing on a ball.

2. In an angular plane-like sitting on a swing.

3. In an orbital plane- sitting on the merry go round which goes round like earth around the sun.

4. In the horizontal plane- sitting in a car or riding a bicycle.

5. Rotation —moving around in rotations as we used to do when we were kids —go round and round and round till the world goes round and fall down and still see the world moving.

Also, we are very clear with our body and also very accurate about which direction and what speed is comfortable. When my son plays on the swings and I swing him fast, he tells me, "So do you want me to fall off the swing?" But when I go slowly, he says, "Am I a baby?" So you can see how well the vestibular system checks the speed and also knows what speed is comfortable.

Another amazing thing that it does tell me when it is enough – so I went to my sister's house and she had a swing in the living room. I kept swinging and chatting for more than an hour and then I could sense an alarm inside telling me to get off the swing and that it was enough for me. This is the body's way to protect the system.

Vestibular system has very strong connections with:

1. **Eyes**– Have you noticed that the world keeps revolving even when we stop going round in circles. That is our vestibular system telling us, "Ok, you have stimulated me enough! Just stop now." Technically, it is called post rotary nystagmus.

2. **Brain** –We feel giddy after we go round in circles – the vestibular system tells the brain, "Come on dear! It's enough for me for now." This is its way to stop excessive input and to prevent what is called "vestibular overload."

3. **Autonomic nervous system** – How many of you have experienced nausea after going round in circles or felt a "weird" feeling in your stomach after that? This is one more connection that needs to stop any excessive input.

4. **Muscles of the back** – Have you noticed that when we sit on a swing, we automatically erect our spine. This is one more connection by which this system maintains the tone in the postural muscles.

5. **Strong connections with the cerebellum** – This is how the vestibular system helps us to balance. So, when we are giddy after a lot of spinning, we lose our balance.

6. **Proprioceptors** – The vestibular system has strong connections with the proprioceptors and they work hand in glove.

7. **Reticular activating system** – This is like a switch which either makes us alert or dulls us down.

One important thing about this system is, the effects of imbalance of the vestibular system is felt in other systems. What do we see if there is vestibular dysfunction?

The system can be hypo- or hyper-sensitive. Individuals may have difficulties with planning or even registering the input. The following things can be seen:

- Visual spatial map – which in simple terms means an understanding of the world and the space around - gets distorted.

- Difficulty learning movements or actions that require timing and sequencing.

- Difficulty in moving in dark places, because such a person would rely on vision for the map. Also, there will be an underlying anxiety and depression.

- Difficulties with visual perception, words are all scrambled, spellings do not make sense. Sequence of spellings is difficult to remember and retrieve giving an appearance of learning disability.

- Overreact, negatively and emotionally, to very simple ordinary movement.

- Some kids may completely avoid movement to some others who would always seek movement.

- Feeling of fatigue and very low stamina or not sensing that the body is tired and needs rest so they seem to be filled with a lot of energy.

- Will avoid playing in the park – on swings, merry go rounds or seek it a lot.

- Will be very cautious and move really slowly

- Gets scared when the head is put upside down or seek this input repeatedly

- Any change of head position causes stress in some kids or individuals.

- Uncomfortable while climbing and descending staircase

- Has motion sickness while riding in a car or plane or sometimes lifts.

- Wants to manipulate the environment and the parent or caregiver and will be very scared

- Needs constant physical support from the parent or a trusted adult

- Has intense fear of falling backwards in space

- May not protect himself if he is falling

- May crave swinging and spinning all the time without getting dizzy

- Needs to constantly keep moving thus has difficulty sitting at one place.

- May be clumsy and keep bumping into things.

- Not able to generalize the tasks that have been learned

- May not understand boundaries and get too close to people

- Difficulty in developing bowel and bladder control

- Takes time to develop hand dominance and may be ambidextrous

Coming to Proprioception, it is a sense which refers to the input we receive about the position, force, direction, and movement of our body parts. It helps to integrate tactile and vestibular sensations. Proprioceptors are present in our muscles and joints. For example, knowing how much pressure is required in removing toothpaste from a tube, how much pressure is involved while writing, all of that is done by our proprioceptors.

Because it is present in the muscles and the joints, it is as large as the tactile system. Vestibular and proprioceptive systems work together and it is not possible to segregate them. You will see similar challenges which you would see in a child who has vestibular processing issues and a few more below:

- Difficulties with touch, balance, and movement.

- Poor body awareness.

- May be clumsy and tip over and fall frequently.

- Does not understand boundaries and may invade body space.

- Uses vision to do even daily and routine tasks.

- Does not understand how much pressure to use while writing.

- Mouths on to collars, T-shirts or pencils or non-eatable items.

- Slaps feet while walking or jumping.

- May choose to do only familiar tasks only and not want to take new challenges

- Has articulation or oral motor problems.

I have stressed a lot on self-regulation (in the part covering parents or therapists) and offering emotional support in my earlier chapters. Most psychologists and even doctors trace emotional problems back to conflicts in childhood, but sometimes the problem can be traced even further back to poor processing of sensory input during fetal life and infancy. I love how Dr. Ayres stressed on this from the beginning. It is extremely important that the child feels safe and secure in his own body. Without this, he will be in a state of fight and flight. Learning and relationships are formed when we feel safe not when we are in a state of stress (fight-flight-freeze mode).

CHAPTER 21

ART OF THERAPY

"Children come into the world exquisitely designed and strongly motivated, to educate themselves. They don't need to be forced to learn; in fact, coercion undermines their natural desire to learn."

-Peter Gray

Typically, there are three ways to address sensory integration dysfunction.

One way of doing this is by creating strategies to compensate for the disorder. So, for a child who cannot learn how to tie his shoelace or button his shirt, we would buy shoes without shoelaces or shirts without a button like a T-shirt. This approach may offer temporary relief from the problem, but the strategy needs further adjustment to meet future challenges.

Another way to address the problem is repetition. Breaking down the skill into multiple steps and implementing repetitions to master the skill. For example, we can teach a child to tie a shoelace with enough practice, but the same child might need additional practice to tie a bow on a different pair of shoes, or a gift box. Therefore, this approach offers immediate practical solutions, but may not offer solutions to other such situations.

A third approach is to provide therapy to improve the basic underlying functions and diminish the actual problem. **Improving function using a sensory integration framework is the primary focus of this therapy.**

The sensory integration approach is a complex process that requires years of specialized training and study. That being said, it still looks like play if provided appropriately. This therapy has no set protocol or regimen.

Hence, in a way, this therapy is like parenting. Each child is different and requires different interactions. There is no set recipe or 'magic trick' for how to be a parent. Parents who know their child well, learn to read their "signs and signals" and they best know how their child responds, behaves, and learns. So is the case with their therapists.

One of the aims of sensory integration therapy is, 'not to teach specific skills such as matching sound identification, or academics, but to enhance the brain's ability to learn how to do these things'. The objective is to modify the neurological dysfunction that interferes with learning.

In the last chapter, we spoke about the tactile, vestibular, proprioceptive, and interoceptive systems. The question is how to work with our kids using this information. Before we get into knowing how to use activities with our kids, it's important to understand what the art of this therapy is.

When I ask a child to participate in an activity, I emphasize both their physical and emotional involvement, without which, the therapy feels incomplete. So, if you want to effectively conduct therapy at home, you must ensure the emotional involvement of your child.

A therapy resembling a set of instructions isn't going to benefit your child. When you and your child are enjoying and emotionally involved with the therapy then things will improve at a faster pace. Remember, children constantly pick-up on what you feel, not on what you tell them!!!

So, what is a child trying to tell us if he is not complying with the task that you want him to do? He is telling us to get more creative, imaginative, and innovative. Use voice modulation or just be excited and animated while playing with your child! Soak yourself in the process completely both physically and emotionally.

Kids are like little scientists and their inquisitiveness fuels them to cross the milestones of development. This is the kind of environment in which we add vestibular activities, proprioceptive activities, and tactile activities. If I'm not enjoying the activity, if I'm doing it with the child just because the therapist has asked me to for the sake of it, the child learns that my parent doesn't enjoy being with me. The child is forming his concepts, belief system, and values; many layers of development form during such activities. Hence, you and your child need to learn and have fun together to make your child feel safe, supported, accepted, appreciated, validated, and connected with you.

Let's now talk about the kind of language we use when we talk to our kids. The first thing to take care of is the use of a positive language. What do I mean by a positive language?

The language that we commonly use is: "Don't jump, don't shout, no screaming, no shouting, no running, no this, no that."

Kids listen to a lot of 'NO'.

So how can we give a positive transformation to these sentences?

Instead of saying, "No screaming", say, "Let's talk softly." Instead of saying, "No running", it's better to say, "Let's sit on the chair." What I'm trying to convey is,   positive instructions are better than saying "no".

I tell the child what I want from him, rather than what I don't want from him.

When your child feels overwhelmed during the therapy, because he doesn't know what's happening then it becomes important to give them words so that they can express themselves. If a child is non-verbal and cannot express herself, I do a parallel talk for her and speak for her by saying things like, "I know you're feeling scared or I know you are not feeling comfortable."

Children usually respond saying, "Mama I'm so uncomfortable" or "my head is hurting, I am not able to sit at one place, it's getting really difficult for me, please help me out!" So, it's better to speak on behalf of the child at a time when the child is getting too overwhelmed with the process.

Another thing to remember is that I don't always clap to encourage a child. Somewhere, over a while, the child has to learn that a therapist smiling or a therapist saying 'wow' are indicators to know that he's doing well. I'm mentioning this because we need to know that saying 'wow', 'very good', 'very nice' over and over again makes the child get into the habit of it for everything that they attempt.

It starts with external praise to an intrinsic motivation, where the feeling that "I did well", is enough to motivate them to continue doing it. We gradually move away from external sources of reinforcement to an intrinsic reference point where they feel good about themselves.

Another important thing to remember is the 'just right challenge'.

What do I mean by the 'just right challenge'?

Ever seen a child learning to climb a slide? He would climb on the slide and slide down. He'll do it for around 10 to 20 times until he masters it. Once he has mastered it, what will he do? Now he will try to climb up from the ramp. He'll hold on. He will try to climb up. After several efforts, he will be ecstatic that he finally did it. So, what was the child actually doing? He was challenging himself, but it's "just right". Now, the child is learning to hold on and climb up, and after he has done that for 15-20 days and he has mastered that, now, it's not a challenge for him anymore. So, what he does now is, he tries to walk up the ramp without holding anything because that's fun for him.

Again, what exactly is he doing? He's creating another challenge for himself. Now, he would again go up and come down the slide and soon, he would realize, sitting is not much fun and then he would try to slide down on his stomach.

In all of these things, the child is constantly trying to pose himself with a challenge. What Jean Ayers observed in terms of the tactile activities, proprioceptive activities, and vestibular activities is, we try to make it fun, we make it playful. Then we provide opportunities for the 'just right' challenge.

When you follow the program at home, you have to observe that your child is in touch with his inner drive. If the child's connection to his inner drive is lost, that's a call for you that you have made that activity too difficult for him.

We have to ensure a child's safety while he plays, but not at the cost of his play and exploration. These little scientists love to explore and it is our job as parents and teachers to take care of their safety while they challenge themselves. Hence, a child shouldn't be stopped from doing things that are difficult for him. They are still trying to come out of their comfort zones because that's going to make them believe in their own abilities. We cannot do it for the child, the child has to do it all by himself. We cannot explore for the child and build connections in his brain. He has to explore himself and play and that's how the connections develop. We can ONLY provide them with opportunities.

Many times, I meet parents who come to me and they say, "I told my child to jump from this little stool and he could not jump. I know that he can do it and it's such an easy task. It is really easy. I don't know why he is doing this. I pushed him, I scolded him." I always tell such parents that it's easy for you, but that does not mean it is easy for your child; the child perceives it as difficult. If it's a stool that is too high for the child, I suggest modifying the activity. It's important that the child is enjoying and feeling confident after doing that activity. If the child comes out of that activity feeling why did he ever do it, it won't help either of us.

So, the aim is to ensure that you go lower if the child feels incompetent, and you go higher if the child seeks a challenge. It is not we who decide what the child should do or not. It is the child who's going to allow us, who's going to lead us and tell us what he wants to do.

When they are doing such activities, there would be noise, they would shout, scream, do various kinds of things and I think that should be allowed. That is their expression. Sometimes, these expressions need to be allowed to shape them into mature forms of self-expression.

The context and the reason for therapy are to ensure that we build the skills with the vestibular-proprioceptive-tactile activities, while the child is in touch with his inner drive. It is also important to create a safe environment and the right challenge for them to develop a particular skill. When the child achieves it, he laughs aloud and starts to believe in himself. We praise him for doing that. That is the whole formula and the whole recipe to make it happen for the child. That is the crux, the essence of sensory integration; that is the essence of play for any child.

So if I'm doing an activity for the child, there will be changes and improvement in the kid, but if I want to make the gains faster, the involvement of the child is really a big factor.

If I'm making a child do something that he doesn't feel safe and secure with, it's not going to help him. It will put his system under fight-flight-freeze mode. The child would go into a stress response. So remember, it's important to not enter into a power struggle and to push only as much as the child can take. It's like a just-right challenge; it shouldn't be too much of a challenge for the child. When these things are balanced well, you will see the child improve at a faster pace.

It is important to end with success; everything has to end with success so the child goes home feeling that he was good. Each day, the aim is to make him feel he was amazing.

The second important thing to do is to sandwich the kids' inabilities between his abilities. So do a very simple activity which he has mastered and then do an activity which we are trying to work upon, which he is finding difficult. If it is not happening, we take a break and do another easy activity again. Then we try the same hard activity again. We keep sandwiching, till we feel the child can do it. And we give support by creating a safe environment that the child needs. We should positively support them with a lot of appreciation, which should be honest praises.

Remember, our intention to provide therapy is to help a child discover his abilities.

The best system to stimulate initially would be the tactile system. Again, the child would lead and we would follow. But it's a very good idea to start with the tactile input without pushing the child too much.

Many times when I apply pressure with my hands, some kids don't like it; so I let them hold their bodies. Touch perception is different when somebody else touches our bodies. So, if the child is not happy with you touching them, you can ask them to do it themselves.

Sometimes, I use equipment because that's even better. I can use a therapy ball to help them touch or rollover, if they are not comfortable with the touch of a hand. Another important thing to remember is that before I start with any kind of input, I give a lot of deep pressure. So, a good amount of pressure, a good amount of rubbing are the kind of things with which I start working with the child.

Another important thing to remember with the touch input is, many parents do a lot of tickling with the kids and say that their child enjoys it a lot. **Tickling always overwhelms the child. Tickling is something that I will definitely not recommend for any child. Ensure that you stay away from tickling your child because that overwhelms them.**

As I work on the touch input with pressure or with rubbing, I keep looking at the child's face. I have to keep checking if the child is comfortable or not. Even if he's a nonverbal or a verbal child; if the body language conveys that he's not comfortable, I move away. I don't want to stress his system. I don't want him to feel that he's not safe. That is very crucial.

Opportunities to provide tactile input are plenty in the context of self-help skills. Use bath time to provide tactile opportunities using soap and body wash. Let the child use a loofah and name the body parts he touches it with. Use oil after bath and provide deep pressure opportunities. Back massage and face massage are great fun things. Shampooing hair and oiling them are great ways to give input in the context of functional activities. If the child has sensitivities, prepare them well in advance. I will be elaborating more on this in the chapter titled TEACCH. Kids may not participate 100% but even 10% is good enough to start with.

Be vigilant for signs of distress which should be taken as a signal to stop doing these activities- changes in heart rate, crying or meltdowns,

excessive sweating, fast breathing, nausea or vomiting, changes in skin color, dilated pupils, disorganized movements, nervous laughing, or escape / avoidance behaviors.

Use mealtime as a tactile opportunity. Eating rice and *dal* or vegetables with hands is a great idea even if the child starts by participating very little. He may want to wipe his hands and that's ok too. But if these opportunities are not given, then, these may not develop at all. These are more therapeutic and can be done in the context of self-help skills.

Take your kids' help or ask them to participate in daily chores. While making chapati ask the child to hold the dough or even roll it, allow him to engage in activities appropriate to his age. They can mix the *dosa* batter with their hands and get exposure to tactile opportunities. Involve them in removing peas, mashing potatoes, and breaking coriander or curry leaves. Let them sort pulses and grains in the context of meaningful activity. Let them wash small clothes and squeeze them, wash bicycles, scooters, and cars. Provide them opportunities to clean bathrooms, broom, and clean the house, clean windows, help to remove cobwebs. This way, they learn to organize the space around them. Rough and tumble play at home, especially with fathers is a great way to provide input and to also build connections.

Use different textured cushion covers and bed sheets and doormats. Be creative and play around with such opportunities. Start with just 10 activities on an everyday basis – it will happen every day for sure if done in the context of self-help skills. Incorporate it into your and your child's routine.

Walking barefeet on grass, sand, pebbles, or soil is a great activity. Picking up fallen leaves and sticks is another great activity. Crushing fallen flowers is an amazing thing that kids love to do. Making sandcastles at the beach is something we enjoyed a lot as kids and such opportunities really help. Allow them to play with mud and puddle. Times change, but children develop the same way and require the same three-dimensional, multi-sensory inputs to integrate their sensations.

Parents often complete their kid's tasks or designate it to someone other than the kids. This really hinders the child's development. Only when the child actively participates in his tasks will he develop. Provide them 'opportunities' to engage in sensory-rich environments. A child will not learn in the first go, but the least we can do is provide numerous opportunities.

Participating in self-help skills such as eating, dressing, grooming, bathing, and toilet needs is extremely important and it is our responsibility that they get independent in these essential skills. It is also very important that they practice this skill. Most of the time, parents teach these skills at a therapy center and do them for kids at home. I feel that it is important to learn from the therapist, but not to steal away that opportunity when the child can practice it in the context of self-help skills

We had a great childhood and our play had rich, multi-sensory opportunities. We hung from banyan trees, ran, climbed trees, jumped, skipped ropes, ran through the water sprinklers, and rode cycles. It was fun and that is how we developed our sitting tolerance and attention. Is your child getting this kind of play or is it very structured, going from one class to another?

We spend about 90 percent of our time indoors. Children need to be moving and playing outdoors where they can inhale fresh air. So, it is a good idea to do activities outdoors as much as possible. The present-day deficiency of Vitamin "N" causes Nature deficiency disorder. It is of utmost importance that they play in nature for as long as they can.

Studies are now showing that playing outdoors and exposure to nature and soil enhances mood, cognition, and quality of life. Outdoor play helps children to have perfect vision than kids who spend the same time indoors. Vitamin D that is absorbed through the skin from the sun promotes immunity in critical ways that oral vitamins cannot fully imitate. The messy and dirty world which we are trying to sanitize is the main element necessary for their robust health. Kids who take walks in the parks or play in green playgrounds have improved attention spans and better test performances. They are happier and calmer than their peers who spend their time in less natural environments.

A sensory diet is a group of activities that are specifically scheduled into a child's day to assist with attention, arousal, and adaptive responses. The activities are chosen for that child's needs based on sensory integration theory. This is specifically made for your child by your therapist. Activities and principles suggested above help to provide you information but do not replace what your therapist will offer after evaluating your child.

CHAPTER 22

INTEROCEPTION

The Interoceptive system gives us the ability to feel what is happening inside our bodies. This system has special nerve receptors all over our bodies including our internal organs, bones, muscles, and skin. These receptors send information to the brain which uses it to determine how we feel. Interoception allows us to feel our internal organs and skin. It gives us information regarding the internal state or the internal condition of our body. So for example, if I'm thirsty, hungry, sweaty, or tired, I will make sense of this input through my internal interoceptive system. Interoception is the key component of our emotional experience.

So for example, when a person is meditating, he would feel pleasant emotions and can understand them through his body markers (sensations which I talk of in the chapter of Triune brain). Those body markers are where the breath and heartbeat start slowing down and the person feels a wave of relaxation all through his body. These body markers (sensations) help a person to understand his emotional state (the language of feelings). So, it's important to again reiterate that interoception which is a key component of our emotional experience.

A well-functioning interoceptive system allows us to understand and coordinate the body state with the emotional state. The purpose of the interoceptive system is to help our bodies stay in a state of optimal balance known as homeostasis.

For example, the body states could be that of feeling hungry, thirsty, having a headache or a stomach ache, and the emotional state would be angry, excited, frustrated, irritated, and so on. It is also important to understand that the body's state will help a person to take action. If I'm very thirsty, which is my body state, I would get up and go to drink water. So, it's the interoceptive system that helps me to understand what I need to do. It helps me to anticipate and understand that water is needed if I need to go for exercise.

145

What I'm trying to convey is that the interoceptive system and the internal state awareness is important because that helps us to identify our emotions. When we understand this, it is very clearly understood that we can self-regulate only when we can control the way we feel and act. The self-regulation is completely related to the interoceptive system. So, when a child is two-years-old, his internal system is changing and when we give names to the feelings he is feeling, he starts developing the body markers and understanding himself even better.

With repeated practice, the child learns to understand a lot of things. In the initial stages, the child completely understands her or his internal state through a process called co-regulation. If the parent is angry, the child learns and associates feelings of anger to himself. It's also important to remember that any emotion we feel is always associated with some changes in our bodies.

So for example, if I run fast, my heart beats fast; my legs feel a little tired. And I know that I am tired because I'm sweating and the muscles in my legs hurt. I know that I feel tired because these are the changes that happen in my body. But if I'm not aware of my body sensations and of the changes that are happening in my body, then I am not able to develop somatic awareness or develop somatic markers in my body. Then interoception does not develop. This happens naturally and automatically in the early years of a child.

Having said that, it's also important to know that we all have so many different shades of feelings. We are not just feeling happy, sad, angry, and scared. Anger can come in the form of jealousy, anger turned inward could be guilt, or it could become hurt. There are so many different types of emotions we feel and each emotion feels different to our bodies.

Many times, it so happens that the body markers (sensations) stay and we sometimes forget the emotion that caused those body markers. So for example, if my muscles are shaking, my heart is racing too fast, and I feel something in my stomach, I know that I'm really nervous. I can think of all those situations when I have been nervous, so I have associated those body states with the state of feeling nervous. When I do that, it is called a somatic marker. In fact, the well-known neuroscientist Antonio Damasio calls these observations as 'somatic markers'. As we grow, we develop connections between the experience and the body sensations and we start labeling the emotion. If any of this raw material that provides us information is faulty, it becomes difficult for a child to learn to develop emotional regulation. Through the formation of these somatic markers, we have a speedy system in place that alerts us to the positive and the negative aspects of the situation.

I would like to repeat that our body state combined with the experience helps us to form an emotion and to understand what it is feeling. These somatic markers are very fast; they help us to make decisions very fast. We have another process, the cognitive process, which is more deliberate but is less efficient as it requires more energy.

As we read about the triune brain, we understand that our sensations and emotions and cognitive processes all happen together. When I feel hungry, I get up and eat something. But what most people don't realize is that hunger is not something that will motivate me to do something. It is a predictor of the future. My body doesn't wait until the last minute to get hungry. Instead, we get hungry much before we are in the danger of running out of energy so that we do not spend more energy finding and consuming food. Hunger is an early warning system.

In the same way, emotions don't give us this motivation to do some action. It gives us information about the future and what we need to do about it. Hence, it's important to understand that if the child doesn't even understand what he is feeling if he does not have a somatic marker which is linked to a particular experience, he is not able to understand what emotion he feels and so that poor interoceptive awareness does not let them develop a good problem-solving skill.

On most occasions, we can be flexible and think very fast. That is because we do not take logic-driven decisions. We rely on a lot of rapid intuitive judgments that are assisted because of our past experiences and somatic markers. So having explained all of this, it becomes clear that if a child lacks interoceptive awareness of the basic things that he's hungry, tired, or sleeping or if the somatic markers do not develop and link up with the experience, the child does not understand what emotion he is feeling.

All this while, you read about how we can help a child with sensory processing issues by bringing about a change in the external environment. We worked on dimming the lights, slowing down the vestibular input, reducing the auditory input, creating a calmer space, all of which include only the external environment; whereas, we also need to work upon creating interoceptive awareness. This means that we need to help them become more aware and understand what the internal body signals are. Just like other systems, the interoceptive system can be over- or under-responsive, and that has an impact on the emotions that the child would display.

So, if the child gets hurt, and if the child is under-responsive to pain, he will not feel the pain at all and he would not be able to respond to the pain. Whereas a child who's over-sensitive to the internal body states like pain, even a small bruise could overwhelm him.

Sometimes individuals who I work with, say that the internal signals that they receive are too confusing or chaotic and they do not know how to sort out those feelings. That is another thing that may happen and will create a lot of internal chaos and can also create an emotion of frustration. In such a case, if I'm going to work on just the external environment, it will not bring about the change that I want to work upon because the source of confusion lies within and the child is not able to understand the changes happening in the internal body environment.

I remember working with a thirteen-year-old boy, Ansh -he was diagnosed with Asperger syndrome. He used to get angry with listening instructions like, "You have to do this, you should be doing this or you can't do this." Any sentence with a 'must' or a 'should' triggered his anger. He knew his triggers but was unable to control their effects on him. In his case, he was unable to pick-up the signal because the signals were too overwhelming for him.

Many parents tell me that their kids could not make out when to stop eating. I know many neurodiverse adults who decide how much to eat based on the number of things they are eating. They do not have an internal body alarm or a somatic awareness marker, which tells them that they are hungry. They are using a cognitive strategy because they are not getting reliable signals from their interoceptive sense.

So, the child may feel hungry very often because even the smallest signal of hunger may be perceived as being too hungry for them. It is about how they perceive hunger or thirst. Many times, kids don't drink water at all, because they pick up the signal that they are thirsty when it has reached up to the peak and the body is going into dehydration mode. That's how the interoceptive signal changes and it affects the child on a day-to-day basis.

As I mentioned earlier about Ansh, he could not pick up on those early signals that his body communicated to him about his anger build-up. He could not notice the subtle changes happening in his body because his body markers could not pick up the signals. He could not pick up that he was getting irritated or frustrated or annoyed. Suddenly, he would explode with anger when the anger reached its peak. At that time, it was very difficult for him to self-regulate.

I am working with a 17-year-old boy, Ishaan. He was diagnosed with global developmental delay at the age of 2.6 years. He attends regular college, but his body is still not able to pick up the signal when he needs a washroom. He only realizes his need when the signal turns urgent. That is the reason why many younger kids have a hard time learning how to get toilet trained.

I remember working with an 11-year-old boy, Ronny who was diagnosed with a learning disability. He would get really tired immediately after doing every small activity. It could be a simple activity where he was asked to jump into the ladder from one end of the room to the other. And just one set of those jumps would cause him to feel immensely tired and sit on the chair. He was hypersensitive to the signals of feeling extremely tired.

Many parents tell me that their kids never get tired. This is mainly for kids who have sensory processing issues or a diagnosis of autism. Parents report that the kids are always jumping, running, or moving and it seems as if they never get tired. I think it is not that they never get tired, but that their interoceptive system is not giving them the signal that it is too much and that they need to take a break.

When there is a poor emotional awareness in children, they will definitely have difficulty identifying and describing emotions. Imagine the kind of stress and chaos they are going through because of the faulty interoceptive system; which is sometimes over-responsive, sometimes under-responsible, sometimes poses difficulty with discrimination. They try to calm their inner chaos and stress by co-regulating with an adult.

If the adult does not come from a place of center and starts reacting then there's a lot of chaos within the child and it gets really difficult for him to co-regulate emotionally or even self-regulate. When there is a difficulty with emotional regulation, we may see them as being more anxious, overwhelmed, having meltdowns, getting aggressive, irritable, and rigid, not wanting any changes in the routine, and wanting to have predictability. When there is so much stress coming from within, if we try to change things in the environment or work on behaviors without going to the root cause, the behaviors stay and they do not improve.

For a child who is getting overwhelmed in a classroom, because of whatever reason, he may start regulating himself by moving or jumping around, which helps him feel calmer. Doing things only on the outside, without addressing the emotional need or without helping him calm down, will not help alone. It's important as an adult to make the child aware of what he is feeling and to help him learn to connect the body state and the experience to an emotion. So for example, if I see that the child is sweating, I talk about it and say, "Look, you're sweating. Notice, your heartbeat is going so fast. It seems that you are tired." The child then learns to understand and connect the somatic marker to the emotion and the more often we label the emotion for them, it becomes easier for them to clear the clutter and the chaos within to help them make sense of what they're feeling.

One thing to remember is that teaching self-regulation takes a lot of time. But with persistence and practice, children learn it. So to summarize, it's important to know that interoception helps us understand our bodies. It helps us to know that, "This is my body and this is what I feel." Many individuals with autism spectrum disorder describe a feeling of disconnect from their physical bodies. They report not feeling and relating to their bodies.

In the book, *How can I talk when my lips don't move*, Tito talks about the brain system fragmentation, he indicates that the different subsystems in his brain do not work together. He has written about a thinking-self and an acting-self. Tito describes his acting self as weird and full of actions. He saw himself as pieces, as a hand or as a leg. He said the reason he spun himself in circles was so that he could assemble his parts as a whole. He recalled staring at himself in a mirror, trying to force his mouth to move. All that his image did was stare back. Tito wrote, adopting a third-person point of view that understood the disconnection between his acting self and his thinking self.

There is a book, *Carly's voice breaking through autism*, which Carly co-authored with her father, Arthur Fleischmann. For the first 10 years of her life, Carly was completely non-verbal. In her book also, she talks about the acting-self. These self-reports by Tito and Carly and how they observe their behaviors demonstrate the difference between the observer's view and the subjective experience between the acting-self and the thinking-self. It is the difference between what the sensory problems look like and what they feel like. Another thing that may happen is, the information that the child or adult with autism receives, maybe over- or under-responsive. If the brain receives too much sensory information, the acting self might look under-responsive, but the thinking self would feel overwhelmed. So, it is difficult for a child to understand these interoceptive signals and to make sense of the world.

The reason I'm sharing all of this is to help you understand, when we are calmer or come from our essence, we can offer the child that zone to be able to co-regulate. So, interoceptive awareness is extremely important. I would like to emphasize again, that children are constantly co-regulating. So we must come from our center and essence while working and helping them.

CHAPTER 23

INTRODUCTION TO PRIMITIVE REFLEXES

Ever since I became an occupational therapy student, I have loved to study and understand about primitive reflexes. However, in my college days, we used primitive reflexes to learn and work with kids who had delayed motor milestones. I still remember the discussions that we used to have about them, with various books in our hands in our college library.

In 2011, I met my friend, primitive reflexes again. I wanted to learn more and more about them. I started voraciously reading about them and also started my search for people who could teach me primitive reflexes. I started with Sally Goddard's book on *Reflexes learning and behavior*. There were many more books by her and I soon became a fan of her program called the INPP program. Her book, *Neuromotor readiness* to learning describes the details on how crucial is the role of these primitive reflexes in learning.

I was also very fascinated by the program which Nancy Green offered called the Brain Highways which really helped me to get a base on primitive reflexes. I found Nancy helpful and loved how systematic she was. I love the way she organized her course and also the way she passes the information, week by week. It was just fantastic and I kept learning and adding to my bank of primitive reflexes and applied the principles to the kids who came to me for therapy.

Then came a time when I attended a series of webinars by Svetlana Masgutova. Somehow, I felt everyone was talking about their perspective of primitive reflexes and with each book, with each webinar, and with each course, my understanding of the primitive reflexes deepened.
I started seeing these reflexes in kids who come for therapy and started blending primitive reflex integration with sensory integration. There are some "aha" moments in our lives and our learning and that happened to me when I did my course on Rhythmic Movement Training (RMT). Since then, there was no looking back and I continued learning with RMT till I became an instructor.

Movements that Heal, is a wonderful book by Dr. Harold Blomberg and Moira Dempsey. Another one called, *Beyond the Sea Squirt: A Journey with Reflexes,* is a great book if anyone wishes to understand and learn more about primitive reflexes.

Primitive reflexes are automatic, stereotyped movements directed from the brain stem and executed without cortical involvement. Moira Dempsey says, "The way we move and organize our world, feelings and thoughts depend, in part, on the foundations laid down by how well the primitive reflex program was able to be completed. The primitive reflex movement patterns set the basics of how we learn to be safe and explore the world in which we live. The very foundation of our ability to learn about the world and how to understand it is the way we learn to organize our postural and physical learning – this is our first learning in the world and, when well established, leads on to a far higher likelihood of being able to organize our feelings and thoughts as we mature. This requires that the primitive reflexes program is allowed to be completed and fulfill its role in establishing our lifelong movement patterns."

I explored and learned with Dr. Svetlana and her viewpoint and approach to primitive reflex integration too. I am still learning, but with each course, I dig deeper into the dimensions of understanding and applying the techniques with kids and adults who come to me. I have witnessed the changes in them because of the eclectic approach that I implement.

To elaborate on this, I would like to talk about Rimzim. I was seeing Rimzim who is a seven-year-old girl with a learning disability and a significant discrepancy in the verbal and performance IQ. In the draw the person test- the results showed that she is very anxious and believes in fantasy rather than real satisfaction and also had feelings of inadequacy and dependency. There was also a lot of restlessness and hyperactivity in her. Her visual-motor age was 5 years. She was tiny for her age and skinny, she shied away from making eye contact and just hid behind her mom when she realized someone was watching her.

I didn't want to discuss her issues in front of her mother, so I gave her a puzzle and asked her to play in the room outside my cabin. Rimzim had changed two schools in the past two years because she was unable to cope with academics and used to get easily frustrated and angry in the class. She was receiving counseling at school, but her behavior was worsening each day. Her mother told me that she cannot copy from the board and also made a lot of spelling mistakes. The major complaint was that Rimzim would hit all her classmates and did not interact with kids. She had motion sickness also. Even though she was seven, she continued to wet the bed, every single night.

After we discussed her issues, we called Rimzim to have a general conversation and evaluated her. I realized she had Sensory processing disorder and unintegrated primitive reflexes.

The unintegrated Spinal Galant Reflex affected her sitting, because of which she constantly changed her position and wriggled in the classroom, it also resulted in bedwetting and difficulties with auditory processing. Auditory processing affected her ability to blend, discriminate, and sequence sounds, and thus her spellings suffered and reading comprehension was also slow. The presence of ATNR (Asymmetric tonic neck reflex) and sensory challenges affected her planning and bilateral integration skills. She had difficulties in crossing the midline which made writing very difficult for her. Her eye tracking was also laborious when it involved crossing the midline. Because the entire task of copying from the blackboard was not automatic and completely done by the cerebral cortex. Also, this slowed down her ability to comprehend.

A cortically directed postural response is far less smooth and effective than one which occurs automatically in response to appropriate sensory input.

The presence of STNR affected her posture because the tone of the upper and the lower body was dependent on the position of the head. It also affected her speed of accommodation (the automatic ability of eyes to converge and diverge for near and far objects) which affected copying from the blackboard. She avoided eating by herself because it was messy in the presence of active STNR.

In 1978, Ayres observed that one of the major symptoms manifested by children in disorders of postural and bilateral integration was 'poorly developed primitive postural reflexes, immature equilibrium reactions, poor ocular control and deficits in a variety of subtle parameters that are related to the fact that man is a bilateral and symmetrical being'. As the primitive reflexes are inhibited, the postural reflexes emerge, which gradually take over many of the functions of the primitive reflexes. **Postural reflexes take up to three and a half years of age to be fully developed.**

The postural reflexes were not developed in her case as the primitive reflexes were still present. Thus, there was a general slowness and clumsiness in everything that Rimzim did. Rimzim had a very intelligent brain that was compensating for the above-mentioned challenges but at the cost of falling grades. Since she is intelligent and only she could see the tremendous herculean effort she was putting to participate in tasks at school and home, she was getting really frustrated. She was falling into a pit of frequent tantrums and hyperactivity which were all seen as behavior problems and non-compliance for which she was given counseling in school. Many even thought that Rimzim did so on purpose.

The cerebellum coordinates and regulates movement activity and develops strong connections to the higher-level cortical areas responsible for speech and language. If the primitive reflexes are unintegrated, the postural lifelong reflexes practice motor patterns from a shaky foundation, and postural organization thus becomes compromised. The cerebellum then does not have a good basis from which to modulate and coordinate everything that needs to work together to complete a task gracefully and smoothly.

It is the cerebellum that is responsible for coordination, smoothness, and rhythm in any movement pattern. It plays a big role in modulating the movement. It is also important in modulating our emotions, thought, and behavior as we mature. The better the foundation the cerebellum has to do with this modulation, the more we can organize our emotions and develop impulse control. This clearly was the difficulty that I was seeing with Rimzim.

Rimzim also stammered at times. The cerebellum coordinates the speed of the thought and the speech which if uncoordinated led to stammering. The connections of cerebellum with the Broca's and Wernicke's areas (important areas for speech and language) help with the coordination in the muscles necessary for speech.

So, we started with Sensory integration, Astronaut training (Approach developed by Mary Kawar to work on the vestibular-visual-auditory triad), Therapeutic Listening (Auditory intervention program developed by Sheila Frick), RMT (Rhythmic Movement training), and MNRI (Masgutova Neurosensorimotor reflex integration) to integrate the presence of active primitive reflexes in Rimzim. We also started EFT (Emotional freedom techniques) with her mother. It is because Rimzim's mom was getting stressed while handling Rimzim's rapid mood swings.

Rimzim came for Sensory integration sessions twice a week and her mother followed the program at home while we worked on her emotional wellbeing sessions once in fifteen days. Even after a month of her training, there was no difference in her at all. I was really sad and wondered what went wrong. Then we changed her therapy targets but worked along with the same systems as above. She took a break for April because of exams and was out of town in May for a few days because of which the therapy was irregular.

Then, we decided to be CONSISTENT for a month and see if things get better. I met Rimzim in July and saw the posture of the mother, it was upright and straight and she looked at me with a twinkle in her eyes. I sensed that something good had happened and was really curious to know what it was. We started filling the follow-up form and here is the list of changes they quoted:

1. She started having sound sleep because of which she can focus better (earlier she had disturbed sleep)
2. She had started eating on her own completely whereas earlier she was fed by her mom.
3. Her tantrums and impulsive behavior reduced by 50-60%.
4. Her motion sickness had gone away. In fact, she also sat on the merry go round which was initially something her parents would not even dream of.
5. She had started copying from the blackboard. She has started writing fast. She has stopped hitting her classmates and not just that, she made friends!
6. Her stammering which came with her anger had reduced by 60%.
7. Self-regulation or in simple words —controlling her behavior which used to take 30 minutes earlier- now happens in just 2-5 minutes.

After 6 months of CONSISTENT work with Rimzim at the therapy center and at home by her mother, she changed completely. Her mom was happy and could resume her work again.

Dr. Ayres mentions that the presence of primitive reflexes is significant and in that they tell the therapist that the higher portions of the brain have failed to integrate some aspects of lower function. They are like a window into the child's mind.

A recent study supports the hypothesis that ADHD diagnosis is closely linked to persisting primitive Moro and Galant reflexes in children in the school age. These persisting developmental stages related to certain motor and cognitive functions may indicate that ADHD presents compensation of unfinished developmental stages related to the diminishing of primitive reflexes that may occur as a response to various stimuli. These changes possibly explain ADHD symptoms as a consequence of a conflict between higher and lower levels of cognitive and motor functions during brain processing. This finding in ADHD patients is in agreement with few reported studies in patients with dyslexia documenting higher levels of persisting primitive reflexes.

Peter Gray, Ph.D., a research professor in psychology at Boston College mentions, "We expect kids to sit for hours and do what they are told to do, and if they can't do it, nobody kindly says, 'I see you're restless, get up and play.' They say, 'You better go get tested for ADHD so we can put you on drugs.'

CHAPTER 24

HOW PRIMITIVE REFLEXES AFFECT SPEECH AND ACADEMICS

Do you know, there is a direct link between the presence of unintegrated primitive reflexes and academic underachievement?

Academics has its roots in the adequate mastery of motor skills. Most of the higher cognitive processes are also rooted neurophysiologically in the systems that are involved in postural control. We saw this in the case of Rimzim in the chapter.

To be able to read, the child needs good control of smooth eye movements. The child must also be able to translate a visual symbol on the page to an auditory equivalent. In addition to control of oculomotor skills, this requires prior ability to discriminate between different sounds, sound blends, and nonsense words such as syllables.

Reading requires us to find a visual "fixation" point on the page. This requires that the two eyes learn to work together so that the two eyes see one image instead of two separate images which are called convergence. Also, like a broom, the eyes have to sweep across the print that is to be read. This is called a saccade. The purpose of saccades is to move the eyes as quickly as possible to the next position, so the point of interest is centered on the area of the eye where the focus is at its sharpest (fovea). After each saccade, the eyes pause (fixate) and they may make a small regressive movement, to check or re-check any relevant information that may have been missed in the previous saccade. Any problems with visual fixation, convergence, or control of saccades can affect fluency, accuracy, and comprehension when reading.

It is also important to know that the vestibular system works as a team with the visual and the auditory system to perform tasks that help us to understand the 3-dimensional space around us. When the vestibular-visual-auditory system works together, our world becomes more meaningful and we learn to orient and explore with people and things. So, reading requires the integration of primitive reflexes and the efficient functioning of the vestibular-visual-auditory triad. I combine the protocol of "Astronaut training" also called the sound-activated vestibular-visual protocol developed by the occupational therapist Mary Kawar in my consultation sessions.

Reading also requires the ability to translate the visual symbol to an auditory equivalent. With many kids, when there are auditory processing issues, I have used therapeutic listening. It is a comprehensive, multi-faceted program that involves much more than just the ears. It is a protocol designed by the occupational therapist Sheila Frick. I use a listening program along with primitive reflex integration on many of my cases.

Many listening programs are available like Tomatis, Auditory integration therapy, Samonas, and many more, but I use therapeutic listening as I am trained in this. I am sure the other programs are effective too.

The reason I wish to share all of this is to emphasize how each system is interwoven and how they work together. Just giving practice in reading or writing by repetition alone does not help to achieve skills, especially if the child has a history of academic underachievement. The emphasis needs to be on developing the systems that are involved in the process. For example, I cannot just work on the gears of a car, or just the brakes or the steering, every single part needs to work in unison and coordination to drive the car. The same applies to our bodies.

Learning math requires good spatial skills and good talking between the two hemispheres (left and right) of the cerebral cortex. Math, especially the first few years of math, is quite closely related to space perception and this does not develop well unless the vestibular system develops well. Most of these skills are rooted neurophysiologically in systems that are involved in postural control. Primitive reflexes play a crucial role in supporting and facilitating stability and flexibility in postural control.

To be able to write, a child needs to have developed good eye-hand coordination which is also a motor skill. Babies naturally put their hands and fingers into their mouths. They are learning to grasp objects and put things in the mouth as the Babkin reflex starts integrating. This helps them to develop the fine motor control which is needed to exercise control on their hands and mouth.

When the hand mouth reflex (Babkin) does not integrate, children have a lot of tension in the temporomandibular joint, or the jaw. They also have poor fine motor ability in their hands which makes it difficult for them to participate in tasks such as buttoning, writing, and so on. When this reflex is active, children have movements in the mouth region when they are participating in any task with hands. They may keep their mouth open or stick out their tongue or bite on the side or under the lips while doing writing or cutting.

By 4 months of age, a baby learns to grasp things and hold them in the midline. This is the beginning of coordination between the two sides of the body. By 6-8 months, the child can do the pincer action to pick up small objects. A child is usually able to carry out tasks that involve crossing the midline of the body by four years of age. Crossing over the midline is important not only for general coordination but for the ability to draw shapes and form letters and numbers. By 3 years of age, a child is usually able to oppose the thumb to each of the four fingers of the same hand in succession. This ability improves between three and eight years of age, although some mirroring of movement may still be observed up to ten years of age. Between the age of 3-7years, a child can use scissors, spoons, forks, crayons, buttons, and shoelaces.

The concept of using motor training programs to improve learning is not new. Kephart, Frostig, Getman, Cratty, Barsch, Ayres, Belgau, Kiphard, Schilling, and others all advocated and developed perceptual and developmental screening and training programs to improve the perceptual-motor skills of young children to enhance learning outcomes. Jean Ayres also mentioned that one of the major symptoms manifested by children in disorders of postural and bilateral integration was 'poorly developed primitive postural reflexes, immature equilibrium reactions, poor ocular (eyes) control and deficits in a variety of subtle parameters that are related to the fact that man is a bilateral and symmetrical being'.

In the present day and age, the screen is impacting the development of visual-motor skills and also stealing opportunities for movement from the child. The formative years are spent staring at a screen instead of looking around in nature or focusing on objects around which does not allow the visual system to develop optimally.

When the primitive reflexes are active, there is inefficient myelination of the corpus callosum (it's like a hairband which is a bridge and helps the two hemispheres of our brain to talk). This may lead to learning as well as reading and writing difficulties. It may also affect reading comprehension where the child reads but is not able to answer the questions on what he read.

When the corpus callosum is myelinated well, the child can read well. The natural activities that help with myelination are the integration of the Asymmetrical Tonic Neck Reflex and then creeping and crawling like a baby.

This is strengthened even more by walking, running, and so on. **It is between four to five years of age that the corpus callosum has matured enough for the child to start working in the midline. And by the age of 7 or 8, eyes develop the ability to continuously follow a moving object across midline easily. Total eye dominance is established by 11 or 12 years of age.**

The child must pass through each physical or motor milestone. Many parents feel happy that their child walked too fast and did not crawl at all. I still remember when my son started standing when he was 8 months of age, I facilitated crawling and was happy when he crawled and did not skip that stage. I ensure that every child who comes to us who has delayed motor milestones passes through the stage of creeping and crawling as this is important. Some kids skip crawling and do more bottom shuffling possibly because of an underdeveloped STNR (Symmetric Tonic Neck Reflex). Crawling is necessary for myelination and strengthening the connections in the corpus callosum.

Children who get easily distracted and have difficulties focusing usually have some retention of Fear Paralysis Reflex (FPR) and the Moro reflex. And when the Moro and FPR reflex is present, children react with tantrums when stressed. This is because they easily slip into survival patterns when stressed out.

So, it is important to add sensory integration along with primitive reflex integration so that the child can make gains in reading, writing, and math skills. It does not just develop by practicing it alone. I want you to understand the role that each of these systems and reflexes plays to lay the foundations for academics.

It is also important that the child gets enough play opportunities and opportunities for movement. In most kids who seem hyperactive and have difficulty sitting still, the Spinal Galant reflex is retained. Sitting still also requires good postural control, balance, and orientation.

A healthy five-year-old has a maximum attention span of only around nine minutes but if we expect them to sit for more than 30 minutes and work on sitting tolerance beyond 9 minutes, then it is not a realistic goal.

Let's talk about speech...

A baby learns to put everything into the mouth when he is born. He is not just refining his fine motors by holding objects but also working on his oral motor system naturally. It is important that the child learns to move his whole body and then the arms and shoulders in gross motor activities because they are important for the development of language skills. When they put everything in their mouth, they are learning to understand the tastes, textures, size, and shapes around the mouth. We first learn to explore using the mouth and then our hands. An infant who is never allowed to put things in their mouth and explore will not gain a good understanding of size, texture, shape and will have difficulty with coordination of the muscles of the mouth, lips, and tongue and will continue to attempt to first understand the world through their mouths.

The more opportunities the child gets to hold and play and explore with different shapes, sizes, and textures of objects, the more he will learn to use tools better. By tools, I mean using a spoon, scissor, fork, and so on. Our articulation is dependent on our ability to control the fine motor skills of our lips and tongue. An important thing to note is that it is also closely connected to the fine motor ability of our hands.

We discussed the hand mouth (Babkin reflex) reflex and how its integration is important to develop oral motor control and efficient fine motor skills. Carla Hannaford in her book, *Smart Moves*, mentions that babies begin to babble and vocalize at around the same time when they begin moving their toes. She feels that there could be a correlation between language delays and having tight immobile legs in early childhood. There is a muscle train connection between the tongue and the big toe. When the big toe does not move flexibly the tongue is also not flexible. This affects how we speak and talk. Thus integration of foot reflexes (Babinski) helps to improve language and speech.

I see primitive reflexes as an important piece to be considered while working with neurodiverse kids and even adults.

CHAPTER 25

ROLE OF PRIMITIVE REFLEXES IN EMOTIONAL REGULATION AND BEHAVIOR

As discussed in the earlier chapter, you must have realized how the presence or absence of primitive and postural reflexes at key stages of development provides a window into the functioning of our nervous system. We now know that when the primitive reflexes are inhibited, they allow the postural reflexes to emerge.

While we look at these reflexes, it is important to understand that none of the reflexes act in isolation. They all emerge at various times, develop at a different time and pace, and are integrated at different stages. Each reflex has a journey to emerge, peak up, and then get inhibited or integrated. They never desert us but stay with us as friends. The process of inhibition puts them to sleep in the brain-stem (lower center of the brain) and they can re-emerge if there is damage or accident to the higher brain centers.

At around five weeks in utero the neural tube - which is the foundation of our nervous system - forms. At this time, the intrauterine reflexes - which are the first group of reflexes - emerge. They are meant to emerge, develop, and transform in utero. These reflexes are rooted in survival and teach the growing fetus to move or not move when stressed. These reflexes lay the groundwork for the fight-flight and freeze responses. At this point in time, it is not a primitive reflex. This is because at this point in time neither the senses nor the neural system has been sufficiently developed to generate any reflex pattern. Instead, the reflex pattern is created by direct transmission of information via electromagnetic frequencies between all the cells of the fetus.

Fear Paralysis Reflex is one such reflex that emerges between 5 weeks to 7 1/2 weeks in utero and develops and peaks by 9 weeks. It is integrated between 9 weeks to 32 weeks. It is also called the withdrawal reflex. This reflex (FPR) is also seen in animals, for example, if a rabbit is caught by the headlights of a car, it freezes at the spot instead of running away from the threat. Potential activators of this reflex are multi-sensory, psychological, and also physical. This reflex can also be activated by thoughts or by external events. It is important to know this because the effects of this reflex on behavior are significant because it appears to reduce the control of the neocortex (higher centers of the brain) and makes the person more susceptible to less mature reaction patterns. The FPR transforms into a Moro reflex. However, if the FPR does not integrate, the Moro reflex stays active.

The second set of reflexes is primitive reflexes. Primitive reflexes emerge in the womb beginning with the Moro reflex at 9-12 weeks after conception. Primitive reflexes are fully present at birth in the healthy neonate born at 40 weeks' gestation. They are then gradually inhibited by the developing brain during the first six months of postnatal life. These reflexes are responses to specific sensory stimulation or change in position. A newborn uses the primitive reflexes to move until the brain matures a little to establish connections to the higher structures of the brain.

Moro reflex has two phases. The first flinging out stage which begins emerging at nine weeks should be established by thirty-two weeks when the lungs are developed and the breathing mechanisms are in place. The second clinging/embracing stage of the Moro then begins to develop. By birth, both stages of the Moro should be established, as it is vital for survival. The Moro works by stimulating the sympathetic nervous system and adrenal glands in the event of stress, releasing a flood of adrenaline and cortisol into the bloodstream in order to excite and alert the system.

What exactly is the Autonomic nervous system?

The autonomic (sometimes also called as automatic) nervous system is the part of the nervous system that supplies the internal organs, including the blood vessels, stomach, intestine, liver, kidneys, bladder, genitals, lungs, pupils, heart, and sweat, salivary, and digestive glands.

It has two divisions – sympathetic and parasympathetic. I really don't know why they are named this because the sympathetic nervous system is in no way related to sympathy. It excites the system when we feel threatened and pushes us into a fight-flight mode. So, it is responsible to stay active for a short while and then to calm down. When the sympathetic system is stimulated, this leads either to fear, panic, and preparation for escape or evasion or it leads to anger, rage, and preparation for aggression.

The parasympathetic response deactivates the sympathetic responses and brings elevated levels to calm and cool things down. It helps in lowering elevated heart rate and slowing rapid breathing, returning the digestive system to normal and the person to an overall peaceful, relaxed state of mind. This response is mediated by the ventral vagus nerve (it is a cranial nerve), meaning it is located towards the front of the body.

When Dr. Stephen Porges introduced the Polyvagal theory, he added a third level of reaction which is the most extreme. In this, the parasympathetic nervous system causes a near-total shutdown of key bodily functions. In this state, a person may become speechless, enter deep depression, faint or go into shock. In the most extreme situations, cardiac arrest may occur, leading to death, if not reversed immediately. This is the freeze reaction. This reaction is adapted and the person may tune out or dissociate.

The ventral vagus is regulated by the parasympathetic nervous system (rest and digest state) which operates when we feel calm and safe. In this state, we are open and engaged with our world. We spend our time growing, healing, and restoring the body. Co-regulation is extremely important it has two phases.

In phase one, there are social engagement behaviors

- Facial expressions
- Gestures
- Prosodic vocalizations
- Listening and
- Reciprocity

The second phase of co-regulation has physical contact while immobilizing without fear. This state maintains a physiological state that supports our health, growth, and restoration. It optimizes the ability to rest, relax, sleep, digest, and perform bodily processes. It also enables feelings of trust, safety, and love and does not require face-to-face interactions.

The vagus nerve is constantly taking information and depending on whether the information coming in is 'safe,' the vagus nerve instructs the body to be parasympathetic (calm, engaged, smiling, open) or sympathetic (argue, move away, shut down) behavior. These two systems are in direct communication; they support each other. When we feel safe, we use the social engagement system to communicate verbally and non-verbally.

Dr. Stephen Porges says, **"These 'social' muscles function as filters that limit and allow social stimuli. Hence they determine the individual's engagement with the social environment."**

We engage with the world socially only when we feel safe. We see the world through the lens of our sensory systems. In this state, we interact socially and make friendships. Thus, this state helps us to be in a calm state for good health and restoration of cells. But the social engagement system does not work well when we are in a fight, flight, or freeze states. It goes offline and we cannot access it when stressed.

The Moro reflex when unintegrated or retained puts a person into a fight-flight state.

The following things are noticed when this reflex in unintegrated:

- Increased tendency to be hypersensitive to sound.
- Insecurity
- Generalized anxiety and/or fearfulness
- Dislike for sudden unexpected events
- Poor adaptability – difficulties with transition to anything new and tend to cling to familiarity.
- Easily distracted
- May be physically timid and may dislike or avoid rough sports; poor regulation of energy levels - either too hyperactive or completely exhausted.
- Mood swings
- Tense muscle tone (body armoring which results in a tendency to 'hold in' emotions, sometimes resulting in emotional outbursts or the development of somatic symptoms such as headaches, digestive problems, or other psychosomatic complaints.
- Lack of confidence & low self-esteem
- Need to control or manipulate events.
- A tendency to suffer from sensory overload in busy or novel environments.
- A discrepancy between verbal, emotional, and social behavior often exists, causing problems with social integration, particularly peer relationships
- Dilated pupils are slow to react to light which causes bad night vision and hypersensitivity to light. There can also be a tendency to be cross-eyed at near and far distances. Some people have to wear dark glasses even when inside
- Vestibular sense: Hypersensitivity to vestibular stimulation, motion sickness and problems with balance
- Hypersensitivity to touch

The behavioral traits and longer-term effects of a retained Moro reflex are not just seen in children. They may also be present in adults who suffer from anxiety and panic disorder. Long-term over-stimulation of the stress hormones thus making them more prone to allergies. This is thought to be the result of heightened sensitivity and is accompanied by biochemical changes in response to stress.

If the FPR dominates, it puts an individual into a freeze response. Symptoms of retained FPR are:

- Low tolerance for stress.
- Flaccid, floppy muscle tone
- Inability to respond to external events despite a high level of internal excitation
- Sleep challenges
- Difficulty swallowing, temporary paralysis of the muscles of the pharynx, and larynx necessary for speech. It does not happen voluntarily but it is a physiological shutdown.
- Anxiety and outbursts when there is a change of routine and things no longer remain the way they are used to.
- Lack of emotional security and flexibility can result in a need to manipulate or dominate their playmates
- Over Sensitivity to sound, touch, light, visual stimuli, or vestibular stimulation. Dislikes being touched, especially light touch. Extreme vestibular sensitivity causing nausea, feeling giddy, or feeling disoriented which overwhelms the person and shuts the system. Difficulty making eye contact because the sensory input is too overwhelming. Sound sensitivity is also very commonly seen.
- Extreme tiredness after being exposed to excessive stimuli and may need to rest or even sleep after school

You must have noticed that many symptoms of a retained FPR are also common symptoms of autism. The reflex will be triggered by eye contact and poor eye contact is a common symptom both of autism and a retained FPR. Children with autism tend to shut themselves from the world around them and stop communicating. Other children may become very shy. Other strategies to avoid challenging situations are things such as obsessively sticking to routines, poor adaptability, and refusal to accept change, all common symptoms in autism. When the child is not able to shut out the world, severe tantrums are common reactions.

It is important to remember that the response of the FPR is to shut the system down whereas the Moro excites the system, so the reaction of the child to stress gives an indication as to which reflex is more prominent. When these reflexes are triggered, the child will go into his survival pattern and become acutely aware of what is going on around him; therefore, accommodation will be obstructed and he will not be able to focus his vision and attention and finds it difficult to learn effectively.

We need to know that an individual can be in a fight-flight-freeze response or social engagement mode. We cannot be in both modes together. We discussed earlier that social engagement more or less goes offline as we are engaged in looking after our safety. No one needs social niceties when you are running or fighting for your life, and you don't need them when you are frozen to the ground in fright. The brain diverts the attention to where it is needed and this social engagement mode has less priority to be active when threat is perceived by the individual. At such times, this system is shut down. The situation or the input may not be seen as threatening by us but the child perceives it as one. Behaviors give us a window to understanding how the senses are registering or modulating the input.

In general, the sympathetic and the parasympathetic systems work in harmony. They thus help us to stay calm and interact with others. We can rest and digest. And in such a state, we can speak to others, give eye contact, and engage in conversations. We repair our cells. In this state, there is enough energy for us to do all that we need to engage in. We learn to modulate our environment.

Dr. Porges thinks that many individuals with autism have their vagal system diverted to the body's safety and this then became the focus of the growing child. It makes it difficult for neurodiverse individuals to interact with the outside world. It brings the ears out into the soundscape, brings the eyes out into the visual scape, and puts them into the peripherals. The individual's focus is turned inward and there is less focus on the outside world and thus the integration of the social engagement system does not take place. This may look like poor or limited social engagement and poor processing of language because the individual is closed and hyper attuned to stress and danger.

The presence of the FPR and Moro reflex makes the incoming sensory input too overwhelming and thus overloads the system.

Temple Grandin in her book *Animals in translation mentions,* "I believe animals have lower pain and higher fear than people do. My other reason for believing this at least provisionally is that it's the same with autistic people. As a general rule, we have lower pain, higher fear, and lower frontal lobe control of the rest of the brain than non-autistic people. Those three things go together". She also says, "Fear is a horrible problem for people with autism- fear, and anxiety. Fear is usually defined as a response to external threats, while anxiety is a response to internal threats. If you step on a snake you feel fear, if you think about stepping on a snake you feel anxiety." Temple says that autistic individuals have so much fear and anxiety that it is universal.

The FPR and Moro reflex make it more likely for individuals to be startled and afraid and that also has an impact on the memory. A happy memory of a birthday party may be a frightening one because of the presence of these reflexes. Our hippo-campus (part of the brain responsible for memory) stores information on the basis of what we see, hear, and sense. It also records the feelings and thoughts associated with memory. So, if a child is scared of a balloon bursting at a birthday party, he stores the memory as scary. Next time, if he attends another birthday party, he will be scared of the same feelings and sensations will be elicited in him. This is how memory gets encoded and is saved under pleasant or unpleasant categories. **When memories are unsafe, we see the world through the lens of stress and fear.**

The scrambled sensory processing does not allow the individual to feel safe and puts them into a fight-flight-freeze response, more often than any neurotypical person. It may feel to us that the individual with sensory processing issues or autism or ADHD is behaving difficult, but in reality, they are trying their best to deal with the hidden difficulties. When Hellen Keller was young, she looked wild and her parents and teachers couldn't get through her. In such a case, the child takes up the responsibility of raising themselves because no one understands them.

Many neurodiverse individuals find it difficult to deal with changes and adapt because they are terrified of so many things. It takes years for them to get rid of the fears for very ordinary events like haircuts, balloon bursting, or nail cutting. If our body is rigid and locked down, so are our emotions and thoughts. But when we are able to organize our movements, we can also organize our emotions and thoughts and that helps us deal with our stress. Reflex integration exercises and rhythmic movements combined with sensory integration helps immensely.

When our reflexes are fully integrated, we have access to the resources to calm down after experiencing or perceiving dangers. We are able to see the bigger picture and understand what is safe and what is not. I have worked with many children and adults, I have seen them getting capable of taking the sensory inputs and not slipping into survival once we help them access the resources within them through therapy.

CHAPTER 26

STAGE OF DEFIANCE

"It is a parent's responsibility to preserve their connection with their children, to preserve the relationship, so that the children can let go and become their own selves."
-Gordon Neufeld.

According to Erik Erikson, there are eight stages of psycho-social development. According to his theory, the successful completion of each stage results in a healthy personality and the acquisition of basic virtues.

The second stage of psycho-social development is Autonomy versus shame and doubt. This stage occurs between the ages of 18 months to approximately 3 years. According to Erikson, every child at this stage is focused on developing a sense of personal control over physical skills and a sense of independence. This is the stage where the child starts learning to assert himself or herself, they start expressing their individuality and to learn, becoming more independent and less dependent on their caregivers to meet all their needs. It is important that the child goes through this stage of defiance which is also commonly referred to as the "terrible twos".

The stage of defiance and tantrums is when the child is learning to explore his emotions and understand the feelings that he is experiencing. The child begins to feel that he can be in command of his own life and he lets others know this. Many children at this age use the word "no" to express their newly found independence. Kids learn to understand emotions and when they do not know what to do, they just react. They also learn to gain autonomy which also means that now they need a little more space to assert themselves. So, it is important to give the child the opportunity to feel their own abilities to recover balance, equilibrium, and dignity and at the same time provide support whenever they need it. This stage is a little frustrating to parents, but it is an important stage in the development of social skills.

This stage is important for the child to develop his individuality, to start understanding his or her own emotions, and to start labeling the emotions. First, they develop an understanding of themselves. Once that is developed, they start understanding themselves in relation to others so that they can start understanding how to relate to others and the world around them.

It is important to note that if the breathing space is not given at this stage, children feel suffocated and have more tantrums. But, it is important to be aware that if we are distracted as caregivers when they need help, they feel disoriented and overwhelmed because they are just learning to explore and make sense of their emotions. Although the child is taking his first steps towards becoming a self-reliant person, he still needs a great deal of support, encouragement, and comfort. Most of this comes from being hugged, cuddled, and held in someone's lap, showered with kisses, and rocked. These inputs help a child to feel more organized when they are faced with overwhelm.

When a child has motor handicaps, developmental delays, or developmental deviant behaviors, they do not go through this defiant stage. So, when they do not go through this stage, they stay in symbiosis and they stay reliant on their mothers or caretakers.

After a month or a few months of starting therapy, most children pass through this stage of defiance. It is here when parents tell me that their child is getting more stubborn, more assertive, and is not listening to their instructions. When I say not listening, it doesn't mean that they do not understand, but they choose to not. Not listening is also important, as a child will understand the meaning of "yes" only when he gets to say "no" to things he doesn't like. So this way, they learn to express their own unique self and their individuality.

So if a child passes through it during therapy, it is a good indication. Dr. Jean Ayers also talks about this phase and she says in her book, *Love Jean* that, **"Sometimes during the second to fourth month of treatment, most individuals go through an upsetting period, during which they may feel less well organized and rebel at the treatment. But once they've passed that stage, treatment can be enjoyable. Academic improvement does not appear usually until around the fifth month."**

I want the reader to be aware of this because when the child goes into this defiant phase of being stubborn and asserting himself, it should not be seen as a behavior problem or as a new challenging behavior. Of course, we need to address that behavior. We have to teach children to discipline themselves; we have to teach them socially acceptable behaviors. But it helps to know that children at the age of two are called, 'terrible twos' because that is when they go through the defiant stage. Any child who has developmental disability or autism would also go through this phase when we work on integrating their primitive reflexes.

But if we keep taking a break from the therapies then those behaviors keep coming back. When we know that the child is passing through the defiant stage, it is important to understand and not let the child's behavior trigger us. We need to come from a space of compassion and understanding to provide a container to hold negative or uncomfortable emotions. We do not have to throw tantrums along with our child because then we enter into a cascade of events where the child feels he is not accepted if he expresses negative emotions. He also learns to suppress his emotions or rebels even more. The only mantra that I tell parents to repeat in their mind is, "Focus on your breath and stay grounded in the storm of emotions." It is extremely important to ground ourselves and provide a sacred and safe space to express and process the emotion completely.

If this opportunity is not given, kids grow up feeling disconnected from their feelings. They do not understand and make sense of the emotions that they were feeling. They never express happiness, grief, anger, or any other emotions. We have to give our child a language to express the emotion that they are feeling else they grow up to be unaware of their feelings. If this understanding of emotions does not develop, these kids stay in a state of overwhelm. Feeling the emotions put their emotional system into overload and they shut those emotions down completely (this is not done by volition but happens automatically).

In his book *Movements that Heal*, Dr. Harold Bloomberg talks about the defiant stage and says, "Emotional and physical reactions and dreams occur in people while we work on their primitive reflex integration. When we do that, it causes the nerve nets of the limbic system to develop and link up more efficiently. These processes cause changes in emotional responses, behavior, and even hormonal imbalance and it is very natural for a child to go through these periods of defiance. They may become more demanding, they may become more babyish. They want to start hanging around their mother, wanting to sit on their lap. Some kids become very afraid to sleep alone. Some have horrible dreams or nightmares, some have difficulties falling asleep. In rare cases, there are kids who may have meltdowns, they may want more attention and support than the parents are used to giving them." This is especially true for children who did not go to the defiant stage.

After doing the rhythmic movements, and the exercises over a period of time, these reactions start getting lesser and lesser. Dr. Harold Bloomberg describes that these periods of defiance are succeeded by periods of emotional development when children become more confident, they're calmer, happier, and independent and their impulsive behavior starts to reduce.

When we deal with our kids and when we enroll them for therapy, especially if they're undergoing the primitive reflexes integration exercises, we may see this period of defiance that could come up not in all but in most of the kids. If it comes up, it needs to be addressed and we need to know that it is a part of normal development. Accordingly, we will be able to react and respond to our children.

I remember a child named Vinit, a six-year-old boy with a diagnosis of Autism. He came to me for therapy and I recommended his parents to take him out and give him the kind of sensory diet he requires. So, his parents took him to places they thought would help him get the required sensory diet. But Vinit experienced frequent meltdowns and found it difficult to settle down as they appeared.

It was difficult for Vinit's parents to manage those behaviors of him, in spite of their efforts, they didn't get the results they wanted. Taking Vinit to a playground was a tedious and emotionally draining activity for them. Every time they took him out, they returned with a feeling of endless struggle, but after three months, the trick seemed to work. Vinit became more flexible and resilient. He was now absolutely fine with trying new things and going to new places.

It helped because the parents were aware of the defiant stage and how the child will assert himself. They knew what to expect, they were explained about what are the possible things that might come up. Again, the reason to know all this is to understand what is expected and what behaviors may come up. When it is clear and we know why the behavior is occurring, it becomes easier for us to manage the child's behavior.

Another boy, Abheer, comes to my mind. He was a four-year-old, strong-headed boy reluctant to make any changes in his life. Abheer has sensory processing issues. He wants everything to happen in the same routine.

When we worked with Abheer, we worked on integrating some of his primitive reflexes and used sensory integration. In two months, he was so compliant that his parents were ecstatic. So, his parents took him to the US for a family function. They thought that now Abheer was ready to attend the function and explore the new city, which was earlier impossible with Abheer.

CHAPTER 27

SELF HELPS SKILLS

"The greatest gifts you can give your children are the roots of responsibility and the wings of independence."

- Denis Waitley

Sruti who is based in Visakhapatnam called me for a Skype session with her 8-year-old daughter Sayuri and said, "You know what Reena, I have not been able to follow the program you gave me since I am not able to manage time. My daughter is so busy"

"Busy!" I asked. "What keeps her so busy?"

"She is in school from morning till 1 in the afternoon. Once she is back home, I feed her quickly so that I can take her for therapy. She is in therapy 6 days a week for 2 hours. By the time we finish the therapy and reach home, it is 5. Then, I sit with her to finish her homework. Since there is so much work that she does not complete in the class, I sit with her till 7:30 or 8 pm. And then, you know how important it is that kids sleep on time. So, I feed her quickly and ensure that she sleeps by 8:30 pm. I really don't know where to fit the time to do the exercises that you suggested."

I was like, "OK, I understand but then if you are not able to follow the program, what do you want me to assist you with? Do you want me to help you to manage time or you want me to help you to prioritize?"

Sruti said that her utmost concern is her daughter's dependency on self-help skills. She asked me to help her in some way so that Sayuri can become independent.

"How many hours in a day do you INVEST working on her self-help skills at the moment?" I asked.

"I do everything for her because we are always in a rush. I brush her teeth, make her wear her uniform, feed her breakfast, and then I do the same in the afternoon and evening as well." Sruti answered.

Sruti paused for a moment, she realized she found the answer to her own question. She was not investing any time on those skills. She was spending around seven hours per day on her daughter's academics, but the results were far from desirable. Sayuri was struggling to write, read, focus, and sit in the classroom. Everything for her was done in the class by a shadow teacher.

"So what do I do? I cannot stop her from going to school, she has to be with other kids too. Therapies are important as she learns skills and completing schoolwork is important too", Sruti replied.

"Are you enjoying parenting your child? Is your child enjoying the time she is with you?" I asked.

"No, in fact, I am struggling with her tantrums and meltdowns and that is another area that I want you to help me with!"

I sensed a lot of anxiety and stress just by listening to all of this. I asked what it is that she does in the therapy and remedial sessions. She told me that they are working on self-help skills. I was really perplexed and asked her if it is possible for her to work on those same skills at home by herself, listening to which she got stressed. She said it is difficult to teach Sayuri anything because she listens better to her therapists.

It took me a lot of time to convince her that the job of the therapist is to teach the caregiver and parents so that the skills can be taught at home in the right context and situation. Skills and techniques can be taught to her and she can practice them at home. Therapy frequency can be reduced to twice a week so that the day can be filled with "sensory diet" and "play" opportunities.

I feel that the diagnosis steals logical thinking from us. The purpose of sharing Sruti's story is to understand how parents get into the flow of therapy and then sometimes miss the important "takeaways" of therapy. The therapist's job is to educate and empower the parent so that the parent can empower the child along with just providing therapy sessions alone. This is why I find occupational therapy so holistic as it works with not just the child but the family. Occupational therapy not just focuses on the body, but also on the connection and correlation of the body with the mind. It is also the job of the therapist to ensure that the parent is in a state of calm and peace to be able to teach skills to the child. The therapist helps the parent to become more aware of their thought patterns. So, all the self-help skills such as eating, dressing, grooming, bathing, communicating for toilet and potty, functional mobility, and functional communication are on the top of my list always.

I always ensure that the child is an "active participant" in the self-help skills at his or her level. The best way to teach this is through backward chaining. So for example, if I want the child to learn how to wear his pants then I break it down into steps. Before I do this, it is important to check the developmental level of the child and you may refer to self-care development charts that are readily available online these days.

So, coming back to breaking down the steps of wearing a pant, I would break it in the following steps:

- Step 1:- Put one foot into the pant while the parent holds it.
- Step 2:- Put the other foot into the pant while the parent holds it.
- Step 3:- Pull the pants from the ankle to the knees.
- Step 4:- Pull from knees to the hips and adjust.

So, if I am teaching this to the child, I will start with teaching step 4 first while the first 3 steps are done by the parent. Once the child masters step 4, I will work on teaching step 3 and now, the child does steps 3 and 4 together. And the parent does steps 1 and 2. And in this way, I go on working each step until the child learns the complete skill.

The same technique of backward chaining can be done for all self-help skills and it is very important that the child "actively participates" in these tasks on a consistent everyday basis. When I told Sruti to work on this for just dressing, she was happy and said that she can manage. It may get too overwhelming for a child to suddenly start doing and participating in everything. So, it is a good idea to start widening the circle of teaching self-help skills.

Over a period of 3 months, Sayuri started actively participating, 50% in eating, dressing, and grooming. That was exciting as Sayuri was teaching that we need to be patient to teach and the kids are always ready to learn. But it is not just these self-help skills that fill our day. We also relax and unwind and that is equally important. Most kids are so busy that they have absolutely no time for leisure.

There are a lot of sensory issues and that makes it difficult for parents to work on self-help skills. An understanding of sensory integration, primitive reflexes, and our own triggers equips us to deal with this better.

I know of a lot of children who do not like brushing, chewing, the taste of toothpaste, wearing certain kinds of clothes and so many more such concerns that come as speed breakers in the journey of making them independent. This coupled with motor planning difficulties, coordination problems, poor fine motor skills, poor interest in participation makes this task really really difficult for parents. I have worked with so many adolescent girls and it was very difficult to teach the concept of private and public behavior to them. Adolescent girls and boys would walk around with no clothes on or suddenly remove their clothes when they were angry. Teaching menstrual hygiene is another major issue that we struggled with. Toilet and potty training is another big block where we get stuck at times.

It has been really difficult but it was not for those who worked and stressed on developing independence in these skills early on and worked on sub-skills. They broke the skills down and worked on one sub-skill at a time. Encouraging participation in eating, dressing, grooming, bathing, and toilet training are the main things that parents of younger kids stressed. Later, cooking, managing money, shopping, organization of the rooms and transportation are important areas that should be stressed on. It is the best gift that a parent can give to their kids- independence in these areas and the confidence to manage themselves.

Along with self-help skills, it is also important to provide opportunities to participate in executive function skills like organizing time and space, planning, prioritizing, and decision making. The best way to do this is to involve them as much as possible in day-to-day activities and allow them to make simple decisions about what to wear, what to eat, and so on. It is also important to allow them to clean up toys after playing, clean up their rooms, and clean the house as a part of daily chores. I also feel that exposure to a variety of social situations with a variety of people helps them to generalize skills. Another important thing to do is to provide them the opportunity to plan a small part of the day, ask them questions like - Do you want to clean the room first or hang the clothes for drying? Do you want to do English first or Arts? Then allow them to plan their day and make a schedule of the day and tick whatever has been done. The only way to do this is with a lot of practice and so to ensure that at least one or two hours a day are invested in doing these tasks is very crucial. It is important to note that these skills are best learned in the context rather than separately. For example, Sayuri was learning to wear clothes and eat food in the context of a therapy environment and did not get the opportunity to participate in the context of the house environment when it was supposed to be done.

Academics are important if the child or the individual can cope but functional academics is extremely important. Such things include the ability to read or write their name, address, phone number, and other personal information. Concepts of handling money and basic addition and subtraction are important too. Reading the signs on the road or instructions at an airport or railway station are important skills too.

Laksh is a 13-year-old boy who was diagnosed with developmental delay at the age of 3. He is in the eighth standard and his parents are happy that he attends a regular school. However, upon evaluation I found, Laksh still finds it hard to identify alphabets and numbers. He is developmentally not ready for class eight. He spends six hours in the school but is completely dependent on others for his self-help skills. He needs to be fed and he cannot button or zip his clothes. His concepts of mathematics are poor, even the basics like counting. His parents run a shop and they do not have the time to help him master skills as they are too busy. Now, Laksh is becoming more assertive and does not wish to go to school. He has no friends and is isolated from his classmates because he does not have the language to communicate with them. He also does not understand "hidden rules" of what to speak and what not to speak.

The reason I share this is to understand how crucial it is to work on these skills early on. Laksh leaves for school at 8 in the morning and is back home by 3 pm. Post this, the teacher comes to teach him academics so that he can cope with the syllabus and there is no time left to work on self-help skills. After 5 p.m. he is either given a screen or a tutor comes to teach him some play skills, but there is no interaction for him with kids of his age. Kids learn best with other kids, of mixed age groups, but Laksh has no such opportunity. I emphasized the importance of teaching him functional academics and working hard on his self-help skills, but the family took time to accept and understand the importance.

I would like to share another example of a boy, Shardul, who is now 19 years old. He was in a regular school and was diagnosed with sensory processing issues and some traits of Autism when he was 3. Shardul found it really difficult to cope with academics- reading and writing were like struggles for him. He somehow managed to till the fourth standard as he changed three schools during this period of time. His parents were clear that Shardul is not keen on academics and was trying to search for a school that would teach him more of functional academics. He joined a regular school again and after reaching eight standards, they realized he could not cope anymore. He was bullied and had huge blows to his self-esteem. His parents ensured that he got opportunities to become independent in eating, dressing, grooming, bathing, toilet, cleaning his own room, and moving around in the neighborhood.

During Shardul's playtime, his mom made sure to always accompany him but pretended to be busy in her routine as he played. She concealed her presence to check if Shardul was able to manage himself and to assess if he is actually capable of taking care of himself. Gradually, their efforts worked to make Shardul believe that he is capable of doing things on his own. He learned to play alone and come back home at a decided time. A lot of emphasis was given on managing time and decision making in the context of his day to day tasks and chores. He was asked to go to the temple every day and buy small things that were needed at home. This was done a zillion times and he failed many times but they persisted and finally, he learned to do so. He was also involved in helping his parents for tasks like cooking, later, he was asked to cook one meal per week. They gave him a lot of exposure to participate socially. Therapy was ongoing, but his parents ensured that they created a balance between school, therapy, and training self-help skills.

Finally, his parents found a school for him which was like NIOS and he got to learn what he needed to become fully independent. Since the school was far away, Shardul traveled by his car initially. His mom wanted him to take the local bus instead. She prepared him for those two months in advance. She explained the name of the bus stop and how to buy the ticket and so on. Shardul's bus trips were accompanied by his mom for the first couple of months, post which he boarded the bus alone.

Shardul completed his high school by doing NIOS and now he is studying in a college and travels independently. He is learning economics which is also his favorite subject and is a confident young boy. He talks to me often about bullying and how he responds to the bullies. I am so proud of him and his parents. It took a 14-years-long journey to get him to where he is today and I respect the hard work and determination of his parents.

Shardul loves to meditate during his spare time. He is not so fond of devices but uses them to communicate with his friends. His written communication is better than verbal and he is still evolving. He is assigned the responsibility of a few household chores and he helps in the community works as well. He also helps his dad in the office with tally and entering data. I am sure that Shardul will find a place for himself in this world as he has been exposed to opportunities to learn skills each passing day.

This is the gift that I pray and intend each parent gives to their kids. Please give them OPPORTUNITIES... They will resist, they will cry, throw tantrums, not comply, may get into a rage, but it is best for them. We must continue to give them the opportunities even if they test our patience. Keep doing it! Small everyday opportunities help to reap huge enormous benefits in the future.

CHAPTER 28

TEACCH

The TEACCH Approach is an abbreviation for 'Treatment and Education of Autistic and Communication Handicapped Children' (TEACCH). It is also called 'Structured teaching'.

We all know that when we have to measure or work on the behavior of any child, we learn about the ABC. Now, the A refers to the antecedent for behavior, which means what exactly happened just before the behavior. So for example, if I talk about a child shouting, screaming, or having a meltdown, then 'A' would be what exactly happened just before the shouting and screaming.

'B' is the behavior. I need to be careful that behavior is measurable. So, screaming is a good way to talk about behavior but saying that the child is throwing tantrums is not a good way to describe behavior because we need to know what he is doing when throwing tantrums. It could be screaming, pacing, flapping, hitting, or biting. The point that I am trying to convey is, if we describe a behavior well, it gives us and the child therapists a clarity on what needs to be worked upon.

'C' is the consequence, meaning what I or the caregiver did to manage the behavior. This is how we understand the ABC of the behavior.

We also check for precipitating events for the behavior. So, if this child is getting aggressive or is biting, I check the ABC but also check if the child slept well, ate well, or had some medical condition that is creating the behavior. The aim is to understand what is precipitating that behavior. When I talk of structured teaching, I am talking about the 'A' or the antecedent. So, we are majorly working on the antecedent or what happened just before the behavior. One of the goals to use TEACCH is to establish predictability so that the child knows what is expected and to prepare the child in advance. Because if the child is prepared well, he complies well.

Structured teaching has various components, beginning with the physical structure at the baseline, followed by the visual schedule, the work systems, and finally the routines and strategies. The physical structure is anything that is adjusted in the environment, to let the child know what is expected. The visual schedule is like a time-table or a checklist. The work systems consist of moving from left-to-right and top-to-bottom.

Let's talk about the physical structure. One of the examples of physical structure in our life is the footpath. We know where to walk as there is a physical demarcation, denoting the space meant for walking and the space for the road. Similarly, jogging tracks let us know where to run. Airport or payment queues, made by ropes, also indicate the place where one is assumed to wait in line. The security check-ups at the airports have a yellow line drawn, which hints us to stop and wait for our turn before entering the security check. During the COVID pandemic, there are circles made on the floor for us to know where to wait so that we maintain social distancing. The physical environment in such cases is structured. It helps us know what is expected of us, as adults. In exactly the same way, the physical structure is needed for kids.

We have no challenges, yet the environment is structured such that it becomes predictable to us, which suggests even strongly that it is highly essential to do the same for kids who would benefit from this added structure in their environment. The physical structure is essentially a form of visual cue. It helps us establish clear visual and/or physical boundaries.

We often tell the children that we will be doing 'some work', without clarifying what work is exactly going to be done. This leads to behavioral difficulties that we may observe while interacting with the child. Sometimes, if there is a group of kids and one child does not understand where to stand, so we can ask them to stand on a particular colored doormat instead. Another thing we commonly do is draw a shape with a masking tape/ washable crayon to indicate the place to stand. This way children are not overwhelmed. So, it is always a great idea to use visual cues rather than just auditory cues.

Let's understand the visual schedule. This tells us what activities will occur and in what sequence. So, it allows the child to predict when, where, and what happens next and when the task starts and ends. It can be used from left-to-right or top-to-bottom. A good way to do this is to draw or show a picture of the activities and number them in order of their performing sequence. This would be a visual schedule in the form of pictures or photographs. This same schedule can be written instead. This is like a timetable that we used at school. It is also like an appointment list that we have or a meeting list which gives us clarity on how our day is going to be structured. Pictures or photographs or texts can be used as per the functioning level of the child. If the child is high functioning and can make his schedule, it will be a good idea to do so as this gives a lot of control. The child feels he has choice and activities can be mutually decided by the parent and the child.

We can add up surprises later once the child has mastered and understands the visual schedule well. Adding an element of surprise at the end of the schedule (surprise cards) can mean adding an activity that the child really likes. This will teach them that a good decision-making process on their part will lead to an activity of their choice when a surprise or a blank card is involved. It helps to make them understand that there are changes in schedule at times and predictability in a routine, but in the structure of predictability, there is change.

Surprise cards can begin with good surprise cards initially, for example, blowing bubbles, getting additional screen time, and so on. Hypothetically, in a schedule of study time, playtime, watching TV, and dinner, some days dinner can be replaced with eating out at a restaurant. This will act as a surprise for the child. Once the child gets used to the changes that are happening, the parent can start introducing surprises that are not so good. For instance, going out to eat at a restaurant can be then replaced with eating at home. There will be a protest and it is expected and is absolutely fine. Imagine if your spouse or your parents say that you will eat out and then without your permission changes the plan. You will definitely be angry and you are allowed to express the feeling or the displeasure. The same is true for a child whose routine is disrupted by us. They are allowed to express their feelings and we offer them the sacred space to contain the emotions.

Let's now understand work systems!!! It is a systematic visual way of answering:

- What work to do?
  For instance, a picture of writing and completing a worksheet.
- How much work to do?
  Depends on the number of worksheets kept.
- When am I finished?
  When the completed worksheets are kept in the 'finished pile'.
- What happens next?
  The next photo will indicate the next activity.

We use a left-to-right or top-to-bottom approach. So it is clear to the child what he is supposed to do. When all the worksheets move over from the unfinished (left or on the top) to the finished pile (bottom or to the right), the child knows that the activity is over.

An example of work systems in our daily lives would be a fast-food joint, where employees stand in line (left-to-right) and complete one step each, passing it on to the next employee in line and finally complete the order. The same logic can be used to teach children efficiently. When parents are trying to teach their children to work independently, they can start by sitting facing the wall and completing the task, using left-to-right or top-to-bottom visual cues. This is called an 'independent work system'. The breaks can be allocated to time or they can be task-based (for example, complete 2 tasks and then take a break). Break cards can be added. Gradually, the time or the number of tasks can be increased as they gain independence in their previous targets. Initially, the parents can supervise the child as they perform these tasks and can eventually leave the room and let the child be independent. I have taught work systems to severe and very low functioning adults too, so we need to know that each child can definitely learn to perform tasks independently.

Incorporating routines help to establish predictability. They compensate for poor organization, sequencing, judgment, and problem-solving abilities. Checking the schedule and following the work systems are two powerful routines that build independence and flexibility. It includes the spatial and sequencing organization of working left-to-right and top-to-bottom. For example, in respite care centers, adolescents or adults stay over the weekend. The main concept of that organization is to follow a 4 step schedule in those two days, teaching the individual to be independent. If a person is confused regarding what he is supposed to do, they are simply asked to refer to the schedule. This schedule is followed so rigorously that the kids eventually learned how to keep themselves occupied, how to perform the tasks, when to perform the tasks, and how much time to spend on each task. Tantrums and meltdowns decrease eventually as it is very clear to the person about what is expected.

I would like to emphasize and stress the need to take a step back and use visual cues more along with auditory inputs to give information to a neurodiverse individual. Often parents instruct the child verbally about the rules for the task, but it is always better to provide visual cues. Something that is shown to the child is retained better than what has been told to him, as he may tend to forget verbal instructions. The instructions can be simply drawn and shown to the child. Visual when combined with auditory input, works wonders for a child.

Some parents tell me that the schedule of the weekday and weekend is different and the child does not understand. In such a case, using a calendar helps. Parents can color Monday to Friday with one color. The visual schedule cards for the same day will be of the same color. Similarly, match the weekend calendar color with the weekend visual schedule cards.

It also depends on the child. You can use different icons, photographs, or different background colors of cards to indicate the demarcation of weekdays from the weekend. Certain parents carry a schedule made of fabric on which the Velcro cards are stitched, which they carry in the child's bag. You can also have two different colored bags, one carrying the schedule for weekdays and the other colored bag carrying the weekend schedule. There are a lot of changes that happen in our lives but using this for a few months will really help kids in adjusting to changes. It needs a significant amount of practice, though. Choose what works better for your child, text, icons, pictures, or objects. I use these strategies for some time and then reduce the structure and predictability. Notice, the word I use is "reduce" not eliminate the structure.

On most occasions, it is a good idea to start using the schedule for ourselves. You could make notes, plan the day for your child. Many parents including me keep changing different books or put the schedule on papers and then lose those papers. It's a good idea to use the same diary or the book to make the schedule for the child. When we are organized, we are teaching our kids to organize themselves. I remember teaching my child and making schedules in different books and then I lost those books and mixed up everything. I also tell my child that we will study at a particular time every day say 5 pm, but would not follow through. And when my son would not come at 5, I sometimes get angry at him for not following instructions. The point that I am trying to make is that we need to also be more organized in time and space before helping our kids. I preached the importance of schedule to everyone but failed to implement it sometimes to my own life. I am just sharing this because it's okay to be imperfect sometimes and work towards exactness by being more aware and mindful.

Parenting is a beautiful journey and parenting a neurodiverse child has special challenges and special joys too. It gives us a chance to care for another human being and to be responsible to provide them opportunities so that they can flourish. More than helping them, it is a bigger call to help ourselves and to explore our feelings, desires, triggers, memories, fears, values, goals, relationships, and beliefs because this is what they pick up energetically from us.

Whether we wish to give or not, our kids are consciously absorbing our conscious and perfect parts. They are absorbing our imperfect parts too. When we accept our mistakes and apologize and show them that we are working towards self-awareness and being mindful, this is what they learn from us.

We often feel guilty that we are not doing enough for our children and that guilt does not allow us to do what we really want to do. Wear the glasses of compassion towards yourself and keep moving forward. We are all a work in progress, so be easy on yourself.

It is important that the child learns self-help skills first and then or along with this depending on the age of the child, we teach them the concept of calendar and time. For time, I usually ask parents to stick a sticker or a symbol on the big hand of the clock. Then I ask parents to put Velcro on each number on the outside of the clock. Once this is done, we use another sticker or a symbol (that we put on the big hand). When I do any task with a child, I show them the placement of the symbol. Like, if the big hand is on 6, then I put the symbol on number 12. So, when I give screen time or work time, I show that the big hand will walk from 6 to 12, and when that happens, the activity is over. Some parents prefer using a digital watch and clock and I do not prefer that. The analog helps the child to understand the "passage of time" which means he will know how much travel the big hand will do to reach a specific number which is not clearly conveyed by a digital clock.

Visual strategies are very powerful and a great tool to use with kids. I strongly recommend you try them with your child.

CHAPTER 29

NUTRITION AND DIET

"The fact that changes in our gut affect our brain's response to negativity or emotionally stirring images is just mind-boggling. But it's also empowering. It means that what we put in our mouths and how we feed our gut bacteria do indeed affect our brain's functionality."

—David Perlmutter

I am writing this chapter on diet, but I want to tell you that I am not a dietitian and a food expert can guide you better on this subject. All that I am trying to do is to bring more awareness about food and how it influences us. I am sure you know this well, but it is important to revisit this area. This is an important topic and I discuss it with parents during my consultations.

Let me give you an example. A parent Renee came to me with her 6-year-old autistic son, Adrian. She spoke to me about her 10-days trip to Europe. I was keen to know how Adrian managed in the new routine and so many unpredictable situations. Renee was happy that Adrian was extremely happy throughout the trip, he ate well and slept well, but was constipated throughout the trip. Renee tried to convince me that Adrian was all good and well behaved even with his ongoing constipation which I found hard to believe.

I am writing this chapter amidst the corona pandemic and the lock down. I am taking consultations online and investing my time in completing this book. The lock down is strict and so many services are hampered. Grocery stores and markets are open only for a specific period and on specific days. The garbage gets cleared once in every 3 days. I ensure that I cut the fruits like watermelon or muskmelon on the days when garbage is cleared, else the peels stink and the house smells horrible. In the same way, if the stool is retained in the gut, it leads to flatulence, bad breath, and increased toxicity. Dr. Maya Shetreat, a Pediatric Neurologist says that the first rule is, "Take out the garbage every day."

Regulated bowels are a key component of the regulated brain and thus regulated behavior.

We have to understand that the gut actually functions as a brain and along with our brains. They both work together as one nervous system. So, it goes on to mean that the digestive imbalances can cause problems in the brain. The gut and gut microbes release more neurotransmitters than the central nervous system. So, it is important to note which food substances cause digestive issues in the child. It does not matter how nourishing the food is, if the child's gut cannot absorb its nutrients, it won't benefit the child. Working with a dietitian or a pediatrician to understand more on this is helpful and I would like to repeat that regulated bowels are a key component of the regulated brain and thus regulated behavior.

As you read in the earlier chapters, the child who has developmental disorders or has a neurodiverse brain is in a defensive mode called the fight-flight-freeze mode. In this mode, the system feels stressed because of a perceived threat or because of sensory differences and that affects digestion. During stress, digestion shuts down and when the stress is over, normal digestion resumes. But if the child is in a state of chronic anxiety, then the digestion goes for a toss. Reflexes such as an unintegrated Moro reflex keeps the child in a state of fight and flight. Sometimes, it is difficult for a child to learn how to get potty trained because of the presence of unintegrated Spinal Galant and Spinal Perez reflex. Poor interoceptive awareness makes it even more difficult for a child to understand the need to use the restroom or even get potty trained.

So, I feel, a team approach helps to understand what food is causing difficulties. Providing sensory integration and working on interoceptive awareness helps too. Also, working on Moro reflex, Spinal Galant, and spinal Perez reflex helps. I have seen great improvements using Chapman reflexes (neurolymphatic points) too.

Making a journal helps. I have seen mood swings to poor sleep patterns improve if we maintain a journal and follow patterns. Use a scale of 1-10, one being no symptoms, and ten means very disturbed. Write down every food that the child eats and co-relate it with the behavior. Your dietitian can help you to understand the pattern.

When I was young, my mom used to take us to Punjab. I loved playing in the fields with my cousins there, we also used to pluck vegetables and eat fresh produce from the farms. When my son was born, I wanted him to experience playing in the soil and eat straight from the farm. When he was around four years old, I asked him, "Do you know where we get tomatoes from?" And his answer shook me. He said, "They come from the mall." I and my husband decided to invest a lot of time traveling to farms and helping my son connect with Mother Nature. I wanted him to know where vegetables actually come from and how the trees look when they are full of fruits like mangoes and apples. I didn't want him to learn this "just from the book."

We are multi-sensory beings and learn by touching, feeling, smelling, tasting, and using all our senses to save an input or to give colors of sensory experience to our memories. Kids nowadays see food coming in packets with labels. We have experienced a different world with papads, pickles, and ketchup produced at our homes. We as kids didn't know the calorie content or labels, but we knew the process of how things that we love to eat were made.

With the industrial revolution, people moved to cities, we became urban consumers and food started coming in jars with labels and a list of ingredients. Labels came to gain our trust as people were skeptical to eat something that came in a jar. But now, we hardly read labels, and sometimes even after reading, we do not fully understand the text. I prefer not buying those products with ingredients like a chemical concoction. Feeding my child a chemical cocktail does not sound logical to me.

The reason I am sharing this here is, our taste buds are hijacked by these processed and artificially flavored foods. It seems like a food war and I am trying to protect my child from the fast-food joints in malls. The junk food giants seem to be winning because consumers are brainwashed and sadly most of us consider those brands and food as a status symbol. The simple relationship of plucking food from mother earth and putting it into our mouth is getting murkier and complicated. If I talk of this relationship, I might be considered the odd one. Such is the propaganda that everyone now believes in. For the developing brain of a child, this food serves no good. Food has become a "product" and is changing faster and beyond the grasp of our physiological evolution.

In England, the government asked food companies to voluntarily remove artificial dyes in products marketed to children by the end of 2009. All companies- including those from the US complied. In 2011, the UK branches of Walmart, Kraft, Coca-Cola, and Mars removed artificial colors, sodium benzoate, and aspartame from their product lines as a result of consumer pressure and government recommendations. When we become aware, we can bring about such changes. Thanks to the awareness that we now have farmer's markets and organic sections for food in the marts.

Dr. David Perlmutter, neurologist and author of *Grain Brain: The Surprising Truth about Wheat, Carbs, and Sugar – Your Brain's Silent Killers,* says, "Increasing numbers of studies are confirming the link between gluten sensitivity and neurological dysfunction."

Many parents who come to me ask me about the GFCF diet and how it helps kids. I found this quote by Dr. Perlmutter which says, "At the root of the problem? That sticky wheat protein, gluten. Although the jury is still out on the connections between gluten sensitivity and behavioral or psychological issues, we do know a few facts: People with celiac disease may be at increased risk for developmental delay, learning difficulties, tic disorders, and ADHD. Depression and anxiety are often severe in patients with gluten sensitivity. This is primarily due to the cytokines that block the production of critical brain neurotransmitters like serotonin, which is essential in regulating mood. With the elimination of gluten and often dairy, many patients have been freed from not just their mood disorders but other conditions caused by an overactive immune system, like allergies and arthritis. As many as 45 percents of people with autism spectrum disorders (ASD) have gastrointestinal problems. Although not all gastrointestinal symptoms in ASD result from celiac disease, data shows an increased prevalence of celiac in pediatric cases of autism, compared to the general pediatric population. The good news is that we can reverse many of the symptoms of neurological, psychological, and behavioral disorders just by going gluten-free and adding supplements like DHA and probiotics to our diet."

We are now understanding that we have lived in this beautiful, symbiotic, self-supportive, and mutualistic relationship with the organisms living within us for millions of years. And now we are threatening that relationship. Not just the food, but the soil in which the food grows is sprayed heavily with pesticides and we have been taught to believe that germs and bacteria are bad and that hand sanitizers are necessary. Children's rapidly growing nervous systems are particularly more sensitive to pesticides. I am not against washing hands with soap and cleaning and maintaining hygiene, but I feel we are overdoing it. The soil in which the vegetables grow is important. "Only when our soil flourishes, our food flourishes, and only then we flourish. What we do to our soil, we do to ourselves." Says Dr. Maya Shetreat.

I remember during my childhood days, there were seasonal fruits and vegetables and now we get most of the fruits all through the year. This is because farming has changed. Our ancestors had a relationship with and understood the science of soil. We have destroyed vital microbes in our gut through overuse of medications like antibiotics, eating processed and artificially colored foods, and also damaged our soils by using chemicals like pesticides, fungicides, herbicides, and by not rotating the crops. Microbes which are in the soil conserve and cycle nutrients and water into the plants and we have sacrificed them along with the abundant biodiversity in soils by overuse of chemicals. So, the same carrot that is grown organically will be vastly different from the one that is grown commercially on a large farm.

Dr. Daphne Miller, board-certified family physician and author of *The Jungle Effect* says, "Nutrients and chemicals in the soil, the weather and the type of seed that the carrot originated from will all change the way that it behaves in our body". So, when we give carrots or vegetables to our kids, it depends on so many factors. Thanks to the growing demand in organic farming and the farmer's market which is changing the awareness of us as parents. The reason I stress this is because parents who come to me are confused because according to them, they are making their child eat vegetables but kids are still falling sick. We need to know where the vegetables are coming from.

The same thing applies to dairy products. I had once been to a safari in Gujarat to see the Asiatic lions and was shocked to see some villagers grazing their cows and buffaloes in the jungle. The guide told us that the inhabitants are indigenous people who have been living for many generations and are allowed to stay in the jungle. Now, imagine the quality of milk produced by this cow and the one produced by the ones who are injected with hormones to produce milk.

Coming to hens, they are forced to spend their lives living in tiny battery cages that are covered with feces, and these spaces are so restricted that it is difficult for the bird to even stretch their wings. These hens have no choice but to urinate and defecate on each other and in such cases, hygiene is addressed by pumping them with antibiotics. On the contrary, free-range hens naturally spend time in the sun and instinctively know what to eat. Such hens lay eggs with yolks 3-6 times higher in vitamin-D than eggs from confined hens. Healthy chickens, healthy eggs, and healthy people.

So, if my child eats an egg every day, it will provide very different nutrition depending on the environment in which those hens were raised and the food they eat. From an antibiotic resistance standpoint, it may be safer to eat eggs than to eat poultry. Broilers (animals raised for meat) are fed more antibiotics than layers (hens laying eggs) since the producer's goal is to increase weight gain over a short period.

When I go to my native place, Punjab, I love eating certain indigenous or native diets, but now, thanks to the growing chain of fast foods with processed and artificially colored foods, these foods are disappearing. It is getting increasingly difficult to find an indigenous or native diet in its purest form now. This was the diet of the ancestors that kept them healthy and fit away from diseases. I used to feel that my mom-in-law is so strict with her eating habits as she always cooks certain foods at certain times of the year, but as I learn more about the diets and their effects on bodies, I realized the immense depth of wisdom our ancestors had and the relationship they shared with food. They would stress eating non-vegetarian foods on certain days only and there is more and more research which is emphasizing how plant-based diets are more helpful. The value of probiotics is getting recognized now. If we see in our culture, we always had probiotic food in some form or the other, like *idlis, dhokla*, and yogurts.

I also know a lot of kids who are picky eaters and have strong food preferences. Working on the sensory issues helps kids and a lot of oral-motor strategies work wonders. Working on the unintegrated primitive reflexes like babkin, sucking, rooting, and palmar grasp reflexes help. I know of many parents who carry their child's food along with them for birthday parties. Some carry their pans and vegetables along with them when they go on a trip because children at times cannot tolerate every food. Some kids want only mashed foods. But slowly and gradually with therapy, I see that they start broadening their preferences and parents get more comfortable with choices around food.

I also feel that it is important to have a relationship with food and to see it with reverence rather than just something that gives us calories. This is because food has a deep intimate connection with our bodies starting from the mouth till it gets absorbed and enters the cells and the mitochondria of every cell in our bodies. It is a good idea to remove foods that have additives, dyes, processed sweeteners, and so on. When we eat these lab-made foods, we are not eating whole foods and are depriving ourselves of the healing powers of real food. Eliminating or avoiding them is a great idea for us and our kids.

Most parents tell me that their kids always want to eat chocolates and chips and not healthy foods. I always tell them to not bring such foods home or eat them if they want their kids to have healthy eating habits. I also believe in taking a middle path which means its okay to indulge once in a while and to not make it too strict. If the child does not have allergies or food sensitivities, then I feel it is okay to allow the child to eat at a birthday party or so. Kids can eat with their friends and that makes them feel accepted in their groups too. But it is important to take care that we set an example and "talk the talk and walk the walk," which means we have fixed times for eating and that we do not eat many times in a day. "Food is a powerful drug. You can use it to help mood and cognitive ability or you can unknowingly make things worse." Says Dr. Daniel Amen.

A few things that can be remembered:

- Hunger is the best sauce – A child will eat best when he is hungry. Most parents offer food because they feel that the child may be hungry. Of course, many children have poor interoceptive awareness and do not understand when they are hungry. They do not register the signal of feeling hungry. But as therapy goes on and kids improve, we need to also check periodically to see if this is developing rather than feed them before they ask. Some kids go on eating and do not know when to stop. I have seen kids on both sides of the spectrum but it is a good idea to keep checking if this interoceptive sense is developing by allowing them to understand their body. Intervene only when you feel that the child has eaten too much or too little but allow that time for them to check and understand the feeling of hunger and satiety once in a while every 10-15 days.

- Cook at home and eat fresh vegetables and salads. We have complicated the entire food dynamics or rather we are brainwashed.

- "Eat foods that love you back," says Dr. Daniel Amen. We have friends and they reciprocate our feelings and the same is the case with other relationships. We do not want to have a relationship with someone who harms us. Eating is also a relationship with food and we decide who we have a relationship with. We do not want to let the food industry or ads decide that for us. Neither do we want to have a relationship with those foods that harm us.

- Try to eat a rainbow of food every day, Make a rainbow meal. Try creating a meal that uses every color — red, orange, yellow, green, blue, purple, white, and brown.

- Offer fruit and vegetable platter mixed with familiar and new items. Allow your child to choose which items he wants to eat and how many so that the kids don't feel pressured to eat the new item but they are just getting exposed to the food.

- Serve fruits and veggies in colorful cups/dishes. Presentation matters and this is why we eat out at restaurants or order food from outside because it is presented in such a way to seduce us.

- Allow playtime that includes fruits and vegetables that do not include eating them -Let your child create fruit and veggie houses, artwork, or simply allow them time to touch them. I feel this works.

- Shop for the ingredients together

- Make the recipe together – let your child mix it, touch it, and smell it while preparing meals.

- Eat one meal together as a family. This does not happen with most families that I see and so I tell them to start slowly and maybe eat once a week, to begin with. It is important to ensure that this time is fun and a great opportunity to bond rather than use it to correct and provide instructions to the child on how to eat and what to eat.

- Offer foods again and again- studies have shown that it takes as many as 15-20 tries to get a child to accept a new taste. So, if your child says no it's okay. You keep trying.

Food choices affect the mood and behavior of our kids. Studies are proving that when we change the diets of our kids, we can change their behaviors. It is a powerful medicine which we need to recognize and use to help ourselves and our kids. We need to be vigilant of what we are eating and where the food is coming from and what our relationship with food is. We see food with reverence as it nourishes us.

CHAPTER 30

POWER OF THOUGHTS

"Your emotions affect every cell in your body. Mind and body, mental and physical are intertwined."

- Thomas Tutko

One parent came to me as she was really unhappy with her son's behavior problems. Her 8-year-old autistic son communicated by using just a few words.

I always try to stay mindful of my energy levels as I sense people around me by the way they influence my energy levels. When a family enters my consultation room, sometimes I feel pins all over my body and I know that the family is really stressed. At times even the most troubled individuals carry a blanket of calm and the peace and tranquility in their presence drenches my soul. Others come and comb my "being" with intense and raw truths about life.

I love to nurture this sense in me and love to sense people by the energies they emit. So, when the door opens, my energy antennae automatically start sensing – is it heavy, light, or sorted or confused or just peaceful. I feel people with my body as a sensor.

Coming back to the parent who was very unhappy with her son, she told me that he keeps coming to her and says the word "smile" and keeps on repeating till she says the word or actually smiles. She wanted me to help her with her son's behavior. We traced back to the source of that behavior, it was arising out of the child's fear that his mom will get angry and so he kept saying "smile" to make sure that mom is happy. In this case, the mom's reaction was affecting the child.

That child's barometer-like sensors beautifully sensed his mom's stress. The days she was calmer, the word "smile" did not come, but the days she was stressed, he would say the word many times. Thus, it was not an issue with the child but with the parent. That little child was just mirroring his parent's state of mind. The next few days after I evaluated this child, a few other children with the same behavior issues came to visit me. They kept repeating things like "are you happy" or just "happy". The energy that I sensed with all of these kids was FEAR- as soon as they uttered those words, my heart felt heavy and tight. Those little kids just wanted their parents to feel happy. All of these kids had the same energy signatures to their words. They were all trying to say "I am sorry, I messed up, but I do not know how to correct my behavior and I am stuck with the negative emotions unable to come out of them, please help me."

On some days I feel that parenting is like an exam. The exam for which we really prepared to the best of our capacities, but when the question paper appears, we turn blank. Everything is there in the mind but nothing comes out on paper. So, even when parents know what to do and how to deal with that behavior, they go blank and REACT instead of UNDERSTANDING their child. Awareness helps us to notice our exaggregated response and reaction immediately and with practice, we can control such reactions from surfacing. The more we are aware, the more we leave the "legacy of love" to our kids and not "the legacy of pain and frustration" which they process when they grow up.

Dr. Bruce Lipton says, "When unthinking or uncaring parents pass on those messages to their young children, they are no doubt oblivious of the fact that such comments are downloaded into the subconscious memory as absolute "facts" just as surely as bits and bytes are downloaded to the hard drive of your desktop computer. During early development, the child's consciousness has not evolved enough to critically assess that those parental pronouncements were only verbal barbs and not necessarily true characterizations of "self". Once programmed into the subconscious mind, however, these verbal abuses become defined as "truths" that unconsciously shape the behavior and potential of the child through life."

Let me tell you a true story of how our thoughts influence others. Dr. Ihaleakala Hew Len worked at Hawaii State Hospital for three years in a ward where they kept criminally insane patients. Psychologists quit the place every month. The staff of that facility suffered frequent episodes of illnesses and their attrition rate was high. It was a depressing place and people walked through that ward in hurry and anticipation, as they were afraid of being attacked by the patients. It was a horrible place to live, work, or even visit.

Dr. Hew Len did not ever see those patients and he never counseled them but agreed to review their files. He looked at those files and upon finding and understanding their psychological traits, he started working on himself. The best part was, as he worked on himself, the patients in the ward began to heal.

After a few months, patients who were shackled were allowed to walk freely. Others who were heavily medicated started receiving lesser doses of medications. And then, some had no chances of being released and were discharged. Things changed fast and beyond anyone's wildest expectations. The staff began to enjoy coming to work there. Absenteeism and turnover stopped. More staff joined in and more patients were released and finally, the ward was closed. The most surprising fact of the above incidence was, Dr. Hew Len never interacted with any of those patients he miraculously treated. When he was asked the magic behind this, he said, "I was simply cleaning the part of me that I shared with them." He did *ho'oponopono* with these patients which is a Hawaiian technique for healing.

Dr Hew Len said, "Simply put, *ho'oponopono* means to make right or to rectify an error. '*Ho*' means "cause" in Hawaiian and *oponopono* means 'perfection'. According to the ancient Hawaiians, error arises from thoughts that are tainted by painful memories from the past. *Ho' oponopono* offers a way to release the energy of these painful thoughts or errors, which cause imbalance and disease."

He says, "*Ho' oponopono* sees each problem not as an ordeal but as an opportunity. Problems are just replayed memories of the past showing up to give us one more chance to see with the eyes of love and to act from inspiration."

You can read more of his work and the four main words of this approach are:

- I love you
- I am sorry
- Please forgive me
- Thank you.

So, for example, if I am concerned about the sleep issues of a child. I can say the above four words till they lose their emotional charge on us. By this, I mean that when I say, "My child has difficulty falling asleep." I feel something in my body – sense it and say those four words till I feel the calmness returning and the uncomfortable sensations settling down.

I was really in awe to see how by just thinking about the problem, we can help and bring about a change. So, you can just imagine the power of a parent's thoughts on the child. The idea that our thoughts can change the physical reality may not fit your current world paradigm, because new ideas are always laughed at. When Nicolaus Copernicus declared in 1543 that it is the sun and not the earth which is the center of heavenly spheres, he was criticized and had to wait to publish this work until he was on his deathbed.

In 1939, a Russian electrical technician named Semyon Kirlian discovered what is now known as Kirlian photography. This photography uses no light but pulsed, high-voltage frequencies to take pictures of radiating energy fields that surround all living things. It is also called gas discharge visualization (GDV). Research on Kirlian photography found out that all things exhibit the characteristic of an energy field, although living things have a much more vibrant energy field than non-living objects.

Dr. George Goodheart, the creator of applied kinesiology developed the technique of "muscle testing". Many physicians worldwide use muscle testing procedures to correct spinal misalignments and other imbalances. Dr. John Diamond applied muscle testing to toxic thoughts. When a person was exposed to any unpleasant thought, the "indicator muscle" would test weak. Diamond called it "behavioral kinesiology" and has tested it on thousands of subjects over many years as a means of instantly taking stock of a person's thoughts and most secret desires. I use muscle testing with all my clients to prioritize my therapy goals and understand what is important and combine it with my clinical reasoning.

I believe that the body knows everything. Every virus, bacteria, or fungus that has ever invaded our body, all our injuries, all our thoughts and feelings, and the entire history of every cell in our body have all been archived. Also, with such great results in my clients, I trust the wisdom of the body implicitly. Many thousands of years ago, the ancient physicians were astute observers of the human body. Energy healing is one of the oldest practices known in the world today. In ancient Ayurveda, this energy is called "*prana*" and in Chinese medicine, it is called "*qi*" or "chi". Imbalances in this energy system affect our physical and mental health. This is something like electricity which we cannot see but feel.

It is important to note that while we like to think that all of our unspoken thoughts are private and that they are confined to our heads, it's not true. We are like a radio station and are constantly broadcasting the energy of our thoughts. These thoughts fill the immense space around us to touch and affect people around us, which includes our kids and loved ones too. I am not saying that we can read the minds but the energy of other's thoughts is detected to some degree by our subconscious minds. Try staring intently at the back of someone's head in a crowd, and inevitably they will turn and look right at you before long. It really works, try it!

Hence, our thoughts about our kids matter as they pick our energies all the time. It's really important to become mindful of our thoughts. Thoughts have immense power to bring about a change in physical reality. Imagine the kind of power you have within you to bring about huge changes in your child. It is easier to live a life of love than to live a life of fear, think about it. It is your choice! If we choose to live the life of love, our body responds by growing in health. If we choose to live a life of fear, our body's health is compromised as we close down in a protective response. Parents are genetic engineers of their kids. Dr. Thomas Verny, a pioneer in the field of prenatal and perinatal psychiatry says, "Findings in the peer-reviewed literature over decades, establish, beyond any doubt, parents have an overwhelming influence on the mental and the physical attributes of the children they raise."

What we think about our kids and what we talk to them really leaves a deep imprint on their psyche. Japanese alternative medicine practitioner Masaru Emoto showed that the structure of water crystals is affected by positive and negative emotions. He claims to have carried out hundreds of tests showing that even a single word of positive intent or negative intent profoundly changed the internal organization of water. Beautiful, highly complex crystalline structures were formed in the water that was subjected to positive intent. However, random, disordered crystals were formed when it was exposed to negative emotions. This made me wonder that our body is 70% water and imagine the power of our thoughts on our kids and our dear ones if the intent alone can bring about such kinds of changes in water alone. Masaru Emoto mentioned that the most positive results occur with feelings of love and gratitude.

Let me explain this with an example of my client. I was working with my team on a 3-year-old child, Shubh, who was given a diagnosis of Autism.

The first day I saw this boy, he did not even acknowledge my presence. I tried to interact with him but he seemed to be in an invisible cylinder around him. His entire focus and energy were directed within that invisible cylinder. I thought of all the tools that are there in my therapy toolbox (my brain) and started working with him. We gave him opportunities to climb on various swings and he enjoyed but kept running away from the swing. He just ran from one corner of the room to the other flapping his hands. His long curly locks fell over his face, obstructing his vision. He was not noticing me, my therapist, or even his mom. I was a little sad and felt bad.

I did a silent prayer and called the source energy to help me and him so that we could connect. I just wanted him to LOOK at me, but it did not work. He was running around with a wall between him and everyone around. I tried my best but all in vain.

I used some more tools for the therapy session to stimulate him. But again, I was not noticed or acknowledged and there was no eye contact at all. The harder I tried, the more he withdrew. My desperation to look into his eyes grew, but that little "guru" taught me to wait and exert patience. I finished the session by praying again and asked angel Metatron to be with him and help him in whatever way the universe feels right. I also prayed for guidance so that I do the best and that the right ideas and tools come to my mind. But I felt rejected by him.

After a month of our efforts, he was still the same and just with marginal improvements. And then, deep down, I felt helpless as a therapist. I prayed hard for any sign that will make me help the family and that little "guru" - as I didn't even know what he was trying to teach me. His curly locks obscured his vision, but because of his sensory troubles, he didn't allow anyone to touch or comb his hair. His clumsiness was oblivious to his surroundings and his walls were difficult to penetrate.

But, as they say, helplessness always brings "hope" with it and that hope told me, the child has "potential" in him. Shubh's parents were both doctors and so the medical part of the challenge was already ruled out. I have worked with kids who did not respond and Shubh was better than most of them. So, I was sure that he would respond, but the question was when and how?

I decided to start with his mother, as she gave up her career to raise the boy. It wasn't hard for me to figure out that she was on the verge of losing her patience. She passed sarcastic comments on him and her frustration and disappointment were evident.

I knew I got the sign I was looking for. So, I gave his mother the much-needed dose of EMPATHY. I told her, it was her choice to have a child & it was her choice to give up her career. I also told her that she was only venting the frustration of her choices on her child and herself.

As expected, she wasn't aware of her situation and upon confrontation, she did what was expected of a mother. That awareness brought in appreciation and affection for her child and herself. Old habits die hard and so that transformation brought in overnight results, neither in his mother nor in Shubh. Gradually the clouds of vagueness cleared and I saw the first silver lining of the positive changes in Shubh when he visited for the consultation after a week. As they entered the room, they brought along a light, fresh, warm, and divine energy. I knew something had changed. Before I could speculate any further,

Shubh came towards me to hold my hand. His almond eyes looked at me to pause for a moment before blinking away with innocence. He giggled and walked away to play. My heart skipped a beat, my throat had a lump of gratitude. I was elated.

Seeing my reaction his mother mentioned, "He started acknowledging people and gave eye contact to everyone around."

That invisible cylinder around him was clearly shattered. He was now available and open to the world around him.

He again came to me to express his keenness on playing with me. His desires and liking were communicated non-verbally, words weren't even necessary for him. Those changes in him were no less than a miracle. That day, I chimed like a schoolgirl. Like a butterfly, I fluttered from room to room to tell my staff about what just happened.

It was no less than a miracle for me. That little "guru" took my hand and moved me from "fear" towards "faith" and told me in his way that "determination, appreciation, consistency, and patience" help to make miracles happen. I was sure that he would make me witness more such miracles.

All that we did was change our attitudes. Self-sabotaging thoughts are important to address. You can take professional help to make peace with your inner emotional wounds so that you can see yourself with compassion and not criticism. There are numerous examples and doctors all over the world who have emphasized the importance of sharing your emotions.

The work of Dr. Gabor Mate, Dr. Peter Levine, Dr. Bernie Siegel and so many more- all of them believe that we have a healing gift within us which should be harnessed. They also guide us not to see the mind and body as two different entities but as interdependent and interrelated systems. Whatever happens in the mind, affects the body, and whatever happens in the body, affects the mind.

CHAPTER 31

MY LITTLE PARENTING GURU

"Don't worry that children never listen to you, worry that they are always watching you."

-Robert Fulghum

After practicing for almost 9 years as an occupational therapist, I was blessed with my baby boy, Neel. He was an amazing baby, he slept on time, he was fed on time and he achieved all his milestones on time. He was a baby who knew the art of self-regulation so I never got to deal with his tantrums. He was a child of my dreams and I felt blessed to have him in my life. Somewhere, I also appreciated myself for being a good mother, a great therapist, and doing my level best at both the fronts. The thought that I know how to manage every single child in this world followed that phase of self-appreciation.

Then at around two and a half years of age - when all kids pass through the stage of defiance - my son Neel started turning assertive. I wouldn't like to call it defiance as it's a stage where children connect with their own selves. This stage is also called "the terrible twos" because that's when kids learn to push or assert their voice. That's when my son just flipped from being calm, settled, and compliant to being defiant and strong-headed. During that phase, he displayed what we term as the "challenging behaviors" like difficulty in sitting in the class and not following rules. Hence, I decided to take him to a developmental pediatrician.

I met the developmental pediatrician and she told me there was nothing wrong with my son, though I thought some kind of behavior modification was needed for him. I thought I was an expert behavioral therapist who knows what needs to be done. Hence, I knew I could do it for my son too.

If you read my book, *The Little Parenting Guru,* I have explained my journey with my son as a parent and how I became more aware as a mother.

The other main thing that helped me to become more aware was when I did a lot of EFT for myself. I got trained to become an advanced practitioner. I went through a series of sessions to release the bags of triggers and to gain mindfulness and awareness. Not just that, I also did NLP (Neuro-Linguistic Programming) and PLR (Past Life Regression) to get more clarity in my life and understand myself better. A lot of internal work was needed in me to clear my internal landscapes and make peace with my inner child.

What was it that I was expecting out of any relationship, especially my relationship with my son?

So, when I witnessed challenging behavior in my son, I started seeing it from both the ends, in short, I wanted to trace the roots of those behaviors on both of us. After much analysis and work, I figured out my contribution towards those behaviors.

My son's bus used to come at 7 o'clock and so, I usually wake him up by 6.30 in the morning. That half-an-hour time was not just enough for us to get ready and catch the bus. This time mismanagement fueled our anxieties and not to mention the subsequent stress. Without realizing it, I vented that stress on my child and also kept directing him by saying things like, "Brush your teeth. Why are you still standing? What are you doing? Why is it taking so long? Come on, do it fast!" And so on.

I bombard him with instructions. It was my way of throwing my emotions, toxic emotions on him. And so, he went to school with the bag of my emotions, and that in turn manifested itself as those challenging behaviors. It was too much for that little soul to understand and regulate. If I could not regulate myself and my emotions, how can I expect my child to do so? After all, his systems were still developing.

Upon addressing this pattern, I started working on myself. I started waking up early and planning the morning routine. I ensured to have enough time and even if we did not have time, I made sure not to stress the situation.

The side effects of positivity and mindfulness are always pleasant and so my son's behavioral issues subsided. As parents, a lot of work is needed for us to make our parent-child relationships healthy. Both of us, the parent and the child, contribute equally to help each other and self-regulate the behaviors. As adults, we need to be in a state of calm so that the children learn to be so.

Dr. Dan Siegel says, "For an infant and young child, attachment relationships are the major environmental factors that shape the development of the brain during its period of maximal growth. Attachment establishes an interpersonal relationship that helps the immature brain use the mature functions of the parent's brain to organize its own process."

Also, another important thing to mention here is, my stress, frustration, and anger with my son made me a different person than who I really was. During my times of distress, I spoke words and said things I would not even use for my enemy. Those moments of anger transformed me into a "monster mom" or a "devil mom". Those harsh words made my little son feel really bad about himself.

Imagine what I was doing to his self-worth and self-esteem, but I don't judge myself or any other parent who does so. I was doing my best with the best that I knew at that time. Now that I know what I need to do I am doing better and I think this awareness is very important for all of us to take care that we come from a place of center, from a state of being grounded and only then we approach our child. Our kids are really our best "gurus" teaching us to get in touch with those core qualities that we don't know exist within us.

If we are coming from a state of anxiety or fear then I do not think that we have a right to have an interaction with the child at all. I think the rule applies to any relationship and not just the child.

When we as parents become aware of our interaction with our kids, the relationship changes completely and beautifully. These changes when coupled with the right kind of therapies systematically followed at home does wonder!

When we appreciate the child's strengths then what comes out is a beautiful and fulfilling relationship between the parent and the child.

CHAPTER 32

LEGACY OF LOVE

"You will never be able to escape from your heart. So it's better to listen to what it has to say."

-The Alchemist

There is evidence that suggests that unexpressed emotions produce over secretion of hormones that suppress the immune system. And kids being kids, they learn these coping patterns from their parents. Allow me to share an example with you.

I worked with one parent Devi who was very concerned that her son needs to learn academics faster. I observed her body language and helped her to become more aware of her body (somatic mindfulness). Her tensed body, heavy voice, spontaneous tears told the tale of her ordeal. I was sure that she was experiencing an implicit memory. Unconscious emotions and conscious feelings, rapid shifts in mood, and rapid physiological changes happen under the impact of implicit memory. Our explicit memory (recall memory) stores facts, figures, and numbers and we have access to them. We can bring them to our awareness and recall them whenever needed. It is an explicit memory that helps us to remember an appointment or a meeting.

Dr. Gabor Mate mentions that implicit memory circuits carry the neurological traces of infancy and early childhood experiences. Encoded in them is the emotional content of those experiences without necessarily having the details of the events which gave rise to the emotions.

When I worked with Devi, we could go down to the deeper layers within her. We confronted her implicit memory of getting scolded by a very strict dad. Her dad always wanted perfection and things to be done on time. As a child, Devi did not have the resources to deal with this memory. She felt traumatic in situations when she was around her dad.

We need to understand here that trauma is not because of a particular situation rather it is on how the situation is perceived, assimilated, and processed by the nervous system. So, a strict parent may not be traumatic for some individuals, but for some others, it may create trauma.

In Devi's case, she did not find a nurturing and calming adult who could hold space and allow her to express her emotions of fear and self-doubt. When uncomfortable feelings are not expressed, they are stored in our bodies. She could not process the feelings and grew up being "stuck" in time. All of us experience uncomfortable feelings of abandonment, rejection, and low self-worth in our lives. The first time we experience them as infants and kids. The younger the child, the fewer resources he will have to protect himself. The child does not understand that his parents are having a hard day, but he personalizes what he feels. This is what Devi did as a child and felt that she was the reason why her dad felt that way. She grew up with low self-esteem and became constantly anxious trying to be perfect in everything to please her dad.

Our bodies store positive and negative events in our lives. Our brain, muscles, breathing, and physical processes start getting fixated into patterns that continue to speak to our brains about old developmental wounds. Instead of staying in the flow, we start getting stuck up in fixed patterns. The past lives through us as Dr. Peter Levine says through our interactions. So, it is important to notice that we do not respond to the present moment but we respond to our perception of what is happening.

Devi's inner self constantly told her that she is not being a good or a perfect mom and thus made her son go through a lot of therapies, classes, rigid routines, and structures. She somehow wanted to get rid of the inner critic who kept playing in her mind. When I worked with Devi and we revisited her implicit memories of freezing up in the events of her dad shouting at her, that is when she helped herself and made her "inner child" work with compassion towards herself. She was able to silence her inner critic which was her dad's voice that she internalized. She also overthrew that constant feeling of guilt that blamed her for her son's poor academic performance. She did all this when she got the help to see herself from the lens of self-compassion and not self-sabotage.

When we narrate our traumatic experiences with an emotionally available, non-judgmental, and reliable person then our brain re-experiences the stress of that trauma in a new way, combining the old stress in the zone of care and connection. As Dr. Steven Porges says, "Safety doesn't come from a lack of threat, it comes from connection". This experience rewires implicit and explicit memories together differently. It was amazing to watch Devi's body shift and relax as she vulnerably expressed what she felt. This is the power of mindfulness and attunement in a healing conversation.

After this work on mindfulness and being aware of the internal landscape of emotions, Devi could settle and relax. When I asked her about her son not picking up academics, she didn't feel uncomfortable. In fact, she told me that she was done sabotaging herself by way of guilt and anxiety. She was learning to flow with the flow and began to love and accept herself no matter what she felt. She learned to develop deeper compassion for herself and her kid.

It is from this space that we start working to help our kids. Does that mean that we do not work with our kids till we are healed ourselves? No, as it is an ongoing process and our kid's behaviors will constantly push the buttons in us which need to be healed. As we become more aware of our emotions, we explode lesser and lesser to situations and we get the messages from them rather than reacting. We see them as opportunities to grow as we slide down into the deeper dimensions of our awareness. The same situation does not make us feel the way it did before and we see the situation from a new lens and a cognitive shift occurs within us.

Therapies and techniques are very helpful, but it also depends on who is using and how are we using them. So, I feel a lot of work on ourselves is extremely crucial and I feel blessed to be living in a world where help and counseling are available which for my parents was not. They had no guidance or help to understand how to be a parent.

To be a good parent to our children, we have to become a better parent to ourselves. We will always be a "work in progress" but our happiness will come from the process of growing internally. Our kids deserve the best version of us and they learn best from us when we model that behavior for them. Our behavior and our ways of coping with life set examples for our kids to deal with their behaviors.

Raising children is much more than providing food, water, education, and therapies. It is a huge responsibility and opportunity to build a legacy of love. The simple mundane day-to-day tasks and chores of brushing teeth, eating meals, cleaning, and mopping give us beautiful moments that can be filled with love and compassion. When we take the time to make thoughtful choices rather than reacting in such daily routine tasks, we help our kids feel safe and loved, and we model healthy habits, which are all part of the true legacy of love.

I want to share what happens if the diagnosis or emotional wounds are not recognized as kids. I was working with an adult - who according to the norms of the society is well- educated, so-called successful, and achieved merits and medals for her works – named Reesha.

Reesha, who is in her mid-forties called me for the first time. She spoke highly of her achievements. She mentioned that she lives in a developed country. She is very reputed and has her name and work featured in elite magazines. She is married to a very successful and famous personality and has two beautiful teenage children. She is at her zenith and her life seemed like the "Perfect" life.

Before I could talk further, she told me to park all those labels aside. She wanted me to see her as a little girl who desperately needed help. She literally begged me to help her out so that she could shine with her truest self. She was diagnosed with Autism at the age of 45.

Reesha's relationship with her husband, her children, her parents, and her colleagues was very strained. She is highly intelligent and knows everything at a cognitive level. But when it comes to expressing herself, she would start screaming, swearing, and throwing things. She could not express herself in a calm manner even when she had the awareness that her ways of expressing are not appropriate. She exploded and reacted to every situation, especially to people who were close to her.

We met and worked together and I realized how her "inner child" was buried under the burden of seeking approvals, assurance, and appreciations from others. She was relying on external validation to believe in herself and had a deficient sense of self. She was using her degrees, her status, and her job as a "label" to identify herself and to make herself feel that she is good. This did not help her to feel fulfilled as the "inner child" within her was not happy. The outer accomplishments were like bandages put on the wounds of poor self-esteem. She desperately wanted to make a connection with her inner compass to feel worthy. She believed that she needed something to be whole and complete and to be accepted for who she was because she identified herself with the deficient self. She just needed the awareness to know that she was already amazing and complete the way she was.

We have this ability to change our minds by putting feelings into words. This helps to develop the neural network in the brain and heal and integrate the trauma which is stored. I was really taken aback knowing how relationships and close connections are disrupted if kids are not treated and if these self-stimulatory behaviors remain unnoticed. It is so important to work on them as kids because later, although they can be treated, the extent of damage can sometimes alter the dynamics of various relationships.

Reesha still used a lot of self-stimulatory behaviors to regulate herself but on the surface, she pretended to appear calm and regulated. She mentioned that in stressful situations, she panicked and felt every muscle shivering with fear and anxiety. Reesha felt a vacuum inside her and always felt that she was not in control of anything. I still remember how she asked me if it was ok for me that she ties a scarf on her chest to feel more secure and in control. We completed the session with her and I asked her if the scarf is still needed. She removed her scarf and felt in control. All that I did for her was to help her find her "inner voice" and to let her express herself – the way she was – her authentic inner self.

Through the process, she gave permission to the "inner child" within her to be a child again. She allowed herself to live in the moment and cherish it rather than think of just the future. She allowed herself to speak what she wanted instead of what others thought she should. She was able to connect to the divine essence, the authentic self within her which made her feel fulfilled. All that she needed from me was to be held in the sacred space of non-judgment and compassion for her. And so, she managed to defuse her own pain and burst that bubble of fragile happiness. She realized that her self-worth is not dependent on someone but her inner springs - something which had unfathomable depths and was forever overflowing. She realized that she is beautifully imperfect and she embraced her imperfections and her dark sides. Her relationship with her husband and kids got better. She started feeling fulfilled.

And the best thing that she realized is that she always did her best with the best of her resources and released herself from the judgment that she held for herself and offered compassion to herself. This took time but the reason I wish to share this is to not see the self- stimulatory behaviors or the challenging behaviors as something to get rid of. It is not just something that we want to get rid of. It is to be seen as a "coping strategy" or a "self-regulating mechanism" that the person has access to. He or she needs to be accepted as it is in the moment and then we work towards the behavior by helping them to re-discover their skills and resources.

Sensory issues and self-stimulatory behaviors need to be seen as a call for help and need to be accepted as they are.

I am not saying that we let the self-stimulatory behaviors stay. What I'm trying to say is, we equip the child with skills but in that particular moment, we accept the child the way he is. While we keep working, we can overcome the obstacles together, with the child.

I have met numerous parents who say that they will not parent their child the way they were parented. Our inner child has these stored implicit memories that impact us, especially the ones from the first seven years of our life. During those initial years, our brain is in Theta state, a very receptive state. Many of our limiting beliefs, fears, and blockages are developed in these critical years, passed down from our parents, which we too can pass on to our children. Our reactions and responses to situations are always connected to this. Depending on our experiences, we may require in-depth work to heal our inner child and to break the cycle and clear our blockages and fears to be fully present.

Only from this space, we can parent consciously and provide the love, compassion, empathy, non-judgment, and understanding our kids deserve.

CHAPTER 33

EVERY BEHAVIOR HAPPENS FOR A REASON, ALWAYS!!!

"Love and compassion are necessities, not luxuries. Without them, humanity cannot survive."

- Dalai Lama

I still remember a boy named Rowan who was diagnosed with Autism and was non-verbal. I first met him in 2003. I was still new to Autism back then with just 3 years of experience in hand.

Rowan was a tall, 9-year-old boy with sleek hair and a smiling face. He always kept playing with his fingers and used to look from the corner of his eyes. He was completely self-absorbed in his own space with these behaviors. But he was extremely calm and very compliant. At times, when things or tasks turned difficult for him, his calm demeanor would change to make him jump on the tips of his toes. He would jump and make weird sounds to regulate his stress.

When calm, he talked in words or used the first letters of the words, else most of the time he expressed himself by taking the person to the object or bringing the object to the person. So, he would get a glass if he wanted water or pull me to the door if he wanted to go home or to stop the therapy session. It was always in a humble way.

One day, while we were working on copying a pattern with blocks, his mom stepped in. She told me that Rowan understands everything – from words to sentences, feelings, and emotions to hidden rules of society and everything. I was not convinced. I have seen the vagueness in Rowan when he constantly flickered things, when he gazed at the light passing through his fingers, and when he played with his spit. We were only through the second or the third session and I was still trying to know him.

His mom understood my disagreement with her statement. She was committed to proving herself because she wanted to stand up for Rowan without intimidating me. She sought my permission to work with him. I had my own doubts, but I also wanted to see the Rowan she just described. She made a design with blocks by stacking them. I thought it was a really difficult task and his mom was expecting too much from him. But I waited to see what finally happened.

She was quiet, calm, and relaxed. She explained Rowan and showed him the tower of blocks and asked him to copy. Rowan was, as usual, flickering his fingers and looking at it from the corner of his eyes. I was sure he didn't listen or understand what he had been told. As soon as the instructions were over, to my surprise, Rowan started copying that pattern. He made some designs that weren't asked for. I was sure that such an outcome was certain. But his mother waited for him to complete when he was done she calmly tapped the table and pointed at the design she asked him to copy. She delicately asked him to take a look at and see if he structured it correctly. I again thought it was too much to expect from him.

Lo and Behold! Rowan broke his tower and made a complete replica of what his mom had made. I was still not convinced and thought that it was a fluke. So, I asked his mom to make another design, and this time again, with the aloofness, flickering, and looking from the corner of the eye deceived me as Rowan replicated the exact pattern.

I was in tears because without his mother's help and guidance, I wouldn't have pushed Rowan as much as he needed. His mother was very clear about what he can do and what he cannot and thus, she wanted me to work along those lines.

Her laser-like CLARITY coupled with her FAITH that her son will learn even with his Autism and her DETERMINATION to follow the program at home were the qualities which I wanted to soak in as well.

I am an expert because of such mothers and such Rowan's who have taught me to look beneath the behaviors. I have learned to wait patiently and help the neurodiverse individuals to find their own skills even while they jump, flicker, make sounds, and do all kinds of strange things. That is their way of self-regulation to fit into our complex world.

They know, understand, and feel everything. It's just that some cannot communicate the way we do, thus teaching us the art of picking up communication from any behavior.

Every behavior is for a reason...

I still remember this child who I saw for the first time, Param. He was given a diagnosis of Autism and was an 11-years-old tall, lean boy who loved to pace around. He would come very close to my face, right in front of my eyes, smile, and then run away. He would make loud noises while pacing from one end of the room to the other and walked on his toes; sometimes jumping on the toes and flapping his hands. This was in 2001. He came with his mom Shobhana. My clinic in those days was on the ground floor and there was a big window from where people could peep inside. There used to be a lot of people waiting out as I shared the space with many other doctors in that polyclinic. Since I was new at that time, I used to get conscious with people peeping in and so, I used to close the windows quite often.

So, one day, I saw Param, I finished my evaluation and started talking to Shobhana to explain to her the home program. Now, Param had free time and my window was open. I was a little conscious that Param was pacing and making sounds. His mom was absolutely calm and relaxed allowing him to do all that he wanted to. Param was getting restless as we talked and Shobhana mentioned that he can go and pace out in the large passage of the waiting room instead of feeling enclosed in that small area. She also told me that the driver will supervise and we can also keep a watch from the window.

Pace out making the sounds and flapping the fingers! I thought.

I got even more uncomfortable because that would mean everyone in the lobby would watch him with their curious set of eyes and some doctors might not like it. But, like always, I decided to park my fears and doubts aside and trust his mom...at least for the moment!

As we talked, my attention was on Param as the magnitude of sounds that he made got higher and higher. From pacing, he went running from one end of the waiting room to the other. Then followed the flickering, jumping, and rocking. Some people got up and looked at us in disgust for not teaching him self-discipline. Shobhana was calm and unaffected by what others thought of her or Param. She told me that she is used to such stares and she just smiled back at them. No explanations came from her, she mastered the art of taking her son the way he is. She also knew that those behaviors were necessary for her son to make him feel calmer and so, nothing else really mattered to her.

I was astonished by her composure and understanding. I thought I was sharing important information with her, but what she shared with me actually transformed me. The color of her wisdom was so intense that it painted away my concerns about WHAT OTHERS WOULD FEEL and made me more peaceful and centered.

You see every behavior happens for a reason...

When I was in Delhi in 2001 to learn more about Autism, I was dropped to the Action for Autism Center by a parent whose son, Nihal, had Autism. Nihal was as old as me and I was 22-year-old then. Nihal had seizures along with Autism. He used to constantly rock while sitting and always flap his hands. Repetition of words and sentences in a sing-song manner was also an issue with him as he didn't know how to communicate effectively. But he was an always smiling and happy boy. One day, Nihal's mom was driving and Nihal was sitting next to her and I was sitting behind. Suddenly, Nihal got angry for some reason and could not self-regulate. He started hitting his mom and the steering wheel went haywire.

Self-regulation is a huge skill where we control our emotions or behavior very easily. Kids and adults with Autism can get sensory overload and that may lead them to have a meltdown. Meltdown means when the system cannot handle any more sensory input and starts to collapse. By sensory overload, I mean that their system perceives the light or the sound or the smell or some input from the environment either too much or too little.

Being an occupational therapist, I was trained to understand and work with such situations. But that day, I froze. I was not prepared for that. I did not know what to do and how to help his mom. One thing was sure, Nihal was trying to communicate something through his behavior which we could not understand. A calm and focused mind is needed for that to be done and I turned "numb" and could not think. His mom took the car to the left. She stopped the car and very calmly looked into my eyes and said, "Don't worry, I will take care of him. You go to the center and inform them that Nihal will be late." I was SHOCKED to see her calm and clear in such a situation. I told her that I will wait and help her if she needs. I also told her that I am fine in being late.

After that, she explained Nihal their plans with the pictures that she carried. It was like a time-table which Nihal understood through pictures. Individuals with Autism understand better when explained through pictures- any visual cue -because they are visual learners. She was calm and cool as a cucumber. She, in fact, apologized to Nihal that she forgot to show the time table, his schedule before leaving. Nihal was definitely settling down and was calmer. His intensity of hitting his mom decreased and he kept touching her now instead of hitting, definitely indicating that the waves of stress hormones in his system were settling, making his behavior settle down. There were people all around the car trying to help in their own way.

Nihal's mom waited for around 15 minutes to explain things to Nihal and then we left for the center. In this process, her dress was pulled, her face was hurt BUT she was smiling like a peaceful warrior who had just won the battle. It takes a lot of EFFORT AND MENTAL STRENGTH to keep calm when your child is not calm but this mother has evolved.

Patience and understanding of the behavior while being CALM is needed in abundance. It was a big learning for me. That day is etched in my memory and my soul bathes into such wonderful qualities now because of individuals like Nihal and his mom. I have been collecting gems of beautiful qualities because of them.

Every behavior happens for a reason. Let me give you one more example. A smart, thin, and tall teenage boy, Akshaj, entered my office along with his mom. His mom wore a sari, *mangalsutra, bindi,* and green bangles. Akshaj sat quietly as his mom talked to me. She asked me for my permission to start the conversation in Marathi and then moved ahead with her conversation. The words she uttered and her feelings and expressions flew like a turbulent river, pouring her heart out like the waves hit the shores.

The intense emotions made me restless. I wished she would stop talking. As she criticized the boy in front of me, the energy around me turned prickly. It was too much to take and the inner child in me pleaded with her to stop. I had made peace with my emotional wounds but the little boy was getting restless and I didn't want him to get any emotional wounds. His body language changed constantly. He looked towards me and to his mom and then decided to dig his eyes into the floor. I was not happy with the conversation and asked her to stop. I took permission from Akshaj and asked him to wait outside. His mother was not happy with his academic performance. He was slow with reading and writing. He was a brilliant boy earlier, but now he had turned defiant. He even back-answered. He didn't have friends and was lonely. Things turned from bad to terrible for them, so she wanted me to do therapy to help him.

I called Akshaj in and requested his mom to wait outside. As soon as she went out of the room, everything changed. That timid looking boy, who sat with droopy shoulders and eyes digging the floor suddenly changed. He looked straight into my eyes. His shoulders and spine were up with chest out, chin up. I was really shocked. He started speaking with me in fluent English with a lovely accent. He was very expressive. He told me, "I know that my parents feel that therapy will help me but I choose not to write. I choose not to read. I will not study no matter how much ever therapy they give me. What do you think of me?"

I thought I was supposed to answer but he went on, "I am intelligent and understand everything that is taught in school. But I will not do anything. I will let my grades suffer". I allowed him to speak. And then when I thought it was right, I asked him how can I help him? He told me that he needs his parent's time and that was all. He again started "My dad is too busy making a career. He took me to Dubai when I was little. I was doing very well there and made good friends. And then they got me to Baroda. I somehow settled in a year's time and adjusted to the change in the learning style and the curriculum. I started making friends. And just as I had settled they got me to Mumbai".Now again, I am not accepted by my classmates and they think differently and behave differently. While the teacher is teaching, I am thinking of how to fit into some group as I feel lonely."

I was now getting to understand what this boy is going through. He told me that his mom is always busy doing household work and does not have time to understand or listen to what is happening in his life. His dad is never available. Whenever he watches TV, he is asked to take care of his younger sister and play with her. He told me that he loves his sister too much but does not always want to babysit.

Once he was done talking, I asked him, "How can I help you?" He begged, "I don't want any therapy to help me. Please ask my parents to give me time and understand me. I just want to talk to them not to get answers or solutions but just talk." He broke down into tears after this statement. I was numb and was starting to wonder what was happening. He was fine immediately and smiled as if everything was fine.

I called his mom in again. This time like a mature adult, the boy told me that he will wait out. His mom agreed to everything that he said and she mentioned that her son didn't need therapy but "time" from his parents. She never saw things from his perspective.

Akshaj was diagnosed with Oppositional Defiant Disorder. All that he wanted to do was to share his pain and frustration but there was no one in his life with whom he could do so, not even his parents!!

Every behavior happens for a reason...ALWAYS!

CHAPTER 34

SETTING LIMITS AND BOUNDARIES

So, we spoke about understanding the sensory processing issues, checking and evaluating for the unintegrated primitive reflexes, and working on ourselves to self-regulate. We work on calming ourselves and evaluate ourselves before we talk to our kids. We give them an environment which as Gabor Mate says tells them - "I welcome your presence. I welcome you to exist in my presence. And I am overjoyed to have you in my presence." And kids can sense the body language and understand us even if they can't name what they are feeling. We allow ourselves to just "be" with our kids and allow us to be trained by them.

Our presence makes them feel safe and they play on their own whereas an anxious child cannot play on his own. Or his way of playing is a way of protecting himself. Play is preparation for life and it happens when the kids feel protected. We have learned and understood that the most important template for the emotional development of the child as well as for the brain's healthy physiological development is a nurturing relationship with mutually responsive adults. This also means that anything that we do that undermines the relationship will undermine the healthy emotional development of the child because it makes the child insecure and pushes them into a fight-flight-freeze mode where they do not learn anything. We want the child to learn that relationships with his parents are stable and reliable even if he has a negative emotion or a tantrum. He is accepted even if he is upset or acting out. He learns that his emotions do matter to us and we are available to help him when he needs us the most.

But does that mean that we are permissive and allow everything that they want?

No, they may want a lot of screen time or may want to have a lot of junk food and those choices are not great choices.

And if we say a "No" to them and reject their demands, it is absolutely normal for them to feel angry about it or for that matter sometimes feel rage. They may want to throw tantrums and make it a big deal because it is actually a big deal for them. The only thing to remember is, "I as a parent do not want to be threatened by that anger or even tantrum myself. I can speak and acknowledge the child's feelings. I know you are so angry because you wanted the second packet of chips and I am not giving it to you. I know, I hear you."

We do not want to teach the child to suppress his feelings rather we want him to regulate his behavior after acknowledging his feelings. It is also very important that we allow enough time for the child to feel his feelings. Sometimes, when my child throws a tantrum and is really angry, I am concerned about my next meeting that is scheduled in ten minutes or concerned about drying the clothes or cooking meals for the day and so I don't want my routine to get upset because of the child's tantrums. So, I prematurely want to stop the anger by raising my voice. And I don't think this is fair.

I was once working with a father who was not able to balance his personal and professional life. He was not able to give time to his kids and his mom. There was a lot of emotional baggage that he was carrying and with every aspect of behavior that we unfolded, he would cry and I would hand over tissue after tissue. When he cried, I allowed him to release and wait until he was ready to process further. It was a one-hour session and he cried for around 30 minutes, trying to process the waves of emotions that kept washing over.

At the end of the conversation, he was better and asked me, "Why does my child (a 6-year-old boy) take so much time to come out of his tantrums? I give him what he wants and that should just settle him down?" I was zapped because sometimes we do not realize the importance and value of processing emotions or even understanding it from the viewpoint of others.

I asked him, "Would you be ok if I told you at the beginning of our session that I understand you cannot balance your life. Now you can STOP CRYING! You needed 30 minutes of crying to process your emotions at the age of 42, how is it possible for your child to process them at a fast speed at 6 years of age. Emotions or tantrums are not like buttons- you do not switch them on and off at will at least in the beginning."

The reason I share this is that most of us as adults want to feel understood and we invest the time at a therapy session to understand and help ourselves to process our feelings because we are so overwhelmed by them. But we do not want our kids to go through this "processing time" and want the crying or tantrums to stop INSTANTLY! That is because it makes us feel uncomfortable or disrupts our routine.

Another thing to remember is we should not use our relationship against them. We should not say things like, "If you don't stop crying, I will stop talking to you. If you don't stop your tantrums, I will not hug you. Mummy's time is canceled. Hugs are canceled."

Let's not take such impulsive decisions. Sometimes, we as parents feel threatened and we do not know how to deal with the situation. This does not mean we project our negative emotions on the child. In the fit of anger, I have seen kids banging their heads or biting their own hands or flinging their arms and legs on the floor, completely unaware of their safety. In such a case, their safety – not just physical but even emotional safety – is our responsibility. But it needs to be managed from a place of calmness. Kids who do not understand language (who are very severe and have severe challenges) understand our energies and the tone of our voices. Little babies who cannot talk or understand language also understand us from the tone of our voices and the energy signatures that we send to them.

So when a child is in the middle of a tantrum and we are centered and talking to them to acknowledge their feelings and thoughts, kids learn to self-regulate. We need to validate that they are having such negative feelings.

So instead, frame your sentences like, "I know you are angry with me right now because you want to watch TV and mummy is not allowing you to, but you can see it tomorrow". We have to allow space for the child's negative feelings without making the child wrong for it. It's easy to just say this but the child is a sensitive person and reads the body language of the parent while he listens to their words. It's that level of non-verbal communication through the body language that sends the message to the child. We don't have to just say that, but we have to be actually "okay" with their anger. Non-acceptance of the child's dark side is one of the biggest wounds that we can inflict on our kids.

We have to give a full invitation to the child to exist in our presence and accept all the emotions that happen to them. If I can't accept the emotion that the child stirs up in me, then I am not able to accept the child. We cannot sanitize our feelings. Kids cannot be only happy, cheerful, kind, and considerate. We have all of the spectra of emotions to be complete and it is important to accept and acknowledge when these so-called negative emotions exist. The first most step is to accept these mixed feelings in us and then in our kids and be comfortable with them.

This does not happen with just one incident but requires many such episodes for them to learn to do so. The child learns that even if he feels overwhelmed and extremely uncomfortable with some emotions, he is safe when his mom or dad is around. He acknowledges that I am not going to stay in this state forever and this will pass and I will be back to my happy, cheerful, and playful self. But if we explode when our children explode, then they fall deeper into the trenches of negative emotions and do not know how to come out of it.

I love the concept of "time in" instead of "time out". I would rather stay with the child and provide the nurturing at an emotional level making him feel that he is understood and it's ok to get washed over by the negative emotions and that I am there with him to help him understand what exactly is happening to him. But in timeout, I give him a message that you need to suppress your emotions or else you are not loved by us. We love you only when you behave well!

Kids want to play video games or be on social media or just watch videos on a screen. The kids are addicted to screens like how an adult is addicted to some of the other things. When the screens are taken away from them, we see a typical addictive protest and anger. Screens affect the developing brain, the more time spent watching screens, the more it depletes the dopamine receptors. Dopamine receptors are the ones that are involved in pleasure, motivation, and the incentive circuitry in the brain. Children learn to develop an attachment and a relationship with the screen. 2- or 3-year-old kids are too little to handle this kind of stimulation. We give the screen to a child when they use it for learning or for its functional use. Using a screen to connect with others using a video call to talk and interact when relatives are far away is amazing. But using the screen as a babysitter is very risky. So, co-viewing and seeing the TV or videos together is good if your child is older and you have given him the screen to just play, he will resist or may even ask for an extension of time when his allotted time with the device gets over. He will get angry, may throw tantrums, and even yell when his demands are not met. But this does not mean that he gets the screen because he engaged in such behavior.

I am only trying to help you understand that we can be lovingly firm and it is okay for a child to feel sad or upset. He may be bullied, may not be invited for birthday parties, his toy might break, he may not get chips or chocolates on a daily basis or he may lose a loved one or a pet. All such situations in the presence of loving emotionally present parents teach kids to self-regulate and become more resilient. They learn that they can manage and handle the "no's", the sad days, the painful days, the bad days and always to bounce back.

It is sometimes difficult for a parent to make a child participate willingly for self-help tasks or for tasks that require managing the space or perform daily chores. There is a lot of defiance, tantrum, and non-compliance that we see in such tasks. Does that mean that we succumb to those needs or we teach our kids that tasks need to be performed even if they are not happy doing it? In such a case, it is important that the parent follows through. Most of the time instructions are given to a child by parents and the kids do not comply. Parents tell me that kids do not follow no matter how many times they are told and that it is really difficult to make them do anything. In such a case, it is important to remember and be aware of the kind of instructions that we are giving to our kids.

Are we giving too many instructions?
Are the instructions comprehended by the child?
Are we putting our kids into a verbal overload?
Are too many people giving instructions?
Do we really want them to follow those instructions?
Was the child prepared before giving those instructions?

Sometimes, instructions are just given for the sake of giving. I remember a child named Darren (an 8-year-old boy diagnosed with Autism). Darren came to us for therapy at the age of 4 and was completely non-verbal. The family came to me from a place which was three hours away from my center. They had to leave early in the morning to visit me. As Darren was young, his parents used to let him sleep in the car when they drove to my center. As time passed by, Darren became more expressive and verbal and could communicate everything that he felt.

One day when Darren was 8 years old, his parents got him to me. They complained about him and mentioned that he does not listen to or follow anything and even argues with them. They spoke of Darren being reluctant to come and meet me that day. I was not prepared for what Darren spoke that day. He said, "Daddy, you know how much I like circuits and I was playing with them. I was not told that we are coming to Mumbai, you and mummy discussed this and did not even think that it is important to let me know. I was reluctant to come because I wanted to finish what I had started. It is our house and I want to be involved in decision making too. You should have told me that you have taken an appointment with Ms. Reena. You did not tell me."

I was happy that he could express and was shocked too. Sometimes, we give instructions and want them to be followed without understanding what our kids are feeling.

We must see things from the perspective of our kids. Instead of taking our children's behavior personally, it is important to understand that children do not want to disobey us and do some of the behavior intentionally. They are only trying to process their feelings and trying to protect their self-esteem. We have to learn to make an infinite eight and keep them in one loop and us in the other and learn to separate ourselves from their behavior.

While setting limits and establishing boundaries for appropriate and inappropriate behaviors, we have to also learn to look at the behavior of our child in general – not just focusing on the negative or the inappropriate behavior. It is important to appreciate the strengths and also talk about the positives while we work on their challenges. And we must see the challenges from the perspective of the child too.

I also feel that we need to be aware of what, why, and when to speak. Sometimes, parents just give a standard statement "no" for everything, when they themselves are not clear on why they are responding this way. This is why it's crucial we only say what we mean, mean what we say, and follow-through

Connecting with our kids is the only key that helps us to shape behaviors. Learning how to behave and shaping behavior happens between 1 to 6 years of age which are the formative years. This is the time to work on self-help skills and set routines and encourage them to help us with household tasks and consolidate their routines. It is important to seize this opportunity and shape our children's behaviors in these years because later it is difficult to work on these areas. Also, it is important to emphasize the importance of "following through"- if you communicate something, see to it that you mean it. Most of the time, as I said earlier, instructions are given and parents are themselves not consistent in following the rules laid down for the house.

There is a root for everything and so there are emotional roots for every behavior. These roots need to be identified instead of working on the surface level behaviors before we set limits for our children!

CHAPTER 35

SSSH.... LISTEN TO SILENCE WITHIN

"It's not important what happens to us or what happens around us. The only thing that really matters is what happens inside of us."

- Ralph Waldo Emerson

When I was in the fifth standard, I was a very talkative little girl. My teacher always scolded me and when she realized that I am not the kind who will sit quietly when told to, she made me the monitor of the class. Now, it was my job to make everyone quiet. "SILENCE PLEASE... KEEP QUIET!" That is all that I would repeat to keep others quiet and silent all the time. While doing so, I would listen to the pin-drop silence outside which also used to push me to the silence within me. I did not understand why staying quiet and following instructions was necessary and we were supposed to not complain and bear it all.

I remember going to the gurdwara during my childhood days, we spent a lot of time just sitting, as the Ragiji (priest) sang melodiously. Sometimes, I used to spend many hours with my eyes closed and just doing "nothing". The gurdwara was a calming place to be in.

I don't know why I did so, but again, the message was, "Listen to the SILENCE within you."

When I was in the eighth standard, my parents took me to trek the mountains. The verdant mountains, untamed rivers, and totally unharmed trees were tranquilizing. The silence of the mountains felt like music to my ears, I spent hours and hours listening to that song of nature.

The song of the rustling leaves,
The song of the blowing wind.
The song of the flowing river,

The song of the chirping birds,
The song of the wind flowing through the mountains,
The song of the animals,
The rhythm of my heartbeats,
The pace of my amazed breaths.

As years flew by, I found myself working with so many parents giving the same message of listening to the SILENCE within.

A parent with whom I worked recently told me that as she wakes up, she catches hold of her smartphone to check her messages and e-mails. The first thing that she does after opening her eyes is, she bombards herself with too many things that her brain finds really hard to PROCESS and DIGEST.

Another parent told me that he tries to spend QUALITY time with his family and when he cannot, he starts staring at his smartphone because sitting in SILENCE is killing.

Another father who came to me for his child mentioned that as soon as he gets into his car, he switches on the music system by default, even though he at times doesn't wish to listen to it. It's just an "automatic response" to just switch on the music system. Sitting in SILENCE is annoying according to him.

Then, another mom spoke to me about her son's sleep issues. She also mentioned her son's screen time and her default response after entering the house to switch on the TV. The TV keeps running even when no one actually watches it.

We have gotten used to receiving so much input all the time from our smartphones and TV commercials. In this age of connecting with our virtual friends and technology, the connection with the self is fading away.

Sitting just alone and just "being" is not a good idea.

Most kids that I work with, have zero resilience skills. They find it difficult to resolve conflicts because the technology and the virtual world is robbing them of the opportunities to develop these skills. That's because more time is spent connecting with technology rather than being INVESTED in people.

As I mentioned in the chapter on Little Parenting, my son's challenging behaviors pushed me to find my answers within me. At the age of 33, for the first time in my life, I met my soul or my core inner being. My soul wasn't about my thoughts or my beliefs but just "me". It is not something that I had ever experienced and I remember having tears of joys and gratitude when I first met my inner divine essence.

The journey started for me when I started training for reflex integration techniques (which I thought I was doing to help my clients). Waves and waves of emotions kept slipping into deeper dimensions of my essence with the training in emotional freedom techniques, neuro-linguistic programming, past life regression, and kinesiology. I was like a voracious caterpillar devouring and digesting all that knowledge to make me more and more aware of my patterns and to discover myself. I saw glimpses of my divine essence and they disappeared to reappear. Because now, I was making friends with myself and shedding off all those beliefs and values that did not allow me to find myself.

I learned to feel my feelings and with each and every tantrum or a roadblock in my child's development, I slipped even deeper into it. I thank my little son for gratitude as we co-created the reality which I live today. I embraced the inner child within me which was longing for love and filled it with so much warmth and healed it. I hugged my soul and I felt embraced in the blanket of infinite love. Resentment and anger slowly were replaced with joy, grace, and gratitude. Discovering newer dimensions within ourselves is limitless and my son helps me to go deeper into it with each passing day.

I learned to slow down to speed up and grow exponentially. This is the most important message that I share with parents to make a deeper and fulfilling relationship with their children. From intention to manifestation and settling down in stillness.

Does that mean that the child will be all fine and "normal"? I really don't know what normal actually means. Every parent who goes within learns to become more and more comfortable with themselves and that helps their child to get more and more comfortable. Parents are okay with the possibilities of the unknown and they can embrace challenges. They know that every difficulty is a portal to grow and evolve.

When I meet parents who have discovered and met their core essence, their acceptance of the situation fuels them to work on their child's challenges. I once asked a parent who had a 7-year-old son, Rohan, who was diagnosed with Autism, "How is your son doing?"

He replied, "He is good and we are taking it each day at a time and working."

He was not sad or even happy but was immersed at the moment with total acceptance. I saw that his little boy was making more progress than he did before. Rohan was the same boy who could not sleep for more than 4 hours three years back. He slept by 2:30 or 3 am and used to be really constipated. There was a lot of self-stimulation and no language for communication even when he could speak. He was in his world of rigid and patterned behavior. And today, he sleeps by 9:30 pm. and can maintain his sleep for 11 hours in one go. He passes motions every day. He uses language for communication but only for his own needs, is connected to his parents, and is able to adapt to new situations. Everything happens the moment parent's start working on themselves and discovering themselves. Parents evolve with their kids. Rohan's parents learned to trust themselves and allow miracles to happen!

Another parent told me, "I know that my child is triggering me with his tantrums and I need to know more about myself. I need to become more aware of my implicit memories, connect with them, and make peace with them. I am in the process and yes I am more aware. I am in my sacred space and ready to accept the perfect and the imperfect (shadow) parts of me and integrate them." I am full of pride when parents talk to me about their children from this space of essence and work on the behaviors of their kids.

The reason I share all of this is to highlight the importance of finding ourselves, discovering ourselves, and working on ourselves before we work with our children. How can we start doing this – by connecting to the silence within and by being more MINDFUL!

We are bombarded with thoughts and hence lose track of a lot of things and the same happens with our kids. Has it ever occurred to you that you pick up your phone to check something and get distracted to check your social profiles or messages? At such times, we often wonder why you picked up the phone in the first place. Has it happened that you tell your child to come for studies or therapy and get involved in the household chores instead? Does it happen that you set screen time for your child and then fail to follow it? We get consumed by our thoughts and release the frustration on our kids for not complying.

I would love to share a few things I do and you can pick them up if they feel right to you. I am a work in progress. I strongly feel that being aware of our own patterns and thoughts is important before we help anyone else.

The morning sets the tone for the rest of the day. I remember my mom's advice here, according to her, the answer to all the problems in my life as a child was to wake up early so that I do not rush and panic. And now, I realize how true that is. It is a good idea to wake up with a grateful heart and set an intention for the day. It is a good idea to refrain from using devices immediately after waking up. It is also a great idea to go off to sleep with a grateful heart too.

As children, we did a lot of yoga and *pranayama*. The only message I got from all my yoga teachers was "stay on your breath", "on your breath", "on your breath" and "on your breath". I am now starting to understand that breath is my constant friend till I am alive and till this air flows into my lungs. It is a powerful life force and I keep coming back to it in the most difficult and the most grateful moments. This is the best barometer to my feelings and to everyone's feelings.

I remember when I was a child, I used to meet a lady at the gurdwara every day. She would always be grateful for everything that she did. While cutting the vegetables, she used to thank her fingers and her body. While singing, she used to thank her breath and voice. While walking, she used to thank her feet. Every day she repeated these words, "*shukrana* (thankful)", "*shukrana*", "*shukrana*" and "*shukrana*". I see this as another powerful tool because it helps me to see things differently in any difficult situation. When parents come to me with a list of complaints and concerns, I tell them, "I will help you with solutions but before that tell me 5 things that are positive in this situation that your child is going through." It really brings in a cognitive shift in them and their body language shifts from being tense to being relaxed. And you know what, they find their own answers after connecting with their core essence. The answers are all within us...ALWAYS!

Reconnecting with nature is the most healing practice for ages. Calibrating our rhythm with that of the earth is the best way to relax and calm down. *Shin rinyoku* means, "forest bathing," it is the staple of Japanese preventive healthcare and it just means to be in a forest. There is a lot of research stating that visiting quiet natural places and walking around has numerous calming and restorative benefits.

Talking and meeting people who resonate and share our bandwidth also helps immensely. Most of our time is spent either in front of the screens or with human beings which are more commercially or work focused thus depriving us of opportunities for genuine connection with others and also with ourselves.

Sometimes, the days are so full and the schedule is so tight that there is literally no breathing space. At such times, creating mini-mindful moments can be created while taking a shower, while dressing up, while eating our meals or even while doing the daily routine mundane chores at home like folding clothes, washing utensils, dusting the house or ironing the clothes.

Another important skill that I feel really helps is the ability to laugh at ourselves and go easy with ourselves. I really encourage and plead with you to find the humor in life itself and not take it too seriously. Laughter produces complete, relaxed action of the diaphragm, exercising the lungs, increasing the blood's oxygen level, and gently toning the entire cardiovascular system. It is like internal jogging. Laughter increases the production of a class of brain chemicals called catecholamines. In addition, they also increase the production of endorphins, the body's natural opiates. Exercise, laughter, and play are closely related and need to be approached with the same spirit as all three produce similar effects on body and mind. Let loose and laugh a bit... Believe me, you will be glad you did it!!

Feel your feelings. Acknowledge them and allow them to come. Take them as messengers who come to convey the internal state of your body. Emotional honesty and self-acceptance lead to better physical health. Dr. Walter Smith and Stephen Bloomfield found that people who can cry freely catch fewer colds than people who always hold back their tears.

Have more tactile experiences- caresses, hugs, kisses, and hand-holding are always possible with the people who matter to us most.

I would like to thank you for investing your time in reading this work and pray that it helps you to grow and find yourself!!!

All the very best to you with everything...

Stay blessed...

REFERENCES

Chapter One
Animals in translation – Temple Grandin
Bright not broken (Gifted kids, adhd and Autism)
Grandin, Temple. Thinking in Pictures
Pretending to be Normal: Living with Asperger's Syndrome - Liane Holliday Willey
Scattered Minds – Gabor Mate
Scholars with Autism – Achieving Dreams by Lars Perner
The Autistic Brain by Temple Grandin ad Richard Panek
The Power of Neurodiversity: Unleashing the Advantages of Your Differently Wired Brain – Thomas Armstrong
https://blogs.scientificamerican.com/observations/clearing-up-some-misconceptions-about-neurodiversity/
https://journalofethics.ama-assn.org/article/spectrum-autism-neuronal-connections-behavioral-expression/2010-11
https://journalofethics.ama-assn.org/article/what-can-physicians-learn-neurodiversity-movement/2012-06
https://www.additudemag.com/adhd-entrepreneur-stories-jetblue-kinkos-jupitermedia/
https://www.cnbc.com/2019/10/07/billionaire-richard-branson-dyslexia-helped-me-to-become-successful.html
https://www.cnbc.com/2019/10/14/people-with-dyslexia-have-the-skills-to-future-proof-the-workforce-ey.html
https://www.forbes.com/sites/dalearcher/2014/05/14/adhd-the-entrepreneurs-superpower/#1e775ab659e9
https://www.theguardian.com/society/2017/oct/09/autism-working-spectrum-capable-employees-talent

Chapter Two
Conversations with a rattle snake- Theo Fleury and Kim Barthel
In the Realm of Hungry Ghosts: Close Encounters with Addiction Gabor Mate
On Grief and Grieving: Elisabeth Kubler Ross, David Kessler
Owen, JB. Ignite Your Parenting: Real life, heartfelt stories to help parents find balance and joy in raising happy children
Scattered Minds – Gabor Mate
Slow Your Roll: Mindfulness for Fast Times By Greg Graber
Stapleton, Dr. Peta . The Science behind Tapping
The conscious Parent (transforming ourselves, empowering our children) by Shefali Tsabary
The Journey: Brandon Bays
https://developingchild.harvard.edu/wp-content/uploads/2005/05/Stress_Disrupts_Architecture_Developing_Brain-1.pdf
https://developingchild.harvard.edu/wp-content/uploads/2004/04/Childrens-Emotional-Development-Is-Built-into-the-Architecture-of-Their-Brains.pdf

Chapter Three
Born for love – Maia Szalavitz and Bruce Perry
Clinician's Guide for Implementing Ayres Sensory Integration: Promoting Participation for Children With

Autism by Zoe Mailloux Roseann C. Schaaf
Inside Out: What Makes a Person with Social Cognitive Deficits Tick? Winner Garcia Michelle
Pedretti's Occupational Therapy: Practice Skills for Physical Dysfunction (Factsbook) Pendleton
Scattered Minds – Gabor Mate
Think Social -Winner Garcia Michelle

Chapter Four
Brain Wash: Detox Your Mind for Clearer Thinking, Deeper Relationships, and Lasting Happiness-Dr.
Perlmutter
Earthing -The Most important health discovery ever – Clinton Ober, Stephen T Cinatra
Energy Medicine: How to use your body's energies for optimum health and vitality Donna Eden and John
Feinstein
Healthy Sleep Habits, Happy Child Marc Weissbluth, MD,
The Healing Power Of EFT and Energy Psychology: Tap into your body's energy to change your life for the
better Donna Eden, David Feinstein
Touch for health: John Thie
https://eftinternational.org/learning-to-sleep-naturally/
https://journals.lww.com/jrnldbp/Fulltext/2019/08000/Sleep_Difficulties_in_Infancy_Are_Associated_
with.4.aspx
https://pubmed.ncbi.nlm.nih.gov/30150906/
https://sciforschenonline.org/journals/neurology/article-data/JNNB-2-130/JNNB-2-130.pdf
https://sleepsense.net/epsom-salt-may-help-kids-sleep-better/
https://sleepsense.net/epsom-salt-may-help-kids-sleep-better/
https://www.aota.org/About-Occupational-Therapy/Professionals/HW/Sleep.aspx
https://www.eftuniverse.com/children-and-adolescents/helping-a-restless-baby-to-sleep
https://www.hindawi.com/journals/oti/2018/8637498/
https://www.ncbi.nlm.nih.gov/pmc/articles/PMC2687494/
https://www.ncbi.nlm.nih.gov/pubmed/23853635
https://www.researchgate.net/publication/326688432_Occupational_Therapy_Practice_in_Sleep_Manage
ment_A_Review_of_Conceptual_Models_and_Research_Evidence
https://www.researchgate.net/publication/50363197_Effects_of_prone_and_supine_positions_on_sleep_
state_and_stress_responses_in_preterm_infants

Chapter Five
Animals in translation – Temple Grandin
Beyond Freedom and Dignity B F Skinner
Beyond the Sea Squirt: A Journey with Reflexes by Moira Dempsey
Born for love – Maia Szalavitz and Bruce Perry
Clinician's Guide for Implementing Ayres Sensory Integration: Promoting Participation for Children With
Autism by Zoe Mailloux Roseann C. Schaaf
Don't Shoot the Dog!: The New Art of Teaching and Training.Khali mouja
Engaging Autism: Using the Floortime Approach to Help Children Relate, Communicate, and Think (A
Merloyd Lawrence Book) Stanley Greenspan
Grandin, Temple. Thinking in Pictures
Hold on to your kids: Gordon Neufeld, Gabor Mate
Love, Jean: Inspiration for Families Living with Dysfunction of Sensory Integration by A. Jean Ayre
Movements That Heal by Harald Blomberg and Moira Dempsey
Post Trauma Recovery: Gentle, Rapid, and Effective Treatment with Reflex Integration Svetlana Masgutova
Denis Masgutov
Scattered Minds – Gabor Mate
Sensory Integration and Learning Disorders by A. Jean Ayres
Sensory Integration and the Child by A. Jean Ayress
The Awakened Family by Shefali Tsabary
The Spark- A mother's story of Nurturing, Genius and Autism by Kristine Barnett
Therapeutic Listening: Sheila Frick and Sally Young
Understanding the Nature of Sensory Integration with Diverse Populations by Susanne Smith Roley, Erna
Imperatore Blanche, et al.

Chapter Six
Love Medicine and Miracles Bernie Siegel
Scattered Minds – Gabor Mate
Born for love – Maia Szalavitz and Bruce Perry
Trauma-proofing your kids – Peter Levine and Maggie Kline
The conscious Parent (transforming ourselves, empowering our children) by Shefali Tsabary
Stapleton, Dr. Peta . The Science behind Tapping

Chapter Seven
Hold on to your kids: Gordon Neufeld, Gabor Mate
On Grief and Grieving: Elisabeth Kubler Ross, David Kessler
Owen, JB. Ignite Your Parenting: Real life, heartfelt stories to help parents find balance and joy in raising happy children
Scattered Minds – Gabor Mate
Slow Your Roll: Mindfulness for Fast Times By Greg Graber
The conscious Parent (transforming ourselves, empowering our children) by Shefali Tsabary
The Journey: Brandon Bays

Chapter Eight
11:11 Time for Abundance by Mana
Hold on to your kids: Gordon Neufeld, Gabor Mate
Scattered Minds – Gabor Mate
Soul song of the new age children by Mana
Waking the Tiger: Healing Trauma Peter A Levine

Chapter Nine
Beyond the Sea Squirt: A Journey with Reflexes by Moira Dempsey
Hold on to your kids: Gordon Neufeld, Gabor Mate
Movements That Heal by Harald Blomberg and Moira Dempsey
Peter O Grey Free to Learn: Why Unleashing the Instinct to Play Will Make Our Children Happier, More Self-Reliant, and Better Students for Life
Sensory Integration and Learning Disorders by A. Jean Ayres
Sensory Integration: Theory and Practice by Anita C. Bundy ScD OT/L FAOTA FOTARA, Shelly J Lane PhD OTR/L FAOTA CSU, et al.
The Psychology Of The Child Jean Piaget Barbel Inhelder
https://www.jpeds.com/article/S0022-3476%2807%2900447-7/abstract

Chapter Ten
Don't Shoot the Dog!: The New Art of Teaching and Training.Khali mouja
Post Trauma Recovery: Gentle, Rapid, and Effective Treatment with Reflex Integration Svetlana Masgutova Denis Masgutov
The Polyvagal theory – Steven Porges

Chapter Eleven
Born for love – Maia Szalavitz and Bruce Perry
Hold on to your kids: Gordon Neufeld, Gabor Mate
Regression Therapy- A handbook for professionals: Wina Fred Blake Lucas
Scattered Minds – Gabor Mate
Trauma-proofing your kids – Peter Levine and Maggie Kline
https://www.ncbi.nlm.nih.gov/pmc/articles/PMC3511633/

Chapter Twelve
Autism: A new perspective by Andrea Libutti and Joao Carlos
Bridges, Holly. Reframe Your Thinking Around Autism
Bruce Lipton : Biology of Belief
Conversations with a rattle snake- Theo Fleury and Kim Barthel
Stapleton, Dr. Peta . The Science behind Tapping

The intention experiment: Lynne Mctaggard
The Polyvagal theory – Steven Porges

Chapter Thirteen
Assessing Neuromotor Readiness for Learning: The INPP Developmental Screening Test and School Intervention Programme by Sally Goddard Blythe
Attention, Balance and Coordination: The A.B.C. of Learning Success by Sally Goddard Blythe, Lawrence J. Beuret, et al.
Beyond the Sea Squirt: A Journey with Reflexes by Moira Dempsey
Born for love – Maia Szalavitz and Bruce Perry
How can I talk if my lips don't move? Inside my autistic mind by Tito Rajarshi Mukhopadhyay
How can I talk if my lips don't move? Inside my autistic mind by Tito Rajarshi Mukhopadhyay
Movements That Heal by Harald Blomberg and Moira Dempsey
Neuromotor Immaturity in Children and Adults: The INPP Screening Test for Clinicians and Health Practitioners by Sally Goddard Blythe
Nobody Nowhere by Donna Williams
Reflexes, Learning And Behavior: A Window into the Child's Mind : A Non-Invasive Approach to Solving Learning & Behavior Problems by Sally Goddard
Sensory Integration and Learning Disorders by A. Jean Ayres
Sensory Integration and the Child by A. Jean Ayress
Sensory Integration: Theory and Practice by Anita C. Bundy ScD OT/L FAOTA FOTARA, Shelly J Lane PhD OTR/L FAOTA CSU, et al.
Soon Will Come the Light: A view from inside the Autism Puzzle Thomas McKean
The Autistic Brain by Temple Grandin ad Richard Panek
The Genius of Natural Childhood, The: Secrets of Thriving Children (Early Years) by Sally Goddard Blythe
Thomas's Journey with Irlen Elloise Scott
Trauma-proofing your kids – Peter Levine and Maggie Kline

Chapter Fourteen
Grandin, Temple. Thinking in Pictures
Nobody Nowhere by Donna Williams
Sensory Integration and the Child by A. Jean Ayres

Chapter Fifteen
An Anthropologist on Mars Oliver Sacks
Clinician's Guide for Implementing Ayres Sensory Integration: Promoting Participation for Children With Autism by Zoe Mailloux Roseann C. Schaaf
Conversations with a rattle snake- Theo Fleury and Kim Barthel
Grandin, Temple. Thinking in Pictures
Scholars with Autism – Achieving Dreams by Lars Perner
Sensory Integration and the Child by A. Jean Ayres
Stapleton, Dr. Peta . The Science behind Tapping
The Spark- A mother's story of Nurturing, Genius and Autism by Kristine Barnett
Understanding the Nature of Sensory Integration with Diverse Populations by Susanne Smith Roley, Erna Imperatore Blanche, et al.

Chapter Sixteen
Born for love – Maia Szalavitz and Bruce Perry
Hold on to your kids: Gordon Neufeld, Gabor Mate
Trauma-proofing your kids – Peter Levine and Maggie Kline
Waking the Tiger: Healing Trauma Peter A Levine

Chapter Seventeen
Sensory Integration and the Child by A. Jean Ayres

Chapter Eighteen
Clinician's Guide for Implementing Ayres Sensory Integration: Promoting Participation for Children With Autism by Zoe Mailloux Roseann C. Schaaf

Love, Jean: Inspiration for Families Living with Dysfunction of Sensory Integration by A. Jean Ayre
Movements That Heal by Harald Blomberg and Moira Dempsey
Neuromotor Immaturity in Children and Adults: The INPP Screening Test for Clinicians and Health Practitioners by Sally Goddard Blythe
Reflexes, Learning And Behavior: A Window into the Child's Mind : A Non-Invasive Approach to Solving Learning & Behavior Problems by Sally Goddard
Sensory Integration and Learning Disorders by A. Jean Ayres
Sensory Integration and the Child by A. Jean Ayress
Sensory Integration: Theory and Practice by Anita C. Bundy ScD OT/L FAOTA FOTARA, Shelly J Lane PhD OTR/L FAOTA CSU, et al.
The Genius of Natural Childhood, The: Secrets of Thriving Children (Early Years) by Sally Goddard Blythe
Understanding the Nature of Sensory Integration with Diverse Populations by Susanne Smith Roley, Erna Imperatore Blanche, et al.

Chapter Nineteen
Beyond the Sea Squirt: A Journey with Reflexes by Moira Dempsey
Bridges, Holly. Reframe Your Thinking Around Autism
Conversations with a rattle snake- Theo Fleury and Kim Barthel
Movements That Heal by Harald Blomberg and Moira Dempsey
Reflexes, Learning And Behavior: A Window into the Child's Mind : A Non-Invasive Approach to Solving Learning & Behavior Problems by Sally Goddard
The Polyvagal theory – Steven Porges
The Spark- A mother's story of Nurturing, Genius and Autism by Kristine Barnett

Chapter Twenty
Grandin, Temple. Thinking in Pictures
How can I talk if my lips don't move? Inside my autistic mind by Tito Rajarshi Mukhopadhyay
Sensory Integration and Learning Disorders by A. Jean Ayres
Sensory Integration and the Child by A. Jean Ayress
Sensory Integration: Theory and Practice by Anita C. Bundy ScD OT/L FAOTA FOTARA, Shelly J Lane PhD OTR/L FAOTA CSU, et al.
The Out-of-Sync Child: Recognizing and Coping with Sensory Processing Disorder (The Out-of-Sync Child Series) by Carol Kranowitz and Lucy Jane Mille
Understanding the Nature of Sensory Integration with Diverse Populations by Susanne Smith Roley, Erna Imperatore Blanche, et al.

Chapter Twenty One
Peter O Grey Free to Learn: Why Unleashing the Instinct to Play Will Make Our Children Happier, More Self-Reliant, and Better Students for Life
Sensory Integration and Learning Disorders by A. Jean Ayres
Sensory Integration and the Child – Understanding hidden Sensory challenges by A. Jean Ayress
Sensory Integration: Theory and Practice by Anita C. Bundy ScD OT/L FAOTA FOTARA, Shelly J Lane PhD OTR/L FAOTA CSU, et al.
The dirt cure: Maya Shetreat Klein
The Out-of-Sync Child: Recognizing and Coping with Sensory Processing Disorder (The Out-of-Sync Child Series) by Carol Kranowitz and Lucy Jane Mille

Chapter Twenty Two
Animals in translation – Temple Grandin
Born for love – Maia Szalavitz and Bruce Perry
Broken Open – Elizabeth Lesser
Carly's Voice (Breaking through Autism) by Arthur Fleischmann and Carly Fleischmann
Descartes' Error: Emotion, Reason, and the Human Brain Antonio Damasio
Graber, Greg. Slow Your Roll: Mindfulness for Fast Times
How can I talk if my lips don't move? Inside my autistic mind by Tito Rajarshi Mukhopadhyay
Interoception: The Eighth Sensory System by Kelly J. Mahler and PhD A.D. "Bud" Craig
Scattered Minds – Gabor Mate
The Feeling of What Happens: Body and Emotion in the Making of Consciousness Antonio Damasio
The Origins Of Neuro Linguistic Programming John Grinder

Waking the Tiger: Healing Trauma Peter A Levine
https://pubmed.ncbi.nlm.nih.gov/32346323/

Chapter Twenty Three
Attention, Balance and Coordination: The A.B.C. of Learning Success by Sally Goddard Blythe, Lawrence J. Beuret, et al.
Movements That Heal by Harald Blomberg and Moira Dempsey
Neuromotor Immaturity in Children and Adults: The INPP Screening Test for Clinicians and Health Practitioners by Sally Goddard Blythe
Peter O Grey Free to Learn: Why Unleashing the Instinct to Play Will Make Our Children Happier, More Self-Reliant, and Better Students for Life
Post Trauma Recovery: Gentle, Rapid, and Effective Treatment with Reflex Integration Svetlana Masgutova Denis Masgutov
Reflexes, Learning And Behavior: A Window into the Child's Mind : A Non-Invasive Approach to Solving Learning & Behavior Problems by Sally Goddard
Sensory Integration and Learning Disorders by A. Jean Ayres
The Genius of Natural Childhood, The: Secrets of Thriving Children (Early Years) by Sally Goddard Blythe

Chapter Twenty Four
Attention, Balance and Coordination: The A.B.C. of Learning Success by Sally Goddard Blythe, Lawrence J. Beuret, et al.
Beyond the Sea Squirt: A Journey with Reflexes by Moira Dempsey
Movements That Heal by Harald Blomberg and Moira Dempsey
Reflexes, Learning And Behavior: A Window into the Child's Mind : A Non-Invasive Approach to Solving Learning & Behavior Problems by Sally Goddard

Chapter Twenty Five
Animals in translation – Temple Grandin
Attention, Balance and Coordination: The A.B.C. of Learning Success by Sally Goddard Blythe, Lawrence J. Beuret, et al.
Beyond the Sea Squirt: A Journey with Reflexes by Moira Dempsey
Bridges, Holly. Reframe Your Thinking Around Autism
Movements That Heal by Harald Blomberg and Moira Dempsey
Reflexes, Learning And Behavior: A Window into the Child's Mind : A Non-Invasive Approach to Solving Learning & Behavior Problems by Sally Goddard
The Polyvagal theory – Steven Porges

Chapter Twenty Six
Beyond the Sea Squirt: A Journey with Reflexes by Moira Dempsey
Erik H. Erikson and Intimacy vs. Isolation (Psychosocial Stages of Development) L.P. Middler
Hold on to your kids: Gordon Neufeld, Gabor Mate
Love, Jean: Inspiration for Families Living with Dysfunction of Sensory Integration by A. Jean Ayre
Movements That Heal by Harald Blomberg and Moira Dempsey
Scattered Minds – Gabor Mate
Trauma-proofing your kids – Peter Levine and Maggie Kline

Chapter Twenty Seven
Clinician's Guide for Implementing Ayres Sensory Integration: Promoting Participation for Children With Autism by Zoe Mailloux Roseann C. Schaaf
Hold on to your kids: Gordon Neufeld, Gabor Mate
Pedretti's Occupational Therapy: Practice Skills for Physical Dysfunction (Factsbook) Pendleton
Sensory Integration and the Child – Understanding hidden Sensory challenges by A. Jean Ayress
Understanding the Nature of Sensory Integration with Diverse Populations by Susanne Smith Roley, Erna Imperatore Blanche, et al.

Chapter Twenty Eight
The dark side of the light chasers: Debbie Ford
The TEACCH Approach to Autism Spectrum Disorders by Gary B. Mesibov Eric Schopler

Chapter Twenty Nine
Attention, Balance and Coordination: The A.B.C. of Learning Success by Sally Goddard Blythe, Lawrence J. Beuret, et al.
Energy Medicine: How to use your body's energies for optimum health and vitality Donna Eden and John Feinstein
Grain Brain: The Surprising Truth about Wheat, Carbs, and Sugar - Your Brain's Silent Killers David Perlmutter
Movements That Heal by Harald Blomberg and Moira Dempsey
Sensory Integration and the Child – Understanding hidden Sensory challenges by A. Jean Ayress
The dirt cure: Maya Shetreat Klein
The End of Mental Illness: How Neuroscience Is Transforming Psychiatry and Helping Prevent or Reverse Mood and Anxiety Disorders, ADHD, Addictions, PTSD, Psychosis, Personality Disorders,and more Dr. Daniel G. Amen
The Jungle effect: Daphne Miller
The Polyvagal theory – Steven Porges
Touch for health: John Thie
https://pubmed.ncbi.nlm.nih.gov/28385512/
https://pubmed.ncbi.nlm.nih.gov/32346323/
https://www.hindustantimes.com/health/antibiotics-use-by-india-s-poultry-farms-endangering-human-lives-says-expert/story-6W6b10gfdUKhOkrTSscDlL.html
https://www.petaindia.com/features/hens-suffer-for-their-eggs/

Chapter Thirty
11:11 Time for Abundance by Mana
Bernie siegel: Love Medicine and Miracles
Broken Open – Elizabeth Lesser
Brown, Brené. The Gifts of Imperfection: Let Go of Who You Think You're Supposed to Be and Embrace Who You Are
Bruce Lipton : Biology of Belief
Graber, Greg. Slow Your Roll: Mindfulness for Fast Times
Siegel, Dr. Bernie S.. A Book of Miracles: Inspiring True Stories of Healing, Gratitude, and Love
Soul song of the new age children by Mana
Stress release Wayne Topping
The Emotion Code by Dr. Bradley Nelson
The intention experiment: Lynne Mctaggard
The Journey: Brandon Bays
The Miracle of Mindfulness Thich Nhat Hanh
The power of your subconcious mind: Dr Joseph Murphy
Waking the Tiger: Healing Trauma Peter A Levine
Zero Limits: Joe Vitale, Ihaleakala Hewlen

Chapter Thirty One
A Mind At A Time: How Every Child Can Succeed – Levine Mel
Bernie siegel: Love Medicine and Miracles
Broken Open – Elizabeth Lesser
Brown, Brené. The Gifts of Imperfection: Let Go of Who You Think You're Supposed to Be and Embrace Who You Are
Descartes' Error: Emotion, Reason, and the Human Brain Antonio Damasio
Hold on to your kids: Gordon Neufeld, Gabor Mate
Regression Therapy- A handbook for professionals: Wina Fred Blake Lucas
Stapleton, Dr. Peta . The Science behind Tapping
Summary of The Whole-Brain Child: 12 Revolutionary Strategies to Nurture Your Child's Developing Mind by Daniel J. Siegel, Tina Payne
The Brain that changes itself: Norman Doidge
The dark side of the light chasers: Debbi Ford
The Feeling of What Happens: Body and Emotion in the Making of Consciousness Antonio Damasio
The intention experiment: Lynne Mctaggard
The Journey: Brandon Bays
The Miracle of Mindfulness Thich Nhat Hanh

The Origins Of Neuro Linguistic Programming John Grinder
The power of your subconcious mind: Dr Joseph Murphy
Zero Limits: Joe Vitale, Ihaleakala Hewlen

Chapter Thirty Two
Broken Open – Elizabeth Lesser
In the Realm of Hungry Ghosts: Close Encounters with Addiction Gabor Mate
Regression Therapy- A handbook for professionals: Wina Fred Blake Lucas
Stapleton, Dr. Peta . The Science behind Tapping
The dark side of the light chasers: Debbie Ford
The Gifts of Imperfection by Brene Brown
The Polyvagal theory – Steven Porges
Waking the Tiger: Healing Trauma Peter A Levine
When the body says no: Gabor Mate

Chapter Thirty Three
Autism Breakthrough (Groundbreaking method that has helped families all over the world) by Raun Kaufman
Autism: A new perspective by Andrea Libutti and Joao Carlos
Conversations with a rattle snake- Theo Fleury and Kim Barthel
Scattered Minds – Gabor Mate
Soul song of the new age children by Mana
The Reason I jump – One boy's voice from the silence of Autism by Naoki Higashida

Chapter Thirty Four
Bernie siegel: Love Medicine and Miracles
Bridges, Holly. Reframe Your Thinking Around Autism
Bruce Lipton : Biology of Belief
Graber, Greg. Slow Your Roll: Mindfulness for Fast Times
Hold on to your kids: Gordon Neufeld, Gabor Mate
Owen, JB. Ignite Your Parenting: Real life, heartfelt stories to help parents find balance and joy in raising happy children
Peter O Grey Free to Learn: Why Unleashing the Instinct to Play Will Make Our Children Happier, More Self-Reliant, and Better Students for Life
Stress release Wayne Topping
The intention experiment: Lynne Mctaggard
The Journey: Brandon Bays
The Miracle of Mindfulness Thich Nhat Hanh
The Polyvagal theory – Steven Porges
Trauma-proofing your kids – Peter Levine and Maggie Kline

Chapter Thirty Five
Anxious (The modern mind in the age of anxiety) by Joseph LeDoux
Bernie siegel: Love Medicine and Miracles
Bobatoon, Star. I Hate Muscular Dystrophy – Loving a Child with a Life-Altering Disease
Born for love – Maia Szalavitz and Bruce Perry
Stress release Wayne Topping
The Brain that changes itself: Norman Doidge
The education of the child and early lectures on education by Rudolf Steiner
The Healing Power Of EFT and Energy Psychology: Tap into your body's energy to change your life for the better Donna Eden, David Feinstein
The Journey: Brandon Bays
The Kingdom of Childhood: Seven Lectures and Answers to Questions Given in Torquay, August 12-20, 1924 (Foundations of Waldorf Education) By Rudolf Steiner ,Christopher Bamford, et al.
The Miracle of Mindfulness Thich Nhat Hanh
The power of your subconcious mind: Dr Joseph Murphy

ABOUT THE AUTHOR

Reena Singh is an Occupational therapist and the founder of Khushi Pediatric Therapy Center. She works for kids & individuals with special needs. With over two decades of experience, Reena works intuitively with families and kids using an eclectic approach. While Reena helped many people as an Occupational therapist, she couldn't help but feel that she was missing something in her methods while guiding the people who came to her with problems.

A turning point came in her life when she became a mother to a very adorable son, Neel. It was then that Reena got hands-on experience of being a parent. Motherhood taught her the importance of raising a child in a holistic and happy environment to later evolve them as a confident and responsible human being. While working with different kinds of people, she realized that most of us are stuck in the self-created emotional cob-webs that stop us from choosing happiness. In her deep desire to help people, she was inspired to learn more and move towards complementary methods of healing.

Her drive pushed her to pursue and learn different techniques within the space of holistic healing. Today, she is an NLP practitioner, Hypnotherapy practitioner, Matrix Re-imprinting Practitioner, Advanced EFT Practitioner, and Touch For health Proficient Practitioner. She combines Occupational therapy with these principles giving the people she works with an all-embracing approach towards parenting.

She believes that her son is truly a parenting guru and each one of us is blessed with these little gurus in our homes. It is just about decoding the messages, learning from them, and evolving.

Made in the USA
Las Vegas, NV
20 June 2023

73688586R00152